01 14

WHO GETS TO BE INDIAN?

WHO GETS TO BE INDIAN?

ETHNIC FRAUD, DISENROLLMENT, AND OTHER DIFFICULT CONVERSATIONS ABOUT
NATIVE AMERICAN IDENTITY

DINA GILIO-WHITAKER

BEACON PRESS, BOSTON

BEACON PRESS
24 Farnsworth Street
Boston, Massachusetts
www.beacon.org

Beacon Press books
are published under the auspices of
the Unitarian Universalist Association of Congregations.

28 27 26 25   8 7 6 5 4 3 2 1

This book is printed on acid-free paper that meets the uncoated paper
ANSI/NISO specifications for permanence as revised in 1992.

Text design and composition by Kim Arney

*Library of Congress Cataloging-in-Publication
Data is available for this title.*
ISBN: 978-0-8070-4496-4; e-book: 978-0-8070-4509-1;
audiobook: 978-0-8070-1823-1

The authorized representative in the EU for product safety and
compliance is Easy Access System Europe 16879218, Mustamäe tee 50,
10621 Tallinn, Estonia: http://beacon.org/eu-contact.

*I dedicate this book to the memory
of my beautiful mother, Rose, from whom
I inherit the gift of my Indianness*

CONTENTS

INTRODUCTION

THERE ARE FEW ISSUES more contentious in Indian country than identity, and no one writes about it to win a popularity contest. The topic is difficult and, for many, painful. For some, this book will be eye-opening, and for others, it may stir up feelings of anger. Still others, I hope, will reexamine any old family stories about the long-lost Indian ancestor. I also want those who are unaware to become sensitized to the abuses of tribal governments that rob people of their tribal status through disenrollment, a topic so fraught that few are willing to confront it publicly. Colonization has been so effective that our very identities as Native people have been usurped, misconstrued, and weaponized. "Divide and conquer" is so internalized that we often can't tell friend from foe, and families are ripped apart in identity-based power struggles. In the United States, no other ethnic identity is as misunderstood as American Indian.

One of the most damaging aspects of the colonial process has been the imposition of the European economic system. The twin forces of colonialism and capitalism resulted initially in the theft of tribal lands, resources, and children. In time, tribal cultures became commodities subject to market forces, eroding our very understanding of who we are as we struggled to survive within this deadly system. Indianness itself became commoditized, resulting in mass confusion about what it means to be responsible to kin and community. As a commodity, Indianness became available to anyone. In time, Indians were sacrificed to protect tribal casino profits. The commodification of Indianness has distorted the way the world sees us—and the way we see ourselves.

The goal of this book is not only to show how we got here but to provide some clarity as we navigate our way through the quagmire. I hope to provide a theoretical intervention into the growing literature on Native identity. My intention, however, is to write not under a pretense of dispassionate objectivity but from an unapologetically personal perspective. I am certain that the story I tell about my own Nativeness will resonate for a great many people; my writing method combines elements of autoethnography, scholarly discourse, and storytelling. Ultimately, my approach is relational, and my goal, more than anything, is to inform.

When I began this project, I thought I was going to write a book about Native American identity that focused on the complexities of Nativeness, the zone of liminality where so many people find themselves. For a variety of reasons, I didn't want to focus exclusively on pretendianism, although it was tempting. I don't love that word or believe it accurately describes those who have thin or even bogus claims to Nativeness. It's not a one-size-fits-all description. It was clear, however, that the issue needs to be confronted with as much accuracy and precision as possible. At the same time, I have observed how disenrollment and enrollment moratoriums have become destructive forces in Indian country, a direct result of tribal indoctrination into capitalism. I see pretendianism and disenrollment as two sides of the same coin, so to speak, of settler colonial capitalism.[1]

First and foremost, I want to build a coherent, compelling analysis to help explain the seemingly intractable problem of Native American ethnic fraud. That is what is missing in our current public debates. The topic gets ever more inflamed with each new high-profile academic, author, or celebrity who gets called out as a pretendian. So much of our discourse on Native identity is emotionally driven reactions within the callout culture of social media; it's hard to avoid getting pulled into those dramas. I also found myself in a situation I couldn't ignore involving Sacheen Littlefeather, best known as a Native American woman who declined an Oscar on behalf of Marlon Brando in 1973. Over a period of ten years, I first accepted her story about who she was, and then came to believe Sacheen Littlefeather was a fraud. I felt unable to disclose what I knew publicly until after her death in 2022. I use the story as a case study to ground this book and introduce this fraught landscape. It serves as an entry point to investigate how Native American ethnic fraud and tribal disenrollment are distinct but interrelated phenomena stemming from the commodification of Indianness, and to understand how a myriad of circumstances have led many people of legitimate American Indian heritage to become disconnected from their tribes.

Sacheen Littlefeather rose to prominence after one seventy-eight-second moment at the 1973 Academy Awards, when she took to the stage in full Native American regalia to decline the Best Actor award on behalf of Marlon Brando for his role in *The Godfather*. It was a seminal moment, the first time the Oscars ceremony had been used as a platform for protest. Littlefeather experienced her Warholian fifteen minutes of fame, which came to define the rest of her life, cementing her legacy as a cultural icon in Indian country. But not long after her death in 2022, it was revealed that, as many had secretly suspected, Littlefeather was not who she said she was. Her image had been built on a single, elaborate lie that lasted half a century. Then, during the writing of this book, almost a year to the day after Littlefeather's death, a bombshell story broke: Buffy Sainte-Marie had also fabricated her life story. It was shocking enough that Littlefeather, one of the most enduring symbols of Native heroism in modern American Indian history, turned out to be a fraud. That someone of Sainte-Marie's stature could also have lied about her identity for six decades was unthinkable. Buffy Sainte-Marie, a rock and roll legend who rose to fame in the Greenwich Village days alongside Bob Dylan, Joan Baez, Joni Mitchell, and others, had become an Indigenous luminary in the US and Canada, supposedly of Canadian First Nations descent. When the Canadian investigative news show *The Fifth Estate* uncovered the facts of her birth and family of origin, the evidence seemed incontrovertible. Sainte-Marie had shared a narrative that she was born Cree but had been adopted during Canada's 1960s scoop era, a time when many Native children were taken from their families and placed in the child welfare system. But contrary to her long-standing and often shifting story, the birth certificate that Sainte-Marie claimed didn't exist was found in the office where such records are stored, in the county of her birth, in Massachusetts. It meant she couldn't have been from a Cree community in Canada, nor a victim of the 1960s scoop. Yet, in one of the biggest moments of her career, Sainte-Marie told children on *Sesame Street* that she was an Indian. She hadn't been adopted at birth, and perhaps most damning, *The Fifth Estate* presented evidence that she had levied threats against her own family if they contradicted her story. Then, at least one social media post emerged, written by her son several years earlier, confirming that his mother was not Indian.

The Buffy Sainte-Marie story punctuated the need for the book I had already been writing for almost a year. The deeper I dug into the research on what constitutes American Indian identity, the larger the phenomenon of pretendianism loomed. The central nagging questions were: How do we explain the persistence of the phenomenon of Native American ethnic fraud? How did it start, and what drives people to claim a heritage they were not born into? I'm not the first to ask such questions, but my perspective growing up outside my tribe of origin, born and raised in Southern California at a particular moment in time and with a certain lived experience, seemed relevant. I was searching for a way to understand Native American ethnic fraud in a historical and structural context. The deeper into the research I went, the clearer it became that Southern California, as the birthplace of pretendianism as we know it today, would be a central animating theme of this book. I trace this back to the nascent film industry in Southern California at the turn of the twentieth century. There are instances outside California of individuals who faked Indian identities before the film era to fraudulently acquire land allotments, but my contention is that Indian ethnic fraud, embedded in the film industry, became normalized, systemic, and uniquely Californian, spreading and playing out in other ways throughout the twentieth century.[2]

My analysis stems partly from Philip Deloria's seminal work, *Playing Indian*, in which he argues that "playing Indian" is tied to European Americans' search for an authentic identity and the need for legitimate belonging as settlers in a land not their own. Deloria drew from early American writers to help make sense of settlers' "desire to extirpate [the Indian] . . . and the contradictory desire to glorify him."[3] Deloria was onto something significant, and his work has inspired new generations of scholarship grappling with the broader questions of Native American cultural appropriation. As my gaze deepened, I began to see different patterns in the growing body of literature on cultural appropriation: *playing* Indian turned into *becoming* Indian, as the research of scholars like Circe Sturm, Darryl Leroux, Kathleen Fitzgerald, Michelle Jacobs, and Brian Haley has shown. "Playing" Indian describes older forms of cultural appropriation characterized by hobbyism as a type of cosplay, superficial and more like a game of charades compared to those who become Indian. "Becoming" Indian takes cultural appropriation to the next level, beyond cosplay when people, sometimes entire families, alter their identities and adapt narratives to fit a persona of "being" Native American without evidence of connection to a legitimate tribal community or lived American Indian experience. It's full-blown ethnic fraud when people intentionally lie about their heritage. This has become such a common phenomenon that since the mid-twentieth century, we see the mushrooming of entire communities and faux tribes composed of what Fitzgerald and Jacobs call reclaimers. Haley is more pointed, using the terms *neo-Indians* and *neo-tribes*, as is Leroux, with the term *self-indigenization.*

The origin of the pretendian phenomenon can be pinpointed to Southern California at a time when the United States was engaged in an Indian policy of forced assimilation. I perceive, however, a gap in the historiography that largely ignores how forced assimilation was not just about the coercive merging of Indians into white American culture but also into its capitalist economic system. Temporally, this period also coincided with the emergence of the film industry, and it is here, in turn-of-the-century Southern California, where we see the emergence of a pattern of Indian ethnic fraud. A study of early film history shows that it didn't take long for the feigning of Indianness to become normalized. I argue that along with assimilation into the capitalist settler state came the commodification of Indianness, first through Indians performing in the popular Wild West shows, giving birth to Show Indians, hired to play themselves in dramatic spectacles that celebrated colonial conquest as the "winning of the West."

For Show Indians, performing indigeneity, initially a survival strategy for veterans of the Plains Wars as they adapted to their new colonized lives, became a viable and lucrative career choice as American Indians merged into the settler capitalist state. The content of early films, meanwhile, was often based on Indian themes, creating a demand for Indian actors, initially filled by Show Indians. With Indianness becoming a marketized commodity in the Hollywood film business, the field opened to anyone who could convincingly adopt an Indian persona.

Throughout the twentieth century, conditions continued to change dramatically for Native people, mediated by coercive federal policy and intensifying capitalist forces. Long before the 1950s relocation program of the termination era, migration from reservations began altering the social landscape for Native people, fueled by the need to escape the poverty resulting from the General Allotment Act of 1887. The relocation program alone drove over a hundred thousand Native people to cities around the US between the 1950s and 1970s.[4] Native people from reservations all over the country found each other and formed new urban-based communities that became centers for ongoing political resistance while also fostering expressions of indigeneity in the context of a new urban pan-Indianism. Because indigeneity is defined by connection to a tribe in which members know each other and are often related, Indian ethnic fraud in reservation communities is highly improbable. But in urban settings, without local relational knowledge, there is space for people to make largely unverifiable claims. Native people also tended to take people at their word for tribal claims.

California became a magnet for what would by mid-century grow into the largest population of Native relocators in the country. Long before the relocation program, as Damon Akins and William Bauer write, Los Angeles attracted Indians seeking economic opportunities in agriculture, defense, oil production, and other industries tied to the real estate boom, including the film business. By 1930, three-quarters of the seven hundred Los Angeles-based Indians counted in a 1928 special census were not California Indians but Indians originally from other states. A thriving network of Native-run organizations sprouted in Los Angeles, and in the relocation years, the Los Angeles

Field Relocation Office oversaw the relocation of thirty thousand Indians from across the West.[5] In Northern California, San Francisco and Oakland didn't experience quite the influx that LA did, though one study estimated the Bay Area population at around ten thousand by 1964.[6] This era of Native American relocation coincided with a broader ethnic renewal movement and changes in census rules in 1960 that allowed for racial self-identification, leading to an explosion of new Native Americans. Through the 1960s and '70s, as the racial pride movement grew, Indianness—being Indian—became desirable in a way it had never been before in the US. With more Indians in urban settings without any of the social mechanisms for regulating identities in reservation communities, the "popularity of being Indian," as Vine Deloria Jr. called it, grew, giving birth to a new type of generic urban Indian identity. I argue this was the social rupture out of which today's pretendianism arose, and nowhere was it more entrenched than California.

The settler capitalist state is the context that shapes Native American identity today for legitimate Native people, pretendians, and everybody in the middle zone of identity liminality. The latter are people who have legitimate American Indian heritage but who for countless reasons have been disenfranchised from official tribal belonging. Driven by economic imperatives, the modern tribe was created out of federal policies designed to foster tribal self-sufficiency, inevitably inscribing the kind of mindsets that come with living in a society governed by capitalism: scarcity, competition, selfishness, individualism, greed. Tribal communities historically characterized by inclusiveness, generosity, trust, and kinship were transformed into federal corporations concerned with the acquisition and distribution of resources, thrusting them into adopting policies that exclude and marginalize their own in increasingly disturbing ways. This is most evident in blood quantum policies, along with disenrollment and enrollment moratoriums that now plague upward of 17 percent of federally recognized tribes, most of which operate casinos. All are genocidal policies imposed not from the outside but self-inflicted.

Blood quantum—the measuring of "Indian blood" in fractions—is a holdover from when Native people were conceived of in a strictly racialized way, outside the framework of today's tribal nationhood. Normalized in federal governing mechanisms first during the allotment years, it later became embedded in federal law and tribal governance frameworks with the establishment of the Indian Reorganization Act (IRA), which created the modern Indian tribe, in 1934. This racial logic infiltrated tribal communities who adopted it with the encouragement of the Bureau of Indian Affairs (BIA) during the creation of IRA tribal constitutions. But tribes have always existed as discrete communities, their interactions with Europeans and then Americans resting on a political nation-to-nation foundation, not on a basis of racial difference. In today's parlance, this relationship is referred to in terms of tribal sovereignty, a legal structure based on distinct treaty-based rights, which US courts have continually upheld. In recent decades a well-funded anti-Indian movement, primarily driven by the religious political right, has mobilized expressly to dismantle tribal sovereignty. This movement uses various strategies with one key argument: American Indian people are unconstitutionally given special rights based on their race, violating the Constitution's equal protection clause, which prohibits discrimination based on race.

As the movement has grown, it has become an existential threat to tribal communities still struggling to survive the onslaught of four hundred years of colonial invasion. A core strategy is to drive legal cases to the US Supreme Court, a dangerous venue for litigating Indian rights in the past few decades, given the court's track record of eroding tribal rights and its current demographic makeup. These legal battles have manifested most seriously in challenges to the Indian Child Welfare Act (ICWA), but similar arguments are emerging against other laws and policies, particularly the Indian Gaming Regulatory Act, deploying the same legal claims about race-based equal protection violations.

The analytical premise of this book rests on the core assumption that legitimate claims to Native American identity are a function of tribal sovereignty and the nation-to-nation relationship between tribes and the US. Focusing on the relationship between federally recognized tribes and the US disavows discourses about Indianness as a racial classification to reinforce the political nature of Native

American identity, in line with canon law and defense strategies to protect ICWA and a broader tribal sovereignty.

The inherent imperfections and contradictions of relying on the ongoing colonial and paternalistic nature of this framework are acknowledged, especially where disenrollment is concerned. At the same time, defaulting to Native identity as constitutive of political status admits of the realpolitik of the tribal and federal relationship, and provides guidance and clarity for understanding Native identity on a spectrum—legitimate tribal belonging on one end, ethnic fraud on the other, and identity ambiguity in the vast middle ground. Building the foundation for a coherent analysis of Native identity and Native ethnic fraud requires historical contextualization to apprehend the structural and systemic nature of the phenomena and to ground it theoretically. Then we can gain a better understanding of how we reached this point and construct more rational, compelling responses, capable of leading to meaningful policies to combat the harms of both pretendianism and disenrollment, both direct results of settler capitalism.

The outline of the book follows a trajectory that mirrors descriptions in the previous paragraphs. I begin by situating myself on the topic of Native American identity as a person of verifiable tribal heritage but without tribal enrollment, thus as an occupant of the vast middle ground of ambiguity on a spectrum of Native identity. Chapter 1 iterates a case study of Sacheen Littlefeather based on my experience with her, with detailed attention to the evidence of her identity fraud, and establishes a basis for how we can cogently identify and discuss Native identity fraud thereafter. Chapter 2 lays out the terms of the debate by substantiating the centrality of tribal nationhood and the federal relationship. This represents the other end of the identity spectrum, with political status as the foundation for measuring legitimacy vis-à-vis the realpolitik of the nation-to-nation relationship within the settler state. This section also explores a discussion on tribal criteria for belonging, especially blood quantum, and examines how it enters tribal vernacular. It also makes distinctions between the numerous ways Nativeness is described. Chapter 3 excavates the origins of contemporary pretendianism in fin de siècle Los Angeles and the nascent film industry and examines this era of federal Indian policy, rooted in assimilation. Interrogating the nature of boarding schools in concert with allotment reveals the ways imposing capitalism on tribal communities and individuals was the central impetus of those policies, ultimately creating conditions of destabilization that impact tribal communities today. The chapter also traces a century-long history of American Indian advocacy in the film industry that was always concerned with Native identity fraud and its theft of jobs from legitimate Indians, bringing us to assess its persistence in Native Hollywood and the art and entertainment world today.

Chapter 4 continues unveiling California as the epicenter of contemporary pretendianism and neo-Indianism, particularly as it expanded and became more normalized during the counterculture era of the mid-twentieth century and infiltrated the New Age movement. Based on Brian Haley's study of Chumash ethnogenesis and neo-tribalism, it opens to a discussion of the proliferation of neo-tribes and identifies ways that neo-tribes in California compete for financial resources in the conservation world based on dubious or outright fraudulent claims to indigeneity. Chapter 5 further investigates the role of settler capitalism in destabilizing tribal communities and individual identities through disenrollment. In the name of nation building, tribes abrogate their own traditional tribal values and "original instructions" rooted in inclusiveness, generosity, and relationality to achieve success gauged by capitalistic standards characterized by scarcity, exclusion, and greed. It highlights the case of the Pechanga Band of Luiseño Indians to expose patterns common to disenrolling tribes and cross-examines the nature of power in tribal politics. Chapter 6 deepens the discussion of Native identity, introducing the idea of its existence on a spectrum. The Native identity spectrum is defined by legitimacy, measured by proximity to a federally recognized tribe, casting light on the many ways individual Native people or tribes can be and have been marginalized and ineligible for official tribal belonging or recognition. I argue that language matters in how people talk about their ostensible Native American heritage, and I probe the ways that Native identity claims take on the character of a personal possession within the logics of the settler capitalist state. Finally, the book returns to the story of Sacheen Littlefeather, offering a culturally based way of viewing Native identity fraud and disenrollment, summarizes the ideas of the foregoing chapters, and offers suggestions for curbing the excesses and abuses of both pre-tendianism and disenrollment.

TELLING A PERSONAL STORY

As a researcher and scholar, I've been trained not to center myself in my research. I'm not trained in autoethnography or memoir writing, so writing at length about my personal experience takes me outside my comfort zone. I don't like to risk being perceived as self-indulgent, but I also know that the story about who I am as a Native person with all my identity complexities could be relatable to many others. It is in the interest of complete transparency with an aim toward accountability that I share my story with you now.

My father, Vince Gilio, was one of six in a family of American-born children to Sicilian immigrant parents. His father, Dominick, was from Messina, and my grandmom, Bessie, was from Palermo, Italy. Both came to the US as youths. Grandpop's name is carved in a wall at Ellis Island. Both were from the old country, people whose English was limited; Grandpop had around a fourth-grade level of literacy and Grandmom could not read or write in English or Italian. It was always up to us family members to write things for her. Grandmom and Grandpop raised their children in Philadelphia during the Depression, but Grandmom's family came in a wave of Sicilian migration through New Orleans in the late nineteenth and early twentieth century. Looking for a new start after a failed marriage in his twenties, my dad hopped on a train to the farthest point west he could go—Los Angeles, California. Most of his immediate family members eventually followed, so I grew up knowing lots of aunts, uncles, and cousins from the Gilio side. In my early years, it was Sicilian dialect and culture I was most exposed to.

My dad met my mom, Rosemarie Burnett Gilio, in Los Angeles sometime in the mid-1950s. My mom's life story was vaguer than my dad's because she kept a lot of secrets. In a profound way, my life has been shaped by my journey to understand my mother, and my mission to uncover the painful history she tried desperately to hide from my sisters and me. I am the oldest of three daughters born to Vince and Rose, and until I was about fifteen, I believed I was the first child for both of them. That was when Mom disclosed to me that she'd had a son before I was born who, she maintained, had been taken from her. She disclosed it one night during one of her epic drinking binges, which were frequent during the days she and my dad were going through a divorce. I would come to know over the course of many years that her son was not the only child she'd given birth to before me—two other children were born after him. It would also eventually come out that my dad had two children from his previous marriage. I was number six out of eight children between the two of them, not as I had always believed, the first child out of three. These details revealed themselves over the span of my entire life. It's been a jarring reorientation of my self-perception. What I've learned has been an inspiring force for this book.

My mom had come to California from Seattle, where she had been living before she met my dad in LA. She was born in Spokane, and she was an enrolled member of the Colville Confederated Tribes, whose reservation is about ninety miles away. She'd spent some of her childhood on the reservation during the Depression while her father worked on roadbuilding projects, likely through the Works Progress Administration. Her father, George Burnett, was white, descended from well-documented lines of settlers stretching all the way back to the earliest New England colonies. One of those ancestors was John Warner, who was a member of the Gortonist religious separatist movement and involved in the Shawomet Purchase of 1643. Shawomet became Warwick, Rhode Island. Another ancestor was Comfort Starr, a well-to-do settler who traveled from England on the ship *Hercules* in 1635 during the Great Puritan Migration and later became one of the founders of Harvard University. I have ancestors from other old English settler families in New England, including the Sages, the Potters, the Warners, and the Formans.

My mom's mother, Mabel Desautel, was born in Republic, Washington, in 1908, which was within the borders of the Colville Reservation just sixteen years before. That's known today as the North

Half in the traditional territory of the Okanogan and Sinixt people.[7] The North Half, over a million acres of fertile valleys and mountainous forestlands in the Columbia River watershed, was taken without consent by an act of Congress in 1892[8] and without proper compensation.[9] Grandma's father was Gilbert Desautel, and her mother was Ida O'Brien. Both descended from long lines of full- and mixed-blood Indians and French Canadian and Scottish settlers. They are traced back at least eleven generations, according to Catholic Church records and journals written by and about David Thompson, the region's first settler and explorer, and his guide, Jaco Finley. Finley, a half-Indian (records vary on whether he was Chippewa or Cree) explorer, founded Spokane House, the first trading post in Washington State, and worked for the Hudson's Bay Company. We are direct descendants of Jaco Finley. The Indians in our family tree were mostly Okanogan, according to census records, and Sinixt, based on oral history, with a few Spokane ancestors sprinkled in, and the Chippewa (or Cree) mother of Jaco Finley. Most became residents on or near the Colville Reservation by the time of its establishment in the nineteenth century.

I met my grandma Mabel only a handful of times because she lived so far from us—and because her relationship with my mom was so damaged. My mother struggled with alcohol addiction, just as her mother did. I did not understand why the relationship was so fractured until the night Mom told me about the son who had been taken from her, which she blamed her mother for. Even then, I couldn't comprehend how something so awful could transpire in a family. All I knew was that my mother believed her own mother never loved her, and I could tell it was related to her drinking problem. My mother's family had suffered a profound breakdown, and alcohol seemed to be at the center of it. One time, our family took a long road trip to the reservation to visit relatives. We spent a week camping in the woods near Republic, hunting and fishing. I was in heaven—even at twelve, all the cells of my body could feel my ancestral connection to the land. I had embraced my Indianness ever since I could remember. But I was keenly aware of the constant fear that excessive drinking instills in a kid, not knowing what will go wrong next, and it always did. Knockdown, drag-out fights. Car wrecks. DUIs. Delirium tremens and psychiatric hospitalization. Jail. All of that happened to my mom, numerous times, during my life as a child and as an adult. My mom's brother, my uncle Jim, contracted a rare brain disorder from his alcoholism, dying in a state of disassociation after years in a mental institution. Alcohol destroyed our family, or so I thought, until I learned about some of our carefully concealed secrets. That's when I realized alcohol was a symptom of even deeper issues.

In my early thirties, I started searching for answers to some of the destructive patterns I had fallen into as an adult, many of which revolved around being a survivor of domestic violence. How had this happened to me? I knew, as the adult child of an alcoholic, I needed to understand my mother better and the circumstances that had shaped her life—and those of my sisters and me. This search led me back to the reservation and my mom's estranged family. My grandmother had long since passed, but her brothers—my great uncles Vern and John—were still there. They welcomed my return, having not seen me since I was a kid. They loved Rosie, as my mom was known in her family. Everyone who knew my mother loved her. Despite all her faults, she was a kind and gentle soul with a heart of gold.

Uncle Vern, in particular, was very accommodating. By then, he was seventy-five, a tribal elder living in a run-down singlewide on the banks of the Columbia River in Elmer City, just down the road from the Colville agency offices in Nespelem. Tough, with a chip on his shoulder, he took pride in still being able to fish and hunt, and provide food for the tribal elders. And he was kind to me, introducing me to relatives I had never met before and acquainting me with our ancestral lands. We went to the July 4 powwow, what he and the other old-timers called the war dances, in Nespelem. In the evenings as the sun set over the ridge across the river, we sat on the porch, watching bald eagles fish for their dinner as we drank his special home brew, and he told me stories. So many stories. Stories about our family. Stories about the olden times before there were cars on the reservation and they still traveled in horse-drawn wagons. He told me how they'd go ice fishing and take the ice from the lakes to icehouses, where they'd pack it with sawdust. They stored food there most of the year. He told me about his mother, my great-grandmother Ida, and how she'd been a logging truck driver in the 1930s. There were stories about salmon fishing at Kettle Falls before the Grand Coulee Dam was built and flooded our sacred falls, and about how he'd helped build that "damn dam" responsible for disrupting so much of Colville life. And then there were stories about the boarding school, Chemawa, in Oregon, that he, Uncle John, and my grandmother had been sent to as children.

In 1991, that first year I was there with Uncle Vern, we did not talk openly about the Indian boarding schools like we do today. Not much was widely known about them. It was common for boarding school experiences not to be shared in families, and it was no different in my family. I remember hearing the word Chemawa, but I don't remember stories about being there. I do remember Mom talking about her uncle Jim O'Brien going to Carlisle during the time Jim Thorpe was there as a point of pride. Uncle Jim came back to the reservation, she said, and later helped bring a lawsuit against the federal government—it took another forty-three years to settle—to compensate the tribe for damage and loss of lands caused by the dam's flooding.[10]

The things Uncle Vern told me about the boarding school were devastating and shocking—having to wear military-style uniforms, being drilled with rifles, receiving corporal punishment, living in isolation—and that was just what he was willing to share. Uncle Vern, Uncle John, and Grandma all tried running away. One time Grandma ran away, got bit by a rattlesnake, and was sent back to the school. For all the things Uncle Vern talked about, I now wonder what kind of things he couldn't talk about. What was the unspeakable? What he told me was what I understand today as a textbook boarding school story. The more I learned over the years about the effects of the boarding schools, the more I was able to make sense of the tragic direction my mom's family had taken. The violence of it all explained the alienation and lack of affection between my mother and her mother, and how it would have generational impact, even in my own life. It explained, at least partially, my mom's alcoholism. The schools were designed, as all federal Indian policy of the time, to destroy Native families and culture. Our family was a living example of how effective it was.[11]

Big unanswered questions about my mom's life still hung over our heads. Then, in the 1990s, my sisters and I found out Mom had given up a second child for adoption. She told us she had received a letter from this daughter through a mediator, requesting contact, which Mom denied. We were upset with her—even if she didn't want contact, we felt it was our right to have a relationship with our sister. I tried to find this sister, who was living in Wenatchee, Washington, but in those days before the internet, it was impossible, without going all the way up there to hunt for her—something out of the question for me, living in Northern California with a new baby.

In early 2022, a woman who had taken a DNA test that led her to us contacted my sister Sissy, asking if she was the daughter of Rosemarie Burnett. She turned out to be Amy, the daughter of our sister in Wenatchee who had contacted Mom all those years before. It was the beginning of our finding answers to the huge remaining questions about our mother's life. Our conversations with Amy led to contact with our missing siblings. We learned about another child our mom had given up for adoption; there were three altogether before I was born. Two of those siblings had found each other in the early '90s when one of them, Amy's mom, was able to access her adoption records in Washington State, which is how they learned about the third sibling, our older brother. But the unsealed adoption records did not provide enough information to reveal the other siblings—my sisters and me. The DNA testing company's database connected us all, including our brother, Robert. All it took was a few emails to connect after a lifetime of believing it would be impossible to find our lost siblings.

It was the adoption records of our brother, Robert, that provided information that has helped me understand my mother's tragic life.[12] His (our) mother raised him until he was five, at which point the state intervened to take him away. He was old enough to have bonded with and have memories of her. Robert grew up believing his mother had abandoned him with neighbors; the unsealed caseworker notes provided to him by the state led him to understand she also desperately but unsuccessfully tried to get him back. The notes indicated that on the day she gave birth to Robert at a Catholic hospital, as a nineteen-year-old married woman, he was declared a dependent of the court and placed under the care of Catholic Community Services. On the papers, his mother's race is listed as "Caucasian and Indian." In our family's records, numerous other historical documents including census records and my own birth certificate ten years later list my mother as white, despite her being an enrolled tribal member her whole life. It is curious, then, that adoption records would identify her as Indian. And it raised the question: Why was Robert made a ward of the court and a dependent of Catholic services the day he was born yet his mother took him home and raised him for the next five years?

The deliberate disruption of Native families, initiated by the federal Indian boarding school policy and enforced at the state level from the early to late twentieth century, was driven by pervasive beliefs in Native cultural inferiority. Social workers in state family services agencies often presumed the unfitness of mothers based on nothing more than being Indian or being poor.[13] They used intimidation and sometimes outright fraud to acquire "consent."[14] Women faced harassment from social workers both before and after giving birth, with pressure to place their babies for adoption. As Margaret Jacobs writes, "Unlike American women more generally, Indian women, whether they were married or not, commonly faced harassment to relinquish their children for adoption."[15] The removal of children from Native women was so widespread that a study conducted by attorney Bertram Hirsch in the late 1960s found 25 to 35 percent of Native children were being taken from their homes. It's been called a scoop because agency officials often entered tribal communities and homes and quickly took as many kids as they could.[16] The crisis led to the creation in 1978 of the Indian Child Welfare Act (ICWA) to help keep Indian children in their homes, families, and communities.

The unsealed adoption records of my older brother provided ample evidence that he was part of the pre-ICWA scoop. The record shows my mom filed for divorce after just a couple of years of marriage. My mother gave birth to two more children during the early 1950s, before birth control pills, and after a failed marriage, as a single working mom, she decided to give them both up—all before turning twenty-five. That's a devastating amount of loss and grief. It explains why my mom suffered from depression, attempting suicide numerous times.

The loss of her children alone was enough to explain alcoholism, let alone her having been born into a family affected by the Indian boarding school experience. In other words, my mother's life was shaped by trauma, a direct result of being born American Indian. It didn't matter that she was mixed-blood and light skinned, or didn't live on the reservation. Being able to pass as white didn't save her from the special abuse reserved for Native people.

My mother's life demonstrates that discrimination toward Indigenous people in the United States was never just about race or skin color. It's always been about what mattered most to the American project: land and resources. Native people were an obstacle to be eliminated—my mother, her mother, the Indian ancestors before them, and those who come after them, including me, my siblings, and all of our children. Indian elimination as an organizing principle is a fundamental thread in the social fabric from which the US has been woven, and as a foundational presumption, it is embedded in the darkest corners of the American mindset, infecting even the most well-meaning people in governmental or family structures. Elimination in today's world means denying people's identity as Indians, even when there is documentation and evidence of kinship relations.

When my mom met my dad in Los Angeles in the mid-1950s, she was struggling to rebuild her life after all she had been through, as was he. Termination was the political force behind federal Indian policy, and while my mom didn't come to LA on a relocation voucher, she was caught up in that wave, inadvertently part of the US effort to solve the "Indian problem." Marrying into a Sicilian family had its own unique challenges; the cultural differences were glaring, despite their love for each other. I grew up close to my large transplanted East Coast Sicilian family, and they loved and embraced my mom. Grandmom understood—and loved—the fact that she had Indian grandchildren. But other family members couldn't understand why I always identified more with my mother's Indian heritage than with our Sicilian and Italian heritage. Maybe it was because I was close to my mom and inherited my looks from her side, or maybe it was because of the happy memories she shared of her Indian childhood. Sadly, though, the message my non-Indian family members conveyed was that my Indianness was not enough to matter, based on their stereotypical views about who is Indian. I have struggled with this feeling of not being enough my entire life.

The truth is I inhabit a painful grey zone of Nativeness, a space of liminality where I am, at least in a legal sense, neither fully Indian nor fully non-Indian. On paper I can't meet the tribe's blood quantum standard, so I am not enrolled like my mother. I possess a certificate of descendancy—a descendant letter—issued by the tribe that entitles me to some tribal and governmental benefits. I inherited fractionated interests of allotment land handed down from ancestors several generations ago. As a legal descendant, I qualify as Indian under some definitions but not others. In a social way, some see me as American Indian while others do not. It is simultaneous inclusion and exclusion, belonging and unbelonging. My descendant letter and fractionated allotment inheritance is a fragile lifeline to my tribal government.

My lived reality is far from unusual. Countless people in the US who descend from American Indians don't meet the standards for full or even partial tribal inclusion. Sacheen Littlefeather, however, was not one of them, as I show in the following pages. Still, the drama of her life and death highlights the endlessly unsettled way we think about indigeneity in the US. Because so much of our national discourse around Indianness centers on personal claims, misinformation, and a long history of stereotypes, Littlefeather's story is an ideal starting point for these discussions. The combination of my personal circumstances and my interactions with Littlefeather are the book's larger story. I add my voice to our collective search for a coherent way to address the issues of Native identity and Native ethnic fraud.

CHAPTER ONE

A PRETENDIAN PRINCESS

The Curious Case of Sacheen Littlefeather

> *Taking on another persona,*
> *you can be anything you want.*
>
> —SACHEEN LITTLEFEATHER, 2010[1]

D ATELINE: SEPTEMBER 17, 2022, Hollywood, California. It was one of the weirdest days of my life, and that's from someone who was born in Hollywood and grew up in Los Angeles, one of the most interesting *and* weirdest places on Earth. LA is the land of illusion, after all, where the fusion of reality and fantasy is a setup for cognitive dissonance at any given moment. But what do you call it when cognitive dissonance is collective, when masses of people believe in a fantasy with little basis in reality, when they have believed a lie for so long that it has become their truth? On this day the discordant culmination of half a century of one person's lies was on full display at the Academy Museum of Motion Pictures, where an event was being held to honor the life of Sacheen Littlefeather. Littlefeather had built a reputation after a peculiar, highly celebrated incident at the 1973 Academy Awards, based on her supposed Native American heritage that helped cement a dubious place in Oscar history. In the infamous incident Littlefeather rejected an Oscar on behalf of Marlon Brando for his role in *The Godfather*, an experience Littlefeather, a budding actress at the time, later claimed ruined her career. The purpose of the museum event was to extend an official apology to Littlefeather for the (supposed) damage. Presiding over the ceremony were director and president of the Academy Museum of Motion Pictures Jacqueline Stewart, former president of the Academy of Motion Picture Arts and Sciences David Rubin, current academy president Janet Yang,

Academy CEO Bill Kramer, and cochairs of the academy's Indigenous Alliance Bird Runningwater and Heather Rae Bybee. It was a celebration of Native culture with all the Indigenous pomp and circumstance—a powwow drum, Native hip-hop artist Calina Lawrence, and Apache Crown Dancers—along with hundreds of attendees at the museum's David Geffen Theater.

I was there with a couple of Native friends who have worked in the film industry—what we might call Native Hollywood—for decades. We knew people at the event and were intimately familiar with the Littlefeather story. I had a personal connection because I had known Sacheen since 2012, when I started working with her as a journalist. My experience with her over the years, however, had shifted my thinking about who she was, challenging the belief that she was Native American. Before that, like most people, I took for granted she was an Indian. In 2016, I began to have nagging suspicions about the veracity of her claims. By 2018, as I shared my doubts with others, who felt the same, I became convinced she was a fraud. Besides all the evidence already publicly available, I had other, more personal evidence, given to me by Sacheen herself. Thus, my attendance at the academy museum event was not as an ardent admirer of Sacheen Littlefeather but as an observer of a bizarre spectacle, gathering material for research. For my companions (also disbelievers) and me, the whole experience was surreal, like a movie where illusion is presented as reality; even the theater's stark red aesthetics reminded me of David Lynch's *Twin Peaks*. Things only got weirder when Sacheen died two weeks later, and then three weeks after that, with the release of an article exposing her false identity. It was the opening of a Pandora's box that had been a long time coming, and the controversy it unleashed is certain to reshape conversations about Native American identity and ethnic fraud in Indian country for years to come. It is an ideal place to start talking about what constitutes Native identity and will serve as a useful reference point throughout this book in our discussions about authenticity and fraud.

The story of Sacheen Littlefeather, born Marie Louise Cruz, cuts deep for many Native and non-Native people who believed her half-century-long deception about being, as she phrased it, "Native

American Indian." Littlefeather's performance at the Oscars, controversial at the time, elevated her to a cultural icon, a hero. She was believable; her appearance was convincing, and her message was on point and timely, solidifying an illusion of credibility. The evidence, however, reveals it was a ruse that people were manipulated into believing. The story of Littlefeather at the Academy Awards has been recounted many times in print, audio, and film over the last half century. Some parts of the story remain the same over time, but taken as a whole, they represent the tip of a much bigger iceberg, hiding a world of inconsistencies, contradictions, and blatant lies. Perhaps most disturbingly, people have been complicit in maintaining Littlefeather's public image over the decades. Most of the untruths can be established by simple fact-checking and the testimony of Littlefeather's family members and at least one former friend, as I will show. Rather than assess every large and small false claim Littlefeather has made over time—there are far too many to cover in a single chapter—I will focus on the most relevant claims and narratives she advanced that turned out to be verifiably untrue, especially relative to being American Indian.[2] What follows is the Sacheen Littlefeather story from the perspective of my experience with her and the information that has become public since her death.

THE OSCARS BACKSTORY

In 1973, Marlon Brando was not just a highly talented, experienced, and celebrated actor; he was an iconoclast. In an industry that punishes those who are too politically outspoken, Brando entered the entertainment world with finely honed political beliefs. He'd studied acting in the 1940s at New York's progressive New School, where he studied under teachers who had survived Nazi Germany and aligned himself with the Zionist movement to build an Israeli state.[3] By the 1960s, Brando was a full-blown civil rights activist, drawn into American Indian causes. He showed up to the Fish Wars protests in Washington State in 1964 at the behest of leaders of the National Indian Youth Council, bringing national visibility to an issue most Americans knew little about: Indian treaty rights.[4] As a Hollywood insider, Brando was attuned to stereotyping and pay inequity, issues that American Indians in the industry had experienced for decades. Using the Oscars to literally stage a civil rights protest was not just confrontational, as some people saw it; it directly defied the industry that had made Brando a star. It also fit with his reputation for irreverence, and Sacheen Littlefeather willingly became his accomplice after accepting his invitation to appear in his place at the Academy Awards on March 27, 1973.

The key facts of the incident are that Littlefeather was a twenty-six-year-old aspiring model and actress living in San Francisco after relocating to the Bay Area from her hometown of Salinas around 1969.[5] She'd been working as the public service director at KFRC radio station when Brando's invitation for her to stand in for him came, about a year after she'd written him a letter. She first contacted Brando when *Godfather* director Francis Ford Coppola connected them.[6] According to her account in the 2019 documentary film *Sacheen: Breaking the Silence*, Littlefeather contacted Brando to gauge his commitment to Native American issues. In the film, she recounts attending the event with Brando's personal secretary and sitting in the second row. When it came time for the Best Actor award, and Liv Ullman announced, "Marlon Brando for *The Godfather*," Littlefeather took to the stage wearing a Plains-style buckskin dress, moccasins, and beaded hair ties. She held her hand up to reject the Oscar statue, her other hand holding the eight-page speech Brando had given her to read. The first thing she said was: "Hello, my name is Sacheen Littlefeather. I'm Apache and president of the National Native American Affirmative Image Committee."[7] It was those two simple words, "I'm Apache," that sparked a controversy that led to the exposure of lies that swirled around her identity after her death in 2022.

The rest of her seventy-eight-second speech, however, raised issues that became the foil for what would prove to be a false claim. She said that Marlon Brando "very regretfully cannot accept this very generous award and the reasons for this being are the treatment of American Indians today by the film industry . . . and on television in movie reruns and also with recent happenings at [the occupation of] Wounded Knee."[8] She had thrown the gauntlet down in front of Hollywood's elite power brokers—and millions of others on live television.

It was a direct challenge to the film industry to confront how it was perpetuating harms to Indian country, whether people were ready to hear it or not. The mix of booing and applause from the audience highlighted the range of reactions to Brando's stunt, with Littlefeather instantly becoming both a pariah and a hero.

The media backlash was swift and severe. The Oscars had never before been used as a platform for protest, so the widespread shock and indignation that followed was to be expected. Brando and Littlefeather were both criticized. Brando was called a coward or an ingrate, and Littlefeather became the target of racist and stereotyped epithets. The irony of some of the media reactions was that Littlefeather's Native identity was called into question, inevitably fueling her story of persecution.[9] She always maintained that after the Oscars she was boycotted in Hollywood, and in *Breaking the Silence*, she claims that the FBI was the source of blacklisting, which she calls "redlisting." "The FBI went around Hollywood and told production companies if they hired me or had me on their show that they would shut down their production. It was highly political and the FBI planted lies about me," she says in the film. No evidence is offered to back the allegation. She claimed that the redlisting made it very difficult for her to get a job, yet her filmography shows that she landed roles in at least seven films between 1973 and 1978, the most significant roles of her short-lived acting career.[10] In another dubious statement in *Breaking the Silence*, Littlefeather posits that after the Oscars, a media blackout on the Wounded Knee occupation was lifted: "All the world's media went to Wounded Knee and broke the media blackout. . . . I believe that changed the tide of history, that lives were saved." It's an extraordinary statement for her to make when historians have typically never connected the two incidents in this way, especially to credit her action with saving lives and "changing the tide of history."[11]

While Littlefeather's acting career didn't unfold as she had hoped after the Oscars incident, for years to come, she did receive a fair amount of media attention. People wanted to know who she was, though no one ever confirmed her claims of being Apache, or if they did, it was not publicized. She never publicly talked about any historical family connections to Apaches. At some point, she added Yaqui to her Native claims but never links to a community or family.[12] Her single-page website states, "Contrary to misinformation which has been published on the internet, Sacheen Littlefeather is indeed of true Native American Indian descent . . . her father was from the White Mountain Apache and Yaqui tribes in Arizona." Littlefeather made a home in the San Francisco Bay Area, living in Marin County with her partner, Charles Koshiway, whom she met in 1990. Koshiway, fair skinned and white-passing, was an enrolled member of the Otoe-Missouri tribe in Oklahoma.[13] Many written sources claimed they were married, but they never legally wed.[14]

Sacheen and Charles had fully blended into the Bay Area urban Indian community, frequently attending powwows and other social events. Charles was a devoted powwow and gourd dancer. Urban Indian communities are spaces of Native American ethnic integration. Throughout the twentieth century, Indian people migrated to cities for many reasons, most often economic. Federal policies throughout the nineteenth century rendered reservations places of devastating poverty as Indians were forced out of their traditional land-based ways of life and into a cash-based economic system. Seeking better lives increasingly meant, as it has for many rural families, migration to cities where economic opportunity promised greater stability and social mobility, especially after World War II when the US economy was deindustrializing and urbanization was growing due to the rise in service, technical, and white-collar work.[15] This is also the era of termination and the federal Indian policy of relocation, which was designed to move Indians into cities and bring about the end of individual Indians, tribes, and reservations—and all related US responsibilities. San Francisco and the East Bay were key destinations for many Native people, leading to an increase in the Indian population. Nicholas Rosenthal documents, based on census counts, a rise in the urban Indian population in the Bay Area from 3,469 in 1960 to 16,959 in 1980, a more than fivefold increase in just twenty years.[16] In urban areas, tribal distinctions easily became muted at places like the San Francisco American Indian Center and Oakland's Intertribal Friendship House, where Littlefeather became involved, and at powwows, which tended to be welcoming to both Indians and non-Indians.

People were not asked at these places to show tribal enrollment cards or otherwise produce proof of Indian ancestry. For someone like Sacheen Littlefeather, who gained instant fame for a deed generally perceived as heroic, there would have been little reason for anyone to question her identity, especially before today's pretendianism. Indeed, because of her performance at the Oscars, she was likely granted greater access to the urban Indian scene than someone with provable Indian lineage or even with just stories about being Indian that would have been relatable to Native people.

However, it was common for Sacheen to talk publicly about coming from a troubled family, as she did in *Breaking the Silence*. She frequently referred to her father as a violent, abusive alcoholic. The story was believable for someone claiming to be Native American. While in many ways it is a trope, alcoholism—which often leads to abusive behavior—is common in American Indian families. Pushing the story helped convince people of her fictional Native American identity.

Sacheen Littlefeather's appearance at the Academy Awards has become legendary in Indian country, though much of US society is unfamiliar with the story. The perfect convergence of circumstances paved the way for Littlefeather to become a cultural icon despite her dubious and unsubstantiated claims, including that she was Apache. Native people were still engaging in armed conflict with the US government. They were still facing the systematic removal of their children through adoption and assimilationist boarding schools, the termination of their reservations, the poisoning of their lands through toxic extractive mining processes, illegal sterilizations, and endless treaty violations, to say nothing of relentless racist stereotyping in popular culture, media, education, and sports. For people barely surviving genocide, Indians needed all the heroes they could get, especially with so few positive media images of them.

This was not the first time in history that desperation drove Native people to extreme beliefs. In the late nineteenth century, for example, as Indians fought against the US government's forced relocation to reservations—often through violent military tactics, including massacres and starvation—new religious movements emerged, especially in the West, where the violence was most prevalent. These dreamer or prophet religions were typically led by a single figurehead who had a vision or prophesy that promised deliverance from misery and suffering, including settlers leaving, Indian people returning to their traditional lives, and a bringing back of the dead. Examples include Smohalla's dreamer religion on the Columbia Plateau, the Bole Maru and Big Head religion in Northern California, the Indian Shakers in coastal Washington State, and the Ghost Dance, which originated among the Paiutes and spread east to the Plains and elsewhere. The new religions tended to be syncretic, blending old spiritual traditions with Christianity, which had been systematically imposed on Indian communities from their earliest contact with Europeans all across the continent. Some scholars have characterized these religious movements as a form of Native resistance to colonialism, comparing them to today's Indigenous social movements.[17] Recall that Wounded Knee itself in 1890 was the site of a massacre where hundreds of Lakota men, women, and children were gunned down in the middle of winter as they performed the Ghost Dance ceremony and prayed for a return to precolonial life.

In 1973, it was all too easy to take at face value a beautiful young woman claiming to be Indian and looking every bit the part, speaking for Indian people on behalf of Marlon Brando. With few victories in the previous four and a half centuries, you could say Native people needed something to celebrate. Along came Marlon Brando and Sacheen Littlefeather, staging an intoxicating, seductive drama that worked to Indian country's benefit. Who in Indian country was going to question it? Claims to Indian identity were becoming more common throughout the twentieth century as Native people migrated to cities and pan-Indianism became more widespread and normalized. Why would people question Sacheen Littlefeather's identity—especially as she played directly to a stereotype—when lots of people were populating urban Native communities with unchecked claims to indigeneity? Ultimately, Littlefeather filled a desperately needed role in 1973 America—Native visibility and voice. On the surface, she represented the idea that Native people could have agency at a time when there was little to be found. Of course people believed her!

As it turned out, not everyone fell for it, and some secretly harbored doubts. Because of the popularity of Sacheen Littlefeather and the characterization of her in historical texts over a couple of generations, it was taboo to question the story she'd been telling. Some tried but were not listened to.[18]

A PERSONAL PERSPECTIVE

In 1973, I was fourteen growing up in Los Angeles as a mixed-ethnicity, identity-confused urban Indian kid from a working-class family. Born at the tail end of the baby boom, I was along for the ride in a generation that played a key role in a seismic changing of society. California and LA in particular were ground zero for much of the social turbulence; it was both an exciting and dangerous time to be a teenager. I'd grown up hearing my mother's stories about the horrible ways Indians had been treated, and back on the reservation, the Colvilles had only recently narrowly avoided termination. I remember dinner table conversations about whether my mom should vote for termination, even though I had no understanding of it.[19] I was aware of news stories about Indians fighting for their rights, and it was drilled into me by my parents to be proud of being Indian. As a young person, I came of age during the Red Power movement.

I don't have any memory of watching the Academy Awards that night in 1973 or the ensuing frenzy. It simply became part of the social landscape of the time while I was paying more attention to rock and roll music and marching band. It was not until I was well into adulthood with a college education that I began to understand the significance of the time I grew up in, of how it had shaped society and who I became. The story of Sacheen Littlefeather declining the Oscar for Marlon Brando came into focus while I was in Native American studies as an undergrad at the University of New Mexico. By the time I was finished with graduate school and working as a freelance journalist, I was well aware of the event and its historical context.

I'd been writing for Indian Country Today, known then as Indian Country Today Media Network (ICTMN). In 2012, I was asked by one of the editors if I'd be interested in writing a story about a recent guest on *The Tonight Show with Jay Leno*, the conservative-leaning comedian Dennis Miller, who had made an offensive joke about Littlefeather. It was related to Elizabeth Warren and her claims about being Native American. Miller said, "She's about as much Indian as that stripper chick Brando sent to pick up his Oscar for *The Godfather*, all right?" The reference was about Littlefeather's nude photos in *Playboy*, which came out not long after the Academy Awards. But much more interesting and relevant today is the questioning of Littlefeather's Indianness almost forty years later. I welcomed the opportunity to write about Sacheen Littlefeather, who had become cemented in my mind as a significant historical figure in Indian country. I interviewed her by telephone, and we became professional acquaintances. By that time, Sacheen, in her mid-sixties, was in remission from breast cancer.

When I wrote that article in 2012, neither I nor the editors at ICTMN had any reason to question Sacheen's identity claims. This was a perfect opportunity to fact-check her claims and hold her accountable, but after four decades of the story being told, and with her declining health and advancing age, challenging her was unthinkable. I now regret not thinking more deeply and pushing my editors to verify her Native identity claims.

My next interaction with Sacheen Littlefeather occurred in early 2016, when she contacted me about ghostwriting her memoir. A literary agent had contacted her, requesting a manuscript. The #OscarsSoWhite campaign had erupted the previous year, and there was reason to believe Sacheen might contribute to the conversation about the lack of diversity in the film industry. She'd been barraged by media requests from all over the world as the Academy Awards approached. I had just finished writing my first book and was open to writing another. We were communicating through her agent, and we had begun the process of developing a book proposal.

I took a trip to visit Sacheen Littlefeather at her home in Marin County in the spring of 2016. She arranged for lodging for me with friends who lived nearby. We spent three days together at her modest two-bedroom duplex in San Rafael, a home she shared with Charles, whom she called Mr. Charles. Our sessions involved hours of me listening and taking notes while she talked. I didn't ask many questions because I thought of it as a preliminary conversation, the beginning of many we'd need to have to write a book together. She was also sick with the flu; I asked her if she wanted to postpone our conversation but she said no, so I just let her talk as I got to know her. We'd agreed how we'd split the book's revenue and discussed titles. My goal for this round of interviews was to put together a decent proposal for her agent. I needed the broad contours of the story the book would tell and later, after we had a signed contract, we'd get into the details. What I knew was that we needed to tell a compelling story about who Sacheen Littlefeather was.

Sacheen spoke first about people she claimed to know during the Alcatraz occupation days—Richard Moves Camp, Charlie Hill, Adam Fortunate Eagle, Lehman Brightman, and Thomas Banyacya. It was the Hopi elder Banyacya, she said, who gave her the name Littlefeather when she was at Alcatraz.[20] These Native people were well-known in the Bay Area's Red Power movement. Sacheen talked about becoming more in tune with her Indian identity as a result of going to Alcatraz and being involved with the Intertribal Friendship House. She said she had taught at D-Q University, an early tribal college in Northern California, where she taught classes on "Native American nutrition" and health.[21] She said she had a bachelor's degree from Antioch University in holistic health education and had attended San Jose State and Cal State Hayward. As we talked about her childhood, she spoke about her deaf father and going to live with her grandparents at eight or nine years old.[22] She did not mention her father being abusive in any way, but did say that when he died of cancer while she was a teenager her mother blamed her. She spoke at length about happy childhood memories related to plays, dance classes, and the 4-H club, which contradicted the many instances on record she said her father was an abusive alcoholic. She never disclosed to me that she had two sisters.

During her teenage years, Sacheen Littlefeather developed obsessive/compulsive behaviors and began hearing voices. At twenty or twenty-one, she said, she was admitted to Highland Hospital, where she was catatonic for three and a half weeks, and then transferred to what was then Agnews State Hospital, a psychiatric care facility in Santa

Clara, for a year. Sacheen spoke at great length about being diagnosed
with schizoaffective and bipolar disorder. She recounted not recognizing herself or her mother and experiencing a recurring dream or
hallucination of her father trying to kill her. She struggled constantly
with internal voices, and I witnessed firsthand an episode in which
she saw things in the room she knew weren't there.

Sacheen talked in depth about Marlon Brando and her friendship
with him. She said that she had stayed at his house at least six times.
The room she slept in was the same room that Brando's son Christian
shot and murdered his sister's boyfriend, Dag Droullet, in the famous
1990 case. Sacheen went on at length about films she'd been in and
famous people she'd met—Tom Laughlin ("hard to work with" on
the set of *The Trial of Billy Jack*), Andy Warhol (the "whitest man I'd
ever met"), Woody Strode (a wonderful man married to a Hawaiian
lady), Tito Puente (taught her how to salsa dance), Celia Cruz (Fidel
Castro's favorite singer, who called Sacheen "their indio"), Jack Nich-
olson (hosted a breakfast with Brando and Maria Schneider, star of
Last Tango in Paris), John Trudell (a genius), and Russell Means (like
a brother—a "cancer brother"). She pulled out piles of memorabilia
and photos, including the *Playboy* images, of which she was quite
proud (in my 2012 interview with her, she had called herself "young
and dumb" when she did the *Playboy* layout). She thought of herself
as something of a celebrity, with access to other celebrities. She explained that "fame magnifies everything and makes you a product"
and that people had treated her as a "footbridge to Brando and other
celebrities. It still happens."

What Sacheen Littlefeather never talked about in my interviews with
her was being Apache or Yaqui. Although in many other interviews
she had claimed her father was half White Mountain Apache and half
Yaqui, she had absolutely nothing to say about her father's supposed
Indian heritage. There were no stories about where her father's people
had come from, no stories from childhood about being Indian or being
connected to a reservation or tribal community, no stories about connecting with Indian family or trying to learn more about her alleged
Apache and Yaqui background. Any talk about her Native identity was
limited to being mixed-race, looking different, or being a member of

the urban Indian community. She had far more to say about her by-gone acting career, being around famous people, being Catholic, and her mental illness than anything about being a connected—or discon-nected—Apache or Yaqui, or an urban Native person.

Sacheen also gave me two hundred photocopied pages of a jour-nal she'd kept from 2011 to 2015. She had been in a writing group, something for which she had a passion, if not a talent. Writing prompts were given, so for at least some of the entries, she expressed her in-nermost thoughts in a directed way. She said that she had always loved writing. I think she wanted to be a writer but knew she didn't have the skills to write a book on her own, which might have been why she asked me to do it with her.[23] Each page of the journal was signed Sacheen Littlefeather or Sacheen Rubio Littlefeather, next to a copyright symbol. Rubio was a name she kept from the only legal marriage she'd ever had, to Michael Rubio in the early 1970s, and it remained her legal last name for the rest of her life.[24] The journal entries were likely written with the hope they would be published at some point. I believe there was also an intent to present only the pic-ture she wanted people to see. Her acting career was not memorable, but her appearance at the Academy Awards had crystalized the way people would remember her over time. The Indian woman declining Brando's Oscar was a performance that replayed itself every time the story was told, decade after decade. It became not only her public identity but her personal identity, regardless of whether she was an Apache. Sacheen Littlefeather was invested in maintaining the per-formance. There was no benefit to any serious genealogy work be-cause she knew there wasn't any actual Apache or Yaqui heritage. A lie told often enough becomes the truth.

Altogether, there were 122 entries in the journal. Much of what she wrote about was related to her health. Many entries—34 percent of the total—reflected struggles with illness, including breast cancer, mental illness, and pain, along with contemplations of death, and many others—46 percent of the total—focused on spirituality, healing, and positive thinking, which makes sense, given her health problems. She seemed to be working on maintaining an optimistic outlook, through Native American cultural practices and Catholicism. But there is also an element of it that seemed to project a rosy, self-aggrandizing view, almost as though she were writing for an audience. The tone matched a carefully crafted public persona. There were only a handful of entries about her childhood, and in general, they shared a history of abuse and violence, particularly at the hands of her father. In one story, before going to school, she had to fix her hair to cover bruises on her face after her father had beaten her and kicked her unconscious. She claimed she had been "physically and verbally abused" and "raped and sexually molested," though she doesn't say by whom. Later in the same entry, she recalled an incident where her father beat her mother, and Sacheen defended her and her mother with a broom: "Then one day when I was 9 years old, my mother got the hell beat out of her and I knew I was next. I took a broom, a big broom, much bigger than myself and I picked it up and I hit my father in the face with that broom as hard as I could—I damn near broke the broom in half. I yelled as I hit him more & more & more. I took the focus off him & off my mother and put it on me. He came at me with a vengeance. I wasn't worth a hill of beans!"

The specific descriptions of severe abuse raise serious questions. On the one hand, Sacheen had told me about recurring dreams or hallucinations about her father trying to kill her. Could the scenes she described in the journal be instances of those hallucinations, the inability to tell reality from fantasy? On the other hand, if the allegations of such violence were true, it would explain the fracturing of her psyche and the development of schizoaffective disorder, as she wrote about in the journal. Are the entries evidence that logically explain her lifelong struggle with mental illness? As time went on, I came to believe that this was not the case because the facts of Sacheen's father's life do not support the narrative, as will be explored. A July 2012 entry recalls a visit with her psychiatrist and a discussion about her diagnosis of "schizoaffective disorder NOS non-specific as related to early childhood traumatic childhood experiences." "Dr._____ and I had an in-depth conversation about that one. Had I not been so abused & traumatized as a child, I might not have a non-specific personality disorder," she wrote in a tone that sounds designed more for an audience than deeply self-reflective.[25]

With regard to the few entries about her childhood, there was one glaring contradiction. In an entry from April 2011, she wrote about her mother coming to live with her in glowing terms: "I might never experience this kind of love again . . . not everyone has a loving mother such as mine." Then, two years later, in May 2013, an entry claimed, "[M]y biological parents were both mentally ill and unable to raise me. I was taken away from by bio parents at age three suffering from tuberculosis of the lungs, child abuse and neglect. . . . It was my maternal grandparents who came to my rescue and raised me from the depths of hell and despair. I felt complete abandonment and betrayal by my mother and father which would live on to paint a distorted picture of life and relationships. There was much pain ahead for me on my journey growing up of feeling unwanted and unimportant, unloved, and that nobody cared—a deep sense of longing—a pain—a frozen need for acceptance that would never be satisfied."[26] These two wildly different accounts of Sacheen's relationship with her mother mirrored a broader pattern of contradictions over many years of her interviews and public statements.

As I reviewed the journal entries on how she wrote about being Native American, the same pattern that emerged in my interviews with her stood out—it was what she didn't say that spoke the loudest. There was no mention of any connection to family or Apache community at White Mountain or other Apache communities, no mention of genealogy or family trees with specific ancestors, and no mention of aunts, uncles, or cousins. There was very little talk of family at all, other than her mother, father, and grandparents on occasion (the ones she said "rescued" her). Two entries addressed Apache culture. One described a Sunrise ceremony that sounded perhaps like something out of a book since it didn't reference being at an actual Sunrise ceremony.[27] She wrote, "I know the blood that runs through my veins is strong in a tribal way and my people the Apache [something unintelligible in parentheses] are strong, even in the face of annihilation." Before the word *Apache* are the words *that the—that* is crossed out, replaced by the words *my people*. It is as though referring to the Apache as *my people* is an afterthought. She then wrote about praying to the sunrise because "we believe our prayers to the Creator are especially strong at the beginning of a new day."

The other entry about Apache culture was a one-and-a-half-page sort of mini-essay about the whipman, a designated discipliner of children in some Native cultures. The entry began: "A man looked at me with no face. He was a holy man. I can feel his essence although I cannot see what he looks like. It is like the whipman I thought growing up [sic]. Grandfather used to tell us stories about the faceless whipman who wore a mask as no one knew who he was. When the children did wrong they were called before the whole tribe or village and punished before everyone by the whipman with no face." It was difficult to determine the inspiration for this entry, whether it stemmed from a hallucination, some other kind of mystical or spiritual experience, or simply creatively writing. Could it have been based on a real experience of a grandfather's storytelling? It was the only entry of two hundred pages where she reflected on a specific ancestor imparting actual Native knowledge. But it felt shallow, disingenuous, and contrived. If she actually had had a grandfather who possessed this kind of cultural knowledge, why wouldn't she have written more stories about him? Why wouldn't she have talked about him in the many interviews where she was asked about her Indian ancestry?[28] Ancestors with these kinds of stories are highly revered in Native families, treasured and frequently spoken of. And the entry didn't say whether it was her alleged Apache (or Yaqui) grandfather; if her father was half Apache and half Yaqui as she claimed, her grandfather would had to have been Apache or Yaqui. In fact, nowhere in the journal was there any mention of Yaqui ancestry.

There were numerous Native American cultural references in Littlefeather's journal, and she often used, as she can often be heard saying in interviews, the phrase *Native American Indian*. It's an odd, redundant phrase not commonly used by Native people, more something outsiders would say. Most Native people of her generation tend to use the simple term *Indian* because that's what they grew up being called and how they referred to each other. The awkward terminology, like some other large and small things about Sacheen's journal and our conversations, never sat right. It felt off, like her other Native

American references, which sounded like what you might have heard in urban pan-Indian communities. I lived in the north Bay Area of Sonoma County for almost twenty years, starting in the 1980s, when the New Age movement was exploding. It was a time when the appropriation of Native American spirituality and the rise of Indian wannabes—more commonly called *pretendians* today—were everywhere. There were clear patterns; wannabes would embrace a narrow view of Indianness, one loaded with stereotypes and focused only on culture, spirituality, and aesthetics. It's a type of spirituality that is Lakota-centric and closely tied to the Native American Church, also known as the peyote religion or tradition. There is a lingo laced with terms like the Great Spirit, the ancestors, *mitakuye oyasin*, *Wakan Tanka*, *inipi*, and *aho*. They know—or want to know—about sweat lodges, vision quests, pipe ceremonies, Sun Dances, and drum circles. Powwows are primary gathering places, as are backyard sweat lodges. They don't know or seem to care about tribal sovereignty or political issues, and their only connections to nonurban tribal communities are summer trips to Sun Dances on reservations open to non-Indians. If they get involved with political issues at all, it's usually through AIM (American Indian Movement), which exists as a shadow of its former self. Living in the North Bay, I saw wannabeism up close and personal for a long time. Too close for comfort in hindsight. I recognized all the signs in Sacheen Littlefeather's journal, peppered with vague references to the Great Spirit, the ancestors, Native American "wisdom" and ceremonies, with Lakota words sprinkled in, which she didn't even get right (she uses the word *Takoshala* for, I think, *tunkashila*, the Lakota word for "grandfather"). In retrospect, these red flags kept popping up for me as I got to know Sacheen through meeting her and reading her journal. It was the beginning of seeing Sacheen Littlefeather's con for what it was.

THE CON REVEALED

After the weekend that Sacheen and I spent working together, she went MIA. I needed to communicate with her about our book proposal, but she mysteriously stopped responding to my emails and phone calls. Finally, after a few weeks of silence, she called and in a very short conversation told me she had "decided to go in a different direction." That was it. No indication of what that different direction was—Did she want a different writer? Or to nix the book idea completely? Or something else? No "I'm sorry, but thank you for your time." No explanation whatsoever. After the time, effort, and expense I'd invested, I felt I deserved at least an explanation. But all I got was a five-minute phone call. I never heard from her again. She had treated me with complete disregard and gracelessness. Still, I had the copy of her journal, and curiously, she never asked for it back.

I was confused about what had happened. I wondered if she didn't like me or the way I wanted to write the book. We were very different people, after all, and I think she probably could see by then that the way I work and write demands an unvarnished, brutal honesty. My gut told me she saw that writing a book, at least with me, would've meant too many details she wouldn't have been able to provide. It was a process of having to be accountable, and I had begun to feel she had something to hide. At first, I thought it might have been about her mental illness, but in time, I realized she hadn't shied away from talking about that side of herself publicly. The only thing left to hide seemed to be her ethnicity. I decided to wait it out to see what would happen, especially if a book would eventually surface.

No book was released, but in 2018, I got word of a documentary film from One Bowl Productions—*Sacheen: Breaking the Silence*. One Bowl Productions has produced a small handful of Native films; its organizational leadership includes prominent and respected Haudenosaunee figures like Oren Lyons and his son, Rex Lyons. By then, I was convinced that Sacheen was not actually Indian at all, and that was what she was hiding. I started seeing her in a different, more critical light. I'd also become aware of a role she played in the 1975 film *Johnny Firecloud*, a cheap, badly done rip-off of the *Billy Jack* films. In the film, she plays a Native American schoolteacher, and there is a scene in which she is brutally gang-raped in her classroom by white cowboys. The scene is so graphic that it was still circulating on porn sites in 2018, and that may still be the case today. Why would a "proud Native American Indian woman" committed to positive and empowering portrayals of Native Americans agree to acting in such a degrading and violent scene? That only added to the questions about why she thought posing for *Playboy* was a good idea. By 2018, American Indian women had risen to prominent leadership roles in every aspect of Native and American life, including tribal and nontribal governments, activist circles, and popular culture. But the problem of missing and murdered Indigenous women, also known as MMIW, and violence against Native women was at crisis levels in the US. I wondered if the makers of the Littlefeather documentary were aware of the rape scene? They must've known about the *Playboy* layout because it was no secret. Sacheen Littlefeather had played an interesting role at an interesting time in history—and became a symbol for the rejecting of stereotypes in film and TV— but what had she actually accomplished in Indian country? What was her list of achievements with lasting impact that went beyond self-aggrandizing narratives? Were the filmmakers going to overlook the ways she contributed to the sexualization of Native women in film? Weren't there inherent contradictions in Littlefeather's rhetoric about the need for positive representations of Native people and the ways she herself perpetuated the opposite? Were the filmmakers going to ask the tough questions about Littlefeather's career and, more importantly, her identity?

I was communicating through social media with one of the film's producers, a California Indian academic who I thought would take my concerns seriously. She didn't. I decided to write to the film's executive producer, Gayle Kelley, to express my concerns about Sacheen's role in media sexual fetishization of Native women and her identity at a time when tribal sovereignty was under attack based on racialized Native identities. I had to be careful with how I worded the letter; I was aware of how taboo it was to question Littlefeather's identity. Although my instincts told me she was a fraud, I had no concrete proof. I simply said I was in possession of information about controversial aspects of her history that would bring troubling issues to light and offered to consult with them. My letter went unanswered.

The film was released and, sure enough, nothing new of substance was covered. It was twenty-six minutes of rehashing the same tired

Academy Awards story told countless times, the same nonsensical claims about Littlefeather's career being ruined from being blacklisted in Hollywood, and the same inflated fantasy of being a "Native American Indian" and suffering as a result—all in addition to the egregious factual errors I've already pointed out, among others.[29] It appeared that not one question was asked about her Native American heritage; there was no new information offered, just the usual nebulous claim to being "Native American Indian." Three years later, however, all hell would break loose.

LIES AND DAMN LIES: PEOPLE COME FORWARD AND THE CONTROVERSY ERUPTS

Sacheen Littlefeather's life came to an end only fifteen days after the academy held their official apology ceremony on September 17, 2022. The ceremony canonized Sacheen Littlefeather into the annals of history, granting her near sainthood status in Indian country. In the audience that night, watching all the dancing and drumming, listening to all the speeches, and seeing all the tears of joy as well as Littlefeather herself reveling in the glory, I knew it was all smoke and mirrors. I also had reason to believe that even those who helped orchestrate the event knew she was a phony, the academy's so-called Indigenous Alliance, run by Bird Runningwater and Heather Rae, whom we'll turn to later in chapter 3.

Three weeks after Sacheen Littlefeather died, an opinion column by Jacqueline Keeler claiming Littlefeather had no Native heritage was published in the *San Francisco Chronicle*. I knew Keeler had done extensive research by September 2022 before Littlefeather died because I'd acquired her report.[30] The report included genealogical profiles from census records, voting registration records, military records, obituaries, school records, and marriage and baptismal records for many of the Cruz family's relatives and ancestors, tracing their roots back to the 1850s in Mexico, where they had migrated from. As Keeler noted in the *Chronicle* piece, none of Littlefeather's ancestors had any documented ties to Apache or Yaqui communities in the US or Mexico. On all the documents Keeler had gathered, they identified as either white, Caucasian, or Mexican—never Indian. Another part of the report showed a timeline of news stories about Littlefeather's claims to being White Mountain Apache. It was obvious that a lot of work had gone into the report, and I was grateful for it because it confirmed my suspicions. The research was thorough, and I acknowledged it in my article for *The Conversation*, an academically inclined journalistic news and analysis site.[31] Jackie Keeler had told me in a phone conversation after she submitted the piece that the research was being heavily vetted by her editor, adding a layer of accountability to the work. But the linchpin of the *Chronicle* article was the testimony from Sacheen's sisters, Trudy Orlandi and Rozalind Cruz. Regarding Sacheen's claim to being Apache on the night of the Oscars, Trudy said, "It's a lie. My father was who he was. His family came from Mexico. And my dad was born in Oxnard." Rozalind said, "It is a fraud. It's disgusting to the heritage of the tribal people. And it's just . . . insulting to my parents." Both were adamant that Sacheen had not only depicted their family inaccurately but slandered them. Their father was not a violent alcoholic—or Indian, as Sacheen had claimed countless times, and their main interest was restoring honor to both of their parents.

I communicated with both Trudy and Roz many times via telephone, email, text message, and Twitter private messages. I copied Sacheen's journal and sent it to both of them. Sacheen had no children; Roz and Trudy were her only remaining kin. Their stories were always consistent. Roz in particular was vocal in her mission to set the record straight.[32] These were some of the most important points the sisters wanted to clarify:

> *Their father was not abusive:* Sacheen's story about their deaf father being abusive was actually describing their father's father, who "was an alcoholic who beat him . . . he [their father] never drank, he never abused us, he wasn't violent," Roz explained in a December 2022 interview on *Latino Slant*. Their maternal grandparents lived in a house on the same property, and when Sacheen said that her grandparents "rescued" her and she went to live with them, it was right next door, a hundred feet away. Roz also debunked the claim Sacheen made at least once, in a 1974

interview, that she was raised in a "shack" in Salinas. Photos show the house was a middle-class sort of dwelling, not a shack.

Their sister didn't grow up with the name Sacheen Littlefeather: The sisters claimed in the *Chronicle* interview that their nickname for their sister Marie was Deb, and that the name Sacheen probably was inspired by the Sasheen Ribbon Company whose products they used in their 4-H Club sewing projects. They reject as pure fantasy the story about their father calling their sister Littlefeather because she danced around with a feather in her hair.

There is no verifiable White Mountain Apache, Yaqui, or other Native American heritage in the family: There were never any family stories about being Native American, and definitely not Apache or Yaqui. Believing her sister knew something she didn't, Roz filed an application for enrollment with the White Mountain Apache; she was rejected because they had no familial connection to the tribe. The application was denied in a phone call with their enrollment office in February 2022, and in her December 2022 interview on *Latino Slant*, Roz said she had not yet received a formal denial letter. Speculating on why Sacheen might take on an Indian identity, Roz said that Sacheen hated their father and hated being Mexican. In a *New York Post* interview, Roz shared when Sacheen took the stage that night to decline the Oscar for Marlon Brando, the family was watching it on TV, and they were "mortified . . . my grandparents and I were blown away. I will never forget how we just stared at each other absolutely awestruck."

Jackie Keeler's article—and the sisters stating in no uncertain terms that their family was not Native was sacrilege to those who believed in Sacheen Littlefeather as a Native American heroine and role model—set Native social media ablaze. It was simply unacceptable to question whether Littlefeather was who she claimed to be for a half century. It was deeply triggering for many people, especially those with ambiguous or tenuous identity claims, or those who felt insecure about their Native identities. They brought up all the reasons why they couldn't be enrolled in their tribes, which inevitably led to conversations about blood quantum. Even for enrolled tribal members, it stirred insecurities about not being perceived as Native enough, based on how they looked or how others treated them. They defaulted to arguments about Native identity being complex, or framed it as a racial issue, or blamed colonialism. These are all real issues, but for many, there was a refusal to simply take the sister's word that she had applied for enrollment as a White Mountain Apache and been denied. Many arguments seemed to hinge on the logic that because Sacheen Littlefeather had done so much good in Indian country, her identity shouldn't matter. One author writing in the Hollywood entertainment paper *Variety*, for example wrote, "I don't presume to know about her tribal connections. What I do know is that she has been a strong voice in the Native community and that she has created space for other Natives to feel empowered in their Indigeneity."[33] Evidently, even if her "strong voice" was based on a complete fabrication, it didn't seem to matter.

People refused to believe that Littlefeather could have been lying for all those years; there was a rush to dismiss the idea and exempt her from any wrongdoing. They criticized and dismissed the sisters for being alt-right Trump supporters or for having a family-based grudge; Roz was accused of "crashing" her sister's funeral, where she stood at the podium and shared stories about her sister being mentally ill and lying about their family and who she was. Jackie Keeler was taken to task for her *Alleged Pretendians List,* created in early 2021. In one of the more ridiculous rebuttals, Daniel Voshart in a self-published *Medium* piece claimed that before their conversations with Keeler, the sisters did believe that they were Apache and Yaqui but that she somehow had convinced them that they weren't.[34]

Sacheen's sisters, Jackie Keeler, and I weren't the only people to come forward with stories doubting or debunking Sacheen's identity claims. I'd heard about a woman named Helene Hagan, a close friend of Sacheen's for over thirty years, who was going to go public with her own knowledge. Hagan had written a letter to the Academy Museum of Motion Pictures, dated December 19, 2022, detailing her long history with Sacheen. She sent the letter on December 30 to eighteen people, including high-profile journalists at mainstream news outlets like the *New York Times*, the BBC, and the *Hollywood Reporter*, as well as the conservative and former Fox-affiliated Megyn Kelly, me, and other lesser known Native and non-Native sources. Hagan describes herself in the letter as "a historian and a cultural and psychological anthropologist specializing in Ritual and Mind, with diplomas from Bordeaux (France) and Stanford Universities, and as President of The Tazzla Institute for Cultural Diversity, Inc. since 1993, with a solid career as a scholar and a defender of indigenous human rights for decades." The letter implored museum officials to not "confuse schizophrenic delusions with history." In nine single-spaced pages, the letter made some new explosive revelations.

Through the years, Hagan had witnessed a life of Sacheen's creation that did not reflect reality. She believed Sacheen's delusional narrative of being an abused Native American child began after her institutionalization at Agnews State Hospital. In interviews and in conversation with me, Sacheen had described undergoing a treatment called psychodrama, which she credited with helping her tremendously. Psychodrama, a form of recovered memory therapy, has been scrutinized for years because of its potential to create false memories, which can lead to people being wrongly accused of crimes, especially childhood sexual abuse by family members. Hagan characterized it as a "carefully crafted tale of her life story, constructing a false identity and claiming a false ancestry." If Sacheen's delusional identity can be traced to psychodrama therapy, it makes sense that she would invent details to fit that narrative. Hagan lists numerous examples of "miscellaneous internet and Academy Museum misinformation," including how people lied to cover for Sacheen Littlefeather. The most significant of those inventions follow here:

Claims by Russell Means about the Academy Awards being watched in the Wounded Knee compound: Helene Hagan recounts she had served on the Dennis Banks Defense Committee and was a consultant to both the American Indian Movement (AIM) and the International Indian Treaty Council. Russell Means had been a close friend since 1982, and she'd attended many AIM meetings in South Dakota and the Bay Area over the years. Hagan pointed out that Sacheen hadn't been present at these meetings and noted that neither Russell Means nor Dennis Banks had ever mentioned Sacheen or any role she may have had in AIM, nor was she mentioned in either of their autobiographies.[35] In the 2009 documentary *Reel Injun* by Cree filmmaker Neil Diamond, Means tells a story about Wounded Knee occupiers having their morale lifted by watching the Academy Awards. The story was first told in a television program conceived and produced by Hagan in 1999 after Means and Sacheen Littlefeather were brought face-to-face for an interview. The story, now being retold, must be maintained. In *Reel Injun*, Means says, "When we were inside Wounded Knee, they're shooting at us every day and night, and there's quite a few people inside in the trading post watching the Academy Awards. All of a sudden we get a call. They start yelling 'Hey, there's an Indian!' And so I rushed in there and saw Sacheen Littlefeather just get to the microphone and she starts making this speech. We don't believe we're going to get out of there alive, and the morale is down low and Marlon Brando and Sacheen Littlefeather totally uplifted our lives."

Hagan noted in her letter that, according to his autobiography and audio archives that kept a running daily sequence of events at Wounded Knee, Means couldn't have been watching the Academy Awards in the compound that night because he wasn't even there. "Both Dennis Banks and Russell Means surreptitiously left the WK compound on Monday night March 26 and traveled along a northern route to adjoining Rosebud reservation, reaching Crow Dog's Paradise where they met family and friends. They returned to Wounded Knee during the March 27th night. Neither of them could have been watching an evening television program in a compound which had its electricity previously cut off by the FBI," Hagan's letter stated.[36]

Claims that Littlefeather's career suffered after the Oscars: Hagan pointed out that Littlefeather's career, in fact, picked up after the Academy Awards as she had few film credits to her name before that. A quick review of her filmography confirms this. Hagan also addressed Littlefeather's claims that she had been targeted by the FBI; she consulted public records that have long since been available in both the FBI online vault and an archive at University of California, Davis, called Native American Activists of the '70s–'80s. In neither source is there a file on Sacheen Littlefeather.

Claims about her marriage to Charles Koshiway: Hagan knew that Sacheen had never been married to Charles Koshiway. She also brought up the very troubling fact that Koshiway was a registered sex offender in California. This is a matter of verifiable public record, and I obtained a copy of the legal document confirming his status.

Helene Hagan's letter seeks to set the record straight on numerous other claims that Sacheen Littlefeather made over the years, including that she had received a bachelor's degree in holistic health and nutrition. Sacheen told me during our interview that she earned her degree from Antioch University. Hagan attempted to verify this claim, and the public release of her letter included a response from the Antioch University registrar's office. The letter, dated December 14, 2022, confirmed that Sacheen Littlefeather Rubio had been a student in 1980–81 but had not completed a degree. In a private communication with me, Hagan shared that Sacheen had constructed a fantasy world where she imagined herself as a medicine woman/healer.[37] She also shared that Sacheen had contacted One Bowl Productions about the documentary project, which made it clear to me that Sacheen had abandoned the book project in favor of a film project. Hagan said that she, too, tried to stop them from making the film. She alleged that One Bowl Productions had used footage from the 1999 television show she created with Sacheen and Russell Means without permission, resulting in legal action for copyright infringement and, ultimately, the end of her thirty-year friendship with Sacheen.[38]

\\\\\\\\\\\\\\\\\\\\\\\\

My experience with Sacheen Littlefeather became a journey into a deeper, much more difficult conversation about what it truly means to be American Indian. Even though I did not know Sacheen well, her presence in my life put me in a position I could never have anticipated. It wasn't a story I sought out; she came to me, and whether intentionally or not, left me with her journal and the choice of whether or not to share it. Because Sacheen Littlefeather has become such a beloved cultural icon—not just for Native Americans but anyone who cares about diversity in the film industry—this puts me in an unenviable position. For years, I wondered why she drew me in to write an autobiography with her, only to suddenly change her mind without so much as a conversation or an apology. I have since learned she treated many others with the same disregard, including people she had long friendships with, such as Helene Hagan.

Let us briefly outline a narrative timeline of Sacheen's Indian "identity" based on verifiable facts, many of which we have already established through various documented sources, her sisters' testimony, and some of Sacheen's own, often contradictory accounts. Marie Louise Cruz was born into a hardworking, middle-class Mexican American family in Salinas, California. She was raised in a small extended family, with loving grandparents and parents who had their own challenges but seemed to care deeply for each other and their children. The ethnically mixed family had no connections to any Native American community or heritage, nor did they have any family stories about Native ancestry.[39] According to her sisters, Sacheen saw her first Indian reservation at seventeen when the family took a road trip through the Southwest on vacation. Within a couple of years, by 1969, she began a modeling career, working with Salinas photographer Ken Cook of Cook's Photography. On March 28, 1973, the day after the Oscars, Cook was quoted in the *Salinas Californian*: "She wanted to capitalize on the Indian thing; she's a big phony." The newspaper article featured one of Cook's headshots of her in a bare-shouldered, sexually suggestive pose wearing a beaded Indian headband. Around this time, she experienced a psychotic break, attempted suicide, and entered a mental health facility, where she underwent psychodrama therapy. She emerged a year later with a story about being a Native

American child of a full-blood Indian father, a violent alcoholic who abused her mentally, physically, emotionally, and sexually. She was diagnosed with schizophrenia.

By 1970, shortly after being released from the hospital, Sacheen became a student at San Jose State University and got involved with Native American activism during the Alcatraz occupation. She may or may not have been one of the occupiers, but this was when she fully immersed herself in the Bay Area urban Indian scene. She was spending time around Indians from reservations who had come to the city on relocation, rebuilding Native community in their newly adopted homes. She frequented the San Francisco American Indian Center and attended powwows. But there were also burgeoning numbers of people like her who were latching onto Indians in search of new lifestyles and new identities; some were hippies, but many were people, like Sacheen, reimaging themselves as Indians for a variety of reasons, mainly because, for the first time in American history, Indians were beginning to be seen in a more positive light. She learned the lingo, culture, and aesthetics of a growing pan-Indianism. Marie Cruz completed her transformation into Sacheen Littlefeather during the year-and-a-half Alcatraz occupation, after her institutionalization. Powwows had become a way of life, and she joined committees and groups to exercise her newfound urban Indian identity. Her father passed away in 1966, at the age of forty-four from cancer, after many years of illness. He never lived to see his daughter adopt a delusional identity, one built on lies about him.[40]

Meanwhile, Sacheen continued to try to break into the Hollywood film industry, landing small modeling gigs, a minor role as a prostitute in an Italian film, and other activities to boost her visibility. While the Alcatraz occupation was still ongoing, in the fall of 1970, she won the Miss American Vampire contest for a role in the horror film *House of Dark Shadows*. She never accepted the part, but was now known by her new stage name, Sacheen Littlefeather.[41] By 1971, she was publicly being referred to as White Mountain Apache.[42] In 1972, she participated in a photo shoot called "10 Little Indians" for *Playboy* magazine, which was initially canceled but was later published as a solo layout shortly after her Oscars appearance. The Academy

Awards incident took place in March 1973, and contrary to her claims of being blacklisted, her career actually saw a temporary boost, with small roles in several American films, the last of which was in 1978. By the late 1970s, her acting career was essentially over, but she has solidified her place in history as Sacheen Littlefeather, the Apache woman who rejected Marlon Brando's Oscar. While her Academy Awards message emphatically scorned Hollywood's stereotypical portrayal of American Indians, ironically, her public persona as a model and actress was built on perpetuating harmful, stereotypical images of Native people. Worst of all, it was based on the misrepresentation of herself as an American Indian.[43] In other words, it stands as one of the biggest hoaxes in both Indian country and Hollywood history. The careful, calculated construction of an ambiguous, racialized, urban Indian identity—built on self-identification—laid the groundwork for the myth of Sacheen Littlefeather.

Littlefeather managed to deceive two generations of people in the US and beyond, even with mountains of evidence of fraud laid out in the open, year after year. People desperately clung to their image of Sacheen as the great American Indian rights champion and collectively ignored all evidence to the contrary. The thing about a good con, though, is that it works because there's just enough truth mixed in with the deception to make the story believable.

By 2022, the Academy of Motion Picture Arts and Sciences was deeply invested in the Sacheen Littlefeather mythology, with its formal apology and the museum's permanent exhibit of the Oscars incident. After Sacheen's death and the release of the *San Francisco Chronicle*'s article, the museum and the academy had more than a little mud on their faces—it was more like a mudslide. Their response was barely a whimper, a feeble attempt to cover their tracks. Their out? The museum released a statement saying, "Native American and Indigenous identity is deeply complex and layered, especially in the United States, and these communities have long battled erasure and misrepresentation. With the support of its Indigenous Alliance—an Academy member affinity group—the Academy recognizes self-identification."[44] But wait, wasn't self-identification exactly what got us into this mess? We'll return to this question in chapter 3.

CHAPTER TWO

INDIGENEITY, NATIONHOOD, RACIALIZATION, AND THE SETTLER STATE

*Why Political Status Matters
to Native "Identity" Formation*

SACHEEN LITTLEFEATHER'S DECEPTIVE identity claims hinged on certain "commonsense" presumptions Americans (and others) hold about who Native Americans are and what Native American identity is. The foundational assumption is the most superficial—appearance. You can tell who an Indian is by looking at them. Sacheen instinctively knew this and played to it. Sacheen Littlefeather, a Mexican American, presented as nonwhite or racially mixed. Her physical appearance easily conformed to a popular stereotype of what American Indians are supposed to look like, especially when she dressed to convey a conventional image of Native Americans as buckskin-wearing Plains Indians. She continued to build on her staged identity for the next five decades by adopting other convincing but superficial markers of Native identity—a shared lingo within the context of urban pan-Indian culture and participation in cultural activities. These elements of presumed Native Americanness rest on the idea that Native American is primarily a racial, ethnic, and purely cultural category, like being Mexican American, African American, or Italian American. The terms *Native American* and *American Indian* are themselves broad generalizations that mask a vast diversity among the hundreds of tribal groups across the United States, leading to the common misperception that Native Americans are one monolithic, homogenous cultural group. While there are shared cultural traits, they are not ethnically or culturally homogenous beyond a surface level.

Seeing Native Americans predominantly as a racialized cultural classification of Americans is an incomplete and inaccurate way of understanding who they are. It's not that American Indians did not look physically different from European settlers; they clearly did, which is one reason why both groups felt the need to classify each other in ways that made sense. However, the differences between Indians and settlers, especially in the early centuries of European arrival, were rooted more in their relationships to the land and in Indians as distinct peoples. Who they were as tribal peoples was inseparable from the land. They were the living, human expressions of their very environments, mirrored in language and spiritual practices. The most obvious distinction from the European perspective was cultural: Indigenous people were not Christians. This difference was used to justify Europeans' violent domination. It remains woven into the legal fabric of the United States, shaping to this day the relationships between American Indians and the settler capitalist state.

Over time, however, American Indian difference became embedded in US legal and social structures in racialized terms, becoming one of numerous mechanisms orchestrating and rationalizing their elimination. However, racialization obscures the fact that the American Indian relationship to the US is at its foundation political—a relationship that came to be coded as nation-to-nation—and individual American Indian "identity" is an extension of it. At the same time, there are countless ways individual American Indians have been cut off from that relationship, and other ways the political ties between individual Indians to tribal nations and the US is ambiguous and incomplete.

AMERICAN INDIAN NATIONHOOD

To fully understand American Indian tribes' national and political status, a geopolitical lens is necessary to examine how their nationhood exists on the historical continuum of the pre- and swiftly changing post-Colombian world. Prior to the disruptive arrival of Europeans, American Indians had been living finely attuned to nature, and within the dictates of ecosystems that ensured their longevity. The term *hunter-gatherers* is a misnomer, depicting Native peoples as primitive societies devoid of complex systems of governance and flattening the vast diversity of lifestyles, often agricultural. Even in migratory (as opposed to nomadic) societies, migration usually occurred within highly defined territories determined by seasonal food acquisition, or seasonal rounds.[1] These often highly managed landscapes and land-use patterns led to the evolution of cultural worldviews and people's conceptions of themselves in relation to those particular places and ecosystems.[2] Their eco-inspired worldviews in turn coalesced sophisticated systems of self-governance and political practice that regulated norms of appropriate social behavior, which includes diplomacy within a tribal national culture.[3] For millennia, Indigenous nations managed relationships with neighbors and occasional interlopers, defined not just by conflict but also by cooperation. The best example is the Six Nations of the Haudenosaunee, or the Iroquois Confederacy. Much has been written about Iroquois political theory and the Great Law of Peace,[4] said to have been created in the twelfth century,[5] but it is not the only example of American Indian diplomatic strategy and political thinking. Vine Deloria Jr. and Clifford M. Lytle in 1983 wrote about several precolonial forms of tribal governments, comparing them to today's tribal governments,[6] and similar treatments can be found throughout American Indian studies literature.

In 1648, while the English and the Spanish made their earliest colonizing voyages to the North American continent and tensions between settlers and Indians in New England, Jamestown, and the Southwest were rising, Europeans were settling generations-long wars over religion, territory, and domination. The Thirty Years' War between Catholic and Protestant monarchical estates within the Holy Roman Empire concluded with the Treaty of Westphalia in Germany, which also addressed to a lesser extent the Eighty Years' War between the Netherlands and Spain,[7] giving birth to the Westphalian state system.[8] The formation of the United States and its Constitution in 1789 occurs just 141 years into the modern state system, with the European Westphalian system conferring the "stamp of legitimacy" on the fledgling US state.[9] The concept of territorial sovereignty, which came to define the modern state, descended from European monarchies; it was the context for how Europeans and later Americans came to deal with the Indigenous nations of what came to be the United States.[10]

When Europeans arrived on the continent seeking religious freedom and economic opportunity, they also brought with them all their histories of conflict, war, and the penchant to dominate others based on Christendom's hierarchical social structures. What became the United States was formed from these modes of historical thinking and being, animated by greed and violence. Indigenous nations then became the targets of Europeans' greed and sense of entitlement to the land, violently superimposing the new state on top of ancient preexisting communities. This process of settler colonialism was repeated all over the western hemisphere, Oceania, and Europe. As Rudolph Rÿser writes, "Nations that would have been free in their own right found themselves under the control of rulers who exercised the central power of a state. Peeking out from beneath the superimposed states' smothering political dominance were thousands of bedrock nations that sought to exercise their right to self-determination and self-government."[11] Settler colonialism as a process thus crystalized into a structure as Patrick Wolfe contends, always with the goal of eliminating the Native population to acquire their territory.[12] This "logic of elimination" means settlers seek to replace original nations and peoples, a process that becomes embedded in all aspects of the settler state psychologically, socially, politically, discursively, and legally. It is an impulse that forces Indigenous people into a position of continual resistance, always fighting for the survival of their rights to exist as collectivities and as individuals.

There was, however, the inconvenient matter of the hundreds of treaties the Europeans and later their American counterparts signed with tribal nations. Treaty-making was one way for Europeans to gain a foothold in the continent early on; they purchased Indian lands and maintained peace.[13] It "brought an air of civility and legitimacy to the white settlers' relations with Indians,"[14] as Deloria and Lytle write, and while they acknowledge that treaty-making was often not an equitable process, it was nonetheless the international practice of state- and nation-craft that established the political relations and mutual sovereignty between European colonists and later the Americans. By 1823, the US began its unilateral, systematic, and unjust erosion of tribal sovereignty with the *Johnson v. McIntosh* decision. The case embedded the doctrine of discovery into the US legal system as the new foundation for US and Indian relations, confining tribes to the will of the US state without their consent. Federal Indian law scholar Robert Miller summarizes the doctrine of discovery: "In a nutshell, the Supreme Court said that, under Discovery, when European, Christian nations discovered new lands, the discovering country automatically gained sovereign property rights in the lands of non-Christian, non-European peoples, even though, obviously, the native peoples already owned, occupied, and used these lands."[15] Miller goes on to argue that the doctrine of discovery morphed into the ideology of Manifest Destiny, which divinely ordained the US to "overspread and to possess the whole of the continent;"[16] full-spectrum territorial domination was always the aim, and Indians were in the way.[17] Still, despite federal law's continual hegemonic attacks on tribal sovereignty, tribal nationhood, however diminished, is an unavoidable reality for the United States.

PRODUCING NATIVE DISAPPEARANCE AND US POLICY

By the latter part of the nineteenth century, the US achieved military dominance over tribal nations, solidifying the settler colonial project to remake the North American continent in the image of Anglo Christian Europe. With Native nations confined to reservations or otherwise out of the way,[18] traditional forms of governance severely disrupted, and populations at record lows, the US's policy approach toward Native people—what Rÿser terms Fourth World nations[19]— could now focus on forcible assimilation into the settler state. The plan for absorption was to be accomplished through numerous social and institutional mechanisms legislated through the General Allotment Act of 1887, also known as the Dawes Act. The law created a network of boarding and day schools, often in partnership with churches, and sought the breaking up of tribal reservation landholdings into individually assigned parcels called allotments. Boarding schools would ensure children's conversion to Christianity, the erasure of their Indigenous languages through enforced English, and indoctrination into capitalism's wage labor system. Allotment would teach the values of personal ownership and selfishness, a social norm Indian agents and legislators noted with angst was missing from tribal communities.[20] The indisputable objective of the Dawes Act was the destruction of tribal cultures through the breakup of families.

As Indians adapted to colonized life during the turn of the century, Americans began to lament the perceived disappearance of a group they had both reviled and romanticized. Narratives of Indian disappearance penetrated popular culture as the manifestation of the settler state's logic of elimination, a kind of self-fulfilling prophecy. The vanishing Indian trope, long present in popular literature like James Fenimore Cooper's 1826 *Last of the Mohicans* and the other *Leatherstocking Tales,* was explicitly articulated in federal policy in this era with Jacksonian removal and the ensuing Trail of Tears. Many more removals followed throughout the nineteenth century across the continent. The idea of Indian disappearance was prevalent in art as well, where the theme adorned the walls of the White House and other state buildings.[21] The vanishing Indian was a predominant topic in the earliest moving pictures such as *The Red Man and the Child* (1908), D. W. Griffith's first western *The Indian Runner's Romance* (1909), and *The Red Man's View* (1909).[22] For Americans, the question was implicit: if Indians—always conceived of in the American imagination as the horse-riding, buffalo-hunting Plains Indian—could no longer live free on the land, wearing buckskins and living in tipis, how could they be "real" Indians?

The tragic half-breed was a facet of the vanishing Indian mythology as well. As a stereotype, the half-breed was seen as tragic not only because he was no longer living a traditional Native life, but because he was now also racially impure. True Indians were expected to be racially pure, untouched by white or other kinds of "blood," conforming to preconceived ideas of what Indians were supposed to look like. The half-breed fit neither the white nor the Indian world as he could not meet the expectations of either society. By the turn of the century, American perceptions about Indians were largely based on the idea of Native people as a race rather than as the distinct nations that the early Europeans encountered and interacted with.[23] American Indian people were treated as racially inferior, thus justifying the ongoing oppressive US social policies aimed at assimilation. If sustained, assimilation as policy would guarantee the elimination of both Indian individuals and tribes as nations.

BLOOD QUANTUM AND THE STATE

Ideas about blood purity and racial mixing have been present in US governance structures since the pre-US colonial era. At least as early as 1705, for instance, a statute in Virginia defined "mulatto" as "the child of an Indian and child, grandchild or great grandchild of a negro" and barred them and others from holding public office.[24] The Virginia statute is an early example of blood quantum, where an individual's ethnicities are parsed into fractions. Scholars often point to this moment in history as the origin of the concept of blood quantum in the US. Blood quantum (BQ) is the fictitious measuring of Indianness based on equating biological material with identity and culture. In theory, the more Indian biological material ("blood") one has, the more culture and identity one is presumed to have—and the less Indian biological material, the less culture and identity. Greater intermarriage outside American Indian lineage or particular tribal groups, at some point, results in a fraction too low to be considered American Indian, depending on institution or even personal opinion. In function, it is a measure of authenticity, determined by institutions and personal perceptions alike. The process, fundamentally subtractive and exclusionary, ignores culture and belonging as dependent on family and community ties, and as such, divides families. Within families it is common for some members who share the same lineage to be recognized as legitimate Indians, while others are not. This is the case in my family, where my mother is an enrolled tribal member, but her children are not. BQ as a sole determinant presumes Indianness is strictly a matter of race. As a concept, race and dividing communities based on racial mixing was foreign to Indian people before Europeans and their American successors introduced it to define Native Americans.

Blood quantum gradually became a central precept for the federal government to deal with American Indian people. It was a way to both limit the number of people the government was responsible to and ultimately phase out its "Indian problem." The infiltration of BQ into federal tribal policy is often assumed to have begun during the Dawes years, but the approach has precedence. As we have seen, anxiety about race mixing is evident in the colonies by 1705, but race mixing between Black and white people was prohibited at least as early as the 1630s.[25] While early anti-miscegenation laws applied to Blacks and Indians, in time, their intent was directed more at policing the boundaries between Black and white populations, as Indian intermarriage with Anglos became viewed as a desirable way to absorb and, therefore, disappear Indians into the (white) American populace.

Establishing clear definitions about who was Indian was also a way to count people and appropriate resources in meeting the US' treaty-based legal obligations. Documenting the history of blood quantum in federal Indian policy, legal historian Paul Spruhan notes that the language of BQ appeared "before the extension of federal authority over tribal territory and was not created for it."[26] The language of blood quantum entered some treaties in the early 1800s to determine allocation of specific property or benefits but not to determine tribal membership, setting as Spruhan contends, an important pattern for later federal uses of blood quantum. In the allotment era, Congress ramped up its practice of defining Indian status based on blood. To determine who was eligible for allotments both full- and mixed-bloods were included, dependent upon tribal membership, a concept not yet fully formalized in most tribes. Enrollment councils were held between tribal leaders and allotment agents to determine membership for deciding who got status,[27] but blood was eventually linked to the right to sell an allotment based on "competency" via the Burke Act of 1906. In 1903, the Supreme Court had affirmed Congress's complete control over Indian affairs with the *Lonewolf* case—later known as the plenary power doctrine—and Indians had long been viewed as wards of the government.[28] The Dawes Act barred allottees from selling their land for a twenty-five-year period. After twenty-five years, an Indian was assumed to be competent to handle their own affairs, and a fee patent was issued making the land fully alienable. The Burke Act accelerated the fee patenting process; in 1913, competency commissions were established, and in 1917, a new rule allowed competency commissions to determine competency based solely on an individual's amount of white heritage. Those more than one-half white were free from the twenty-five-year restriction placed on the allotments of those with more than half Indian blood, prohibiting the land's alienability.[29] Allotments were lost to sales due to poverty, but land was also lost to fraudulent land sales and tax and other liens.[30] By 1934, with the passage of the Indian Reorganization Act (IRA), which rejected assimilation in favor of returning some governing power to tribes, the term *Indian* was clearly defined as members of federally recognized tribes, all descendants of tribal members living on a reservation, and people with half or more Indian blood.

In his historical examination of blood quantum, Spruhan maintains that the US handled Indian affairs based originally on Indians as political entities (citizens of autonomous nations) but increasingly throughout the nineteenth century and into the twentieth as "biological wards" (in other words, wards of the state who were racialized). Yet despite Congress's growing tendency to racialize Indians, he explains, it never completely abandoned the political conception. Why did Congress adopt BQ as such a prominent method for determining Indian identity? Spruhan does not offer an explanation, but clues are evident.[31] After the passage of the IRA, which provided a template for newly reorganized tribal governments' constitutions, blood quantum became the standard criteria for tribal membership. Following the federal model, tribes thus adopted a predominantly colonial, nontraditional way of defining Indianness. Later in the twentieth century, however, blood quantum also came to have new meaning in post-IRA-era tribal governments. In her study of tribal enrollment criteria, Kirsty Gover discovered after 1970, tribes were increasingly adopting lineal descent or "tribal blood quantum" (i.e., "blood" inherited from a specific tribe as opposed to overall "Indian blood" that might include blood from multiple tribes.) The change was more a move toward a genealogical rather than racialized understanding of tribal belonging. It was also a way to repair the historical discontinuity of tribes that may have been terminated or otherwise lost their political relationship to the state.[32]

Legal analysts David Wilkins and Shelly Hulse Wilkins are more straightforward about their understanding of the purpose of BQ. They contend that, in the early twentieth century, with the government's plan for assimilation, officials were motivated by the desire to control costs in meeting their fiscal responsibilities to tribes. Lowering the number of Indians became the sole purpose for applying blood quantum. As Wilkins and Wilkins write, "In essence, the federal government actively sought, in disregard of treaties, agreements, and countless statutes to rid itself of its financial and moral obligations to those Native individuals if considered 'white Indians.'"[33] In other words, if we understand the settler state as a structure bent on the elimination of the Native, then the production of Native disappearance is not just ideological but a practical matter of economics—and the reliance on blood quantum serves both objectives.

Reorganization as federal policy moving toward tribal self-governance did not last long. By the postwar 1940s under the Democratic Truman administration, assimilation was back on the table, and by 1953, it was codified with House Concurrent Resolution 108, or the Termination Act, signed into law by President Eisenhower. The heavy-handed goal was the literal termination of tribes as nations and individuals as legal Indians, and the dispersal of Indians into the general American populace through an organized program of relocation. Indians left their impoverished reservations with promises of jobs in cities all over the country. The jobs were typically low-level factory and other blue-collar jobs, and the housing was substandard, but census figures show that between 1940 and 1970 the American Indian population in cities increased from 8 to 45 percent.[34] Homesick, some returned to their reservations, but most stayed in their newly adopted urban homes and formed new kinds of urban-based American Indian communities. Urban Indian centers organized as nonprofit entities or less formal social clubs served a variety of purposes, including help finding jobs and other kinds of social services as well as providing cultural activities like arts and crafts, dance classes, and annual powwows.

Termination lasted two decades, and it was not officially over-turned until the 1970s after a lot of damage had been done. Don-ald Fixico Jr. documents that between 1945 and 1960 nearly twelve thousand people lost their legal status as Indians, 1,369,000 acres of land were removed from trust status, and 109 tribes lost their federal recognition and treaty-based services.[35] Of those 109 tribes, at least 44 were California tribes that became subject to Public Law 85–671, the 1958 California Rancheria Termination Act.[36] In addition to ex-tensive disruption of tribal cultures and loss of land, political status, and treaty-based services, the net result of termination was the de-mographic shift of relatively large populations of American Indians moving to cities and suburbs from their reservation communities.[37] Native people are largely invisible in the US social landscape for many reasons: they live on geographically isolated reservations, and they don't always conform to stereotypes about what Native Amer-icans look like. Native disappearance is intentionally produced (or engineered) through historically genocidal federal policies and dis-courses in the social sphere. Native invisibility is based largely on the artificial racializing of Native people and the unilateral destruction of tribes as nations.

INDIGENEITY: WHAT IS IT?

Native Americans have been referred to in many different terms, often changing with the tenor of shifting social moments. For example, the term *savage*, widely used until the nineteenth century, has long since been considered derogatory. The term *Indian*, the oldest and most commonly used term since 1492, reflects not how Native people iden-tified themselves but how settlers referred to them. As earth-centered and place-based people, Indians often refer to themselves with words tied to geographical formations like mountains, rivers, valleys, or coasts. Or they may describe themselves as "the humans" among many other forms of life, often conceived of relationally as people. *Indian* is a comparative term that centers settlers as it frames Indians as for-eign "others." It is also a term that aggregates hundreds of separate nations and cultures into one monolithic Native American culture, despite their vast cultural and linguistic diversity. Eventually "Indian" was adopted by Native people to distinguish themselves within settler society. For most, "Indian" is not offensive but nonetheless remains a misnomer for the ways it flattens, homogenizes, and erases tribal diversity. However, the term is most problematic for how it racializes people who exist first as citizens of nations that predate the United States and who never willingly ceded their sovereignty.

Over the latter twentieth and early twenty-first centuries with the rise of civil and minority rights awareness and changes in federal Indian policy, new terms emerged. During the 1960s and '70s, *Native American* replaced the misguided term "Indian," but the inclusion of "American" in the term was a constant reminder of tribal nations' nonconsensual subjugation to the US. Other terms were rejected as well. *Eskimo* was replaced by Alaska Native, Inuit, and Yupik, depending on what part of Alaska one is from. In Canada, the terms *Aboriginal* and *First Nations* became preferred self-referents.[38] As Native rights issues gained greater currency in the international arena, especially in United Nations forums, *Indigenous* became an umbrella term for original peoples and nations within UN member states. The International Labour Organization (ILO), the first specialized agency associated with the UN, began paying attention to Indigenous issues in the 1930s, framing Indigenous peoples as "native workers." In 1953, the ILO published a study on Indigenous peoples, and in 1957, it adopted Convention No. 107 and Recommendation No. 104, which were revised in 1989, becoming ILO 169.[39] In 1982, the United Nations Economic and Social Council (ECOSOC) formed the UN Working Group on Indigenous Populations (WGIP), and by 1986, the WGIP began developing the UN Declaration on the Rights of Indigenous Peoples.[40] Hence, by the early 1980s, *Indigenous* was the term of art describing Fourth World/Indigenous nations internal to states. In the following decades, American Indians increasingly adopted *Indigenous* as a way to emphasize their pre-constitutional tribal nation status. Now even some US policy documents use the word *Indigenous* in place of Native American or American Indian. These terms for Native people are often used interchangeably, though they don't always have the same meanings and can easily lead to misunderstandings when used incorrectly, especially the term *Indigenous*.

"Indigeneity" describes the condition of a people being Indigenous, or native, to a specific place, land, or territory. While no United Nations body has adopted an official definition of "Indigenous" due to the vast diversity of Indigenous peoples, key characteristics nonetheless include 1) a historical continuity with precolonial and/or pre-settler societies; 2) a strong link to territories and surrounding natural resources; 3) distinct social, economic, or political systems; 4) distinct languages, cultures, and beliefs as nondominant groups within state societies; 5) a resolution to maintain and reproduce their ancestral environments and systems as distinctive peoples and communities; and 6) self-identification as Indigenous peoples at the individual level and accepted by the community as their member.[41] There are three notable aspects of this understanding of indigeneity in relation to American Indian people: First, self-identification on the individual level depends upon community acceptance, not just individual claims. Second, a key aspect of indigeneity is being part of a community with a distinct political system; in the Unites States federally recognized tribes are political systems with a distinct political relationship to the US state.[42] Third, nowhere in the United Nations' list is indigeneity tied to race. In the international arena, indigeneity hinges on political status, historical ties to territory, histories of colonization, and difference from dominant societies rooted in culture, language, and knowledge systems. Indigenous peoples may be minority populations within states, and they may be racially different, but it is not racial difference that defines their indigeneity.

Indigeneity is, in other words, a relational concept contextualized by the modern state system, colonial though it may be—a condition Jonas Bens refers to as the "Indigenous paradox." It exists only in relation to something else, paradoxical because within state-based legal systems Indigenous peoples simultaneously reject state domination and depend on the state's recognition to assert their rights.[43] Prior to colonial invasion and the processes of foreigners establishing societies on top of the territories of original inhabitants, the concept of indigeneity would have been meaningless to Indigenous communities. The condition of indigeneity is thus inseparable from the states Indigenous peoples find themselves within. That is why the term *Indigenous* is not always synonymous with American Indian, Native American, or Alaska Native. One can be an Indigenous person of Canada, Mexico, Guatemala, Colombia, or any country living in the United States without being Native American by US definitions; although exceptions exist, they possess no political status within the US state and any claims to being "Indigenous" are contingent upon their relationships to the state they are indigenous to.[44] They may be considered racially Indigenous (however problematically) but lack the political status. Legally, their relationship to the US is based on rules of citizenship and immigration status.

PAN-INDIANISM, NEO-TRIBALISM, AND GENERIC "INDIANS"

As noted earlier, the federal government's termination policy produced a dramatic demographic shift in the American Indian population between 1940 and 1970 because of the relocation program. As Native people increasingly migrated and adopted new lives away from their tribal communities during the twentieth century, they formed new distinctly Native communities in their urban spaces. Indians from many tribes intermingled in ways that reinforced their tribal cultures and enabled them to create coalitions to fight termination and advance Indian rights during the burgeoning Red Power movement era. The Red Power movement, and its articulations of Native nationalism, grew out of the reservation-based activism that began at least in 1964 with the fish-ins in the Pacific Northwest, but by the late 1960s, was also firmly rooted in urban Indian experience in Minneapolis, Seattle, Los Angeles, the San Francisco Bay Area, New York, and other cities.[45] It wasn't the first time Indian people had coalesced across tribal boundaries. In the early twentieth century, the Society of American Indians (SAI) had set that precedent, laying some of the groundwork for what would become the Indian Reorganization Act of 1934 as well as being the precursor of today's National Congress of American Indians, the largest, most important Native American advocacy organization in the US. But the American Indian demographic upheavals brought on by relocation coupled with shifting attitudes in the American social landscape exacerbated an already existing pattern of American Indian cultural appropriation, making the phenomenon of extreme fakes like Sacheen Littlefeather, the actor Iron Eyes Cody, and many others not only possible but far more common.

In *Playing Indian*, Philip Deloria convincingly argues that as far back as the Boston Tea Party, the American compulsion to appropriate Indianness was connected to a need to belong on land that wasn't theirs and to forge a new kind of collective, explicitly American identity. With the anxieties of modernism driving much of the social revolution of the 1960s and '70s, the anti-racist sensibilities of the civil rights struggle ironically made it even easier for non-Indians to appropriate Indianness in the name of political solidarity.[46] It was in this historical moment that for many of the counterculture generation, the impulse to *play* Indian morphed into the impulse to *become* Indian.[47] This concept is reflected in census numbers. Between 1960 and 2010, the American Indian population jumped from 551,591 to 5.9 million.[48] By 2020, that number had increased to 9.7 million. This increase is explained largely by changes in census rules that allowed people to racially self-identify; there was not a new baby boom. The sharpest increase—72.4 percent—occurred between 1970 and 1980,[49] as ethnic revival became more popular.[50] The increase in self-identified Indians coincided with an explosive urban Indian population growth. While Native American people were experiencing greater freedom · and safety with important changes in law, policy, and changing attitudes about race and culture, it also grew easier for non-Indians to exploit Native cultures and their tendency to be inclusive. Into the social ruptures created by the cultural revolution and new census rules stepped the race-shifters, the spiritually hungry, and the charlatans.[51] Joining urban Indian centers, attending powwows and other Native cultural events, enrolling in American Indian studies programs, just emerging in this period, publishing books, and following "medicine men" were just some of the opportunities for people to reimagine themselves as Indians and also to deceive in new ways. We also see the creation of hundreds of new "tribes," especially Cherokee, mushrooming in the Southeast and elsewhere in what Circe Sturm describes as neo-tribalism.[52] As Sturm writes, these new groups, organized as clubs, nonprofits, or state-recognized tribes, began forming neo-tribal communities for those who couldn't meet enrollment criteria in any of the three federally recognized Cherokee tribes. They also pose significant challenges to the sovereignty of federally recognized tribes.[53]

How we talk about the collective political organizing, activism, cultural expression, and social world of Native people has undergone changes in recent decades. The older term *pan-Indianism* describes American Indian people and cultures collectively. In writing about SAI, Thomas Constantine Maroukis contends that pan-Indianism is contested and confusing because Native people did not give up their tribal identities to work with each other. Some argue that the term *intertribal* is far more common and appropriate today and Maroukis concurs, but with the caveat that "[i]f Pan-Indianism is defined as diverse individuals with regional and cultural differences working together toward common goals, such as *self-determination* [my emphasis], then there is no problem with the term."[54]

In 1984, Deloria and Lytle wrote about what they called the "consolidated Indian movement," which they assert emerged in urban areas. They explain there was a need to forgo tribal differences, which gave rise to an ethnic Native American identity because Americans could recognize ethnic Native Americans more than they could grapple with specific tribal affiliations. They write: "The merging of many tribal identities and histories in the urban setting meant the adoption of a common, albeit artificial heritage," with names like the American Indian Movement, United Native Americans, and Indians of All Tribes as evidence of homogenizing nomenclature.[55] Writing about the urban Indian centers, Renya Ramirez has called these sites of multilayered functions Native hubs, where tribal belonging could be experienced within cities. Ramirez writes that powwows and sweat lodges are also places where Native hubs occur.[56] Powwows and urban sweat lodges are similar to other intertribal networks that reinforce individual tribal identities. However, they are also places where tribal identities can become diffuse and largely unverifiable.[57] Urban sweat lodges, Native American Church (NAC), and other spiritual ceremonies became particularly problematic opportunities in the mid-twentieth century for breeding tribally diffuse pan-Indianism, New Age cultural appropriation, and blatant Indian ethnic fraud. It is a topic we will delve more deeply into in chapter 4.

Less discussed in the literature are the negative impacts of pan-Indianism, especially in California. Rose Soza War Soldier's study of the California-based American Indian Historical Society, which existed from 1964 to 1986, examines some of the tensions between California Indians and relocated urban activist Indians during the Red Power movement. The society existed to improve education, communication, and cultural development of American Indians through support for tribal self-determination, explicitly rejecting pan-Indianism. War Soldier's study reveals many California Indians disagreed with the militant activist tactics of urban Indians during the Alcatraz Island occupation, from 1969 to 1971, taking issue with the inconsistency of out-of-state, relocated Indians claiming ancestral Ohlone land under a Lakota treaty while California Indians were fighting for the return of lands to their own tribes.[58] Much activism also, she contends, perpetuated the ongoing erasure of California Indians in their own ancestral lands.

Intertribal organizing did exist, however, and may better express the collaborative nature of the goals and aspirations for tribal self-determination of people with connections to legitimate tribal nations. Whether on reservations or in cities, these were the same groups of people who had been directly impacted by oppressive federal Indian policy and working on behalf of their tribal nations for generations. Even if they had relocated, they were firmly rooted in specific tribal cultures and communities, and were the vanguard of the inner-city Indian populations. But what about the mid- to late-twentieth century self-identifying race-shifters who had no legitimate tribal connections or only flimsy claims to Cherokee or other tribal heritage?[59] Does the term *intertribal* apply to people with no ties to actual tribes, like Sacheen Littlefeather? Or do they represent a type of generic "Indian" within a new kind of urban neo-tribal pan-Indianism? What patterns might emerge between individuals in urban spaces who make questionable claims to Indianness and those with clear ties to tribal and reservation communities? And one of the most important questions this book poses: What does generic urban Indianness mean for tribal sovereignty?

These questions are contentious and provocative, with no easy answers, yet they must be addressed if we are to explore issues of American Indian authenticity and fraud in post-relocation urban settings. With only a few exceptions, qualitative sociological studies on Native American identity have avoided the topic of ethnic fraud, focusing instead more broadly on what defines Native identity. Invariably, in these studies, claims to Native heritage are taken for granted. A few studies have focused on what Michelle Jacobs and David Merolla have called "new Indians," those newly claiming Indian identity after the 1970 census.[60] Following the work of Kathleen Fitzgerald,[61] Jacobs has applied the term *reclaimers* to describe those who adopt an Indian identity to recuperate indigeneity long ago ejected from the family tree. Jacobs, Merolla, and Fitzgerald note that new Indian reclaimers are often people who present as racially white but reframe themselves as Indian, mixed-blood, and multiracial. Usually there are assertions of Indian "blood" in the family genealogy, without hard evidence, which means the reclaimers can rarely prove tribal connections but ironically reinforce a racialized understanding of Indianness as they simultaneously reject their own whiteness. Unmoored from a specific tribal culture or nation, they rely on an Indianness conceived of in stereotypical ways. Indianness is reduced to an enactment of values perceived to be "Indian," such as generosity or the belief that what's in a person's heart is what makes one Indian.[62] It is also asserted by "actively seeking out and learning Indian traditions"[63] and performing Indianness ("doing Indigeneity" and "becoming" Indian, in Jacobs's terms), such as crafting, making tobacco offerings and "spirit plates," sage smudging, pipe ceremonies, powwows, and sweat lodges.[64] There is a romanticized desire to return to the "old ways," which can be taught by sought out mentors. Fetishizing "Native American spirituality" is a core defining element. In these ways, specific tribal cultural practices are flattened and homogenized into an idealized, monolithic, neo-tribal Native American culture. Intertribalism is reduced to generic pan-Indianism in a cultural free-for-all, regardless of individual tribal status or lack thereof.

In Jacobs's book-length treatment of her research on urban Indian communities, *Indigenous Memory, Urban Reality: Stories of American Indian Relocation and Reclamation,* we find the biggest clues for what separates the new, generic Indians from tribal Indians. Jacobs studied two urban Indian centers in the Northeast Ohio area of Cleveland, diving deeply into the distinctions between people whose Indian identities emerge from experiences of relocation on one hand and reclaiming on the other. Relocators are people and their descendants who came to the area from reservation communities during the relocation era. Despite their urban residence, they tend to be enrolled tribal members with ties to reservation communities and families. Younger people may not qualify for enrollment due to not meeting blood quantum requirements, the result of generational intermarriage outside tribal "bloodlines," but they nevertheless maintain kinship ties to tribal communities. Reclaimers are a community of newly Indian-identified people (and their children). People with stories about Indian ancestors who escaped the reservation system explaining why their Indian heritage is not documented are common.[65] Jacobs identifies tensions that have existed between the two urban communities for years, where one community perceives the others' Indian identity claims as inauthentic and fraudulent. Besides reclaimers' tendency to see indigeneity as an open field for all and that being Indian is a matter of what you believe,[66] they also believe that relocators judge them as fake based on "Indian politics."

The deployment of Indian politics conveys the most significant difference between reclaimers and relocators: the level of importance each community attributes to tribal nationhood. Reclaimers downplay the power and relevance of government and tribal documentation to validate Indianness, often to the point of contempt. As Jacobs writes:

> Nonenrolled reclaimers consistently said things that illustrated their lack of engagement with issues of Indigenous nationhood, citizenship, or sovereignty. They maintained, for instance, that they *knew* they were Indian and did not need a "piece of paper" or "plastic" (Certificate of Degree of Indian Blood, tribal identification card) or "number" (tribal identification number) to prove it. They dismissed

so-called political Indians as people who took pride in being certified as Indian by the US government but rarely mentioned Indian
nations' roles in determining tribal citizenship. They said things like
"being Indian is a state of mind"; "it's not the blood that counts,
it's the heart"; and, what really matters is "walking the red road"
and "walking the walk" . . . In this way, many reclaimers defended
their Indian identities while invalidating the identities of "political
Indians," whom they accused of acting like settlers.[67]

For reclaimers, the boundaries of community are expansive and inclusive; for relocators, pretendianism must always be contended with
and results in a certain level of boundary policing. Self-identified reclaimers seem oblivious to Indianness arising from ancestral connection to place, tribe, clan, and family as the definition of indigeneity,
which may explain why Indianness then becomes superficial, artificial, and largely performative. Yet reclaimers understand the role of
community in validating Indian identity, and relying on the community of other reclaimers fills that need.

Jacobs's study of reclaimers and relocators is particular to Northeast Ohio; there may be aspects of it that would not be applicable in
other contexts, for example, the area's century-long history with the
racist Cleveland Indians baseball team. It is reasonable to presume,
however, that the study is typically representative of other contemporary urban Indian communities, especially the distinctions between
Indians who relocated to cities from reservations and those who
self-identify through performative acts of reclamation. In this regard,
there is nothing unique about the Cleveland urban Indian communities. We can expect the same patterns of behavior and discourse to
travel across all urban Indian spaces.

In the book's conclusion, Jacobs illuminates the problem of fraudulent Indianness, stating that the "collective remembrances of reclaimers . . . are concerning. Many reclaimers' Indian identities likely
are based on incorrect interpretations of the past."[68] Here she refers
to the erasure of accurate knowledge about American Indians in
US education systems that have led to pervasive stereotypes driving
the distorted claims to Indianness of non-Native people. Culture is

perceived as disconnected from sovereignty, slipping into the realm of personal possession, where Indian identity is claimed as a right. Arguably, it is these complex processes of miseducation and distortion about who Indians are that set up the preconditions for rampant Indian ethnic fraud. Meanwhile, through their misguided assertions of racialized Indianness and dismissal of tribal sovereignty, neo-tribal urban self-identifiers contribute to the erosion of tribal sovereignty.

ATTACKS ON TRIBAL SOVEREIGNTY: WHY TRIBAL NATIONHOOD MATTERS

As we have seen, the United States established itself and its relationship with tribes as nations. It was the recognition of mutual political sovereignty, though under conditions of thinly veiled contempt and perpetual aggression. As federal Indian policy became more coercive and one-sided throughout the nineteenth and twentieth centuries, the US adopted race as a metric for determining who Native people were to limit the number of individuals it had obligations to. This situation of the federal government's own making is still being used against Native people not only to limit its financial trust-based responsibilities, but by malevolent governmental and nongovernmental actors, to undermine or completely overturn tribal sovereignty through attacks on important tribal sovereignty-based legislation such as the Indian Child Welfare Act and the Indian Gaming Regulatory Act.

A particularly evil aspect of Native disappearance through forced assimilation involved the intentional destruction of Native families. The story of my family's experience with boarding schools and adoption is a classic example of how federal policies targeted tribal families and how the forced removal of children from homes for multiple generations impacted families. It also demonstrates how federal policy influenced policy at the state and local levels. The boarding school mandate of the Dawes Act, for instance, whose motto was "Kill the Indian to save the man," used a widespread belief in Indian cultural, spiritual, racial, and intellectual inferiority to rationalize systematic abuse. Indian inferiority at the state level parallels deeply entrenched patterns at the federal level. These views drove the behavior of social workers in state family services agencies who presumed the unfitness of mothers often based on no more than being Indian.[69] They employed methods of intimidation—at times outright fraud—to acquire "consent" for their children's adoption, sometimes with forms that didn't even clearly state intent.[70] Women were pressured by social workers before and after their children were born to relinquish their babies. In other instances, women living under precarious conditions due to poverty or abuse (my mother's experience) didn't have or were not offered access to resources that could have enabled children to remain in the birth family. Research shows that Native women didn't even have to be unmarried to be subject to the harassment and taking of their children. As Margaret Jacobs writes, "Unlike American women more generally, Indian women, whether they were married or not, commonly faced harassment to relinquish their children for adoption."[71] The removal of children from Native women was so pervasive, a study in the late 1960s found that 25 to 35 percent of Native children were being removed, 85 percent of which were placed in non-Native homes.[72] What happened to my brother Robert was part of what's been called the pre-ICWA scoop, as agency officials entered tribal communities to quickly take as many kids as they could.[73] The crisis of American Indian child snatching led to the creation of the Indian Child Welfare Act (ICWA) in 1978.

ICWA adds greater protections to families and tribes to keep Indian children in their homes, families, and communities. An "Indian child" is defined as a child enrolled in a federally recognized tribe or eligible for enrollment. Blood quantum is not part of the equation, except to the extent that enrollment is dependent upon it.[74] With involuntary out-of-home adoption, foster care placement, or termination of parental rights, ICWA requires state courts to notify the tribe, transferring jurisdiction to tribal court.[75] Among the law's greatest mandates are that:

> ICWA requires "active efforts" to provide socially and culturally congruent "remedial services and rehabilitative programs designed to prevent the breakup of the Indian family" . . . ICWA additionally requires testimony from a "qualified expert witness" knowledgeable of the "prevailing social and cultural standards" of the child's Tribe,

documenting whether continued parental custody would likely "result in serious emotional or physical damage to the child" . . . ICWA mandates that unless there is "good cause" to deviate, the prioritized foster care and pre-adoptive placement preferences are with: 1) an extended family member; 2) a foster home licensed, approved, or specified by the child's Tribe; 3) an Indian foster home licensed or approved by an authorized non-Indian licensing authority; or 4) a children's institution approved by the Tribe or operated by a Tribal organization that can meet the child's needs.[76]

ICWA is widely hailed as the "gold standard for child welfare policies."[77] As federal Indian law scholars Matthew Fletcher and Wenona Singel maintain, ICWA is "likely the most comprehensive and far-reaching, acutely needed, and successful civil rights law that Congress has ever enacted in the history of Indian affairs."[78] They also point out that ICWA was not designed to be a comprehensive statute but a baseline for state courts.[79] Because it is an uncomprehensive, unfunded mandate, there is no mechanism to oversee implementation at the federal, state, or tribal level,[80] and in in-state courts, "compliance is often low to nonexistent."[81] Native children are still four times more likely than white children to be removed from their families, even compared to white families with similar issues.[82] Yet even with its shortcomings, ICWA is a powerful affirmation of tribal sovereignty, based on a long history rooted in constitutional principles, Supreme Court decisions, Indian rights legislation, and federal statutes.

The purpose of the Indian Child Welfare Act is "to protect the best interest of Indian Children and to promote the stability and security of Indian tribes and families."[83] But it's also important to understand that ICWA exists within the broader context of adoption and foster care as a multibillion dollar industry,[84] dominated by the evangelical Christian right, with ever-receding numbers of children available for adoption.[85] ICWA makes it more difficult for non-Native people to adopt Indian kids, which has led to a highly organized anti-ICWA movement. ICWA has been targeted by extremely well-funded conservative interest groups for over a decade to undermine or completely overturn it.[86] Their strategy has been to challenge the law's constitutionality by driving ICWA cases to the Supreme Court, beginning with *Adoptive Couple v. Baby Girl*, aka the Baby Veronica case, in 2013 and *Brackeen v. Haaland* in 2022. The Baby Veronica case, which resulted in the loss of a Cherokee tribal member's custody of his biological daughter in favor of a white adoptive couple, weakened but did not overturn ICWA. *Brackeen* was a more direct attack on ICWA based on three arguments: (1) it discriminates based on race, violating the Fifteenth Amendment equal protection clause; (2) it violates the Tenth Amendment anti-commandeering principles (infringing state sovereignty);[87] and (3) it exceeds federal authority.[88] That is, ICWA critics contend that ICWA is reverse racism against white people and that it violates state's rights.[89]

In November 2022, the US Supreme Court heard oral arguments in *Brackeen v. Haaland*. The case was a source of intense anxiety for Indian country, and it received a fair amount of media attention. Indian rights cases generally fly under the radar of most mainstream media, but those who were paying attention understood what was at stake. Legal analysts pointed out that the case presented a very real threat to tribal sovereignty, arguing that if the Supreme Court agreed with the plaintiffs that ICWA violates equal protection as a race-based law, that logic could be applied to virtually all other Indian rights laws, putting the entire doctrine of tribal sovereignty at risk. Tribes could lose not just ICWA but the legal framework that protects tribal nationhood and what remains of their lands. The Supreme Court is a dangerous place for tribes in the modern era; since the Rehnquist court, they prevail in less than a quarter of cases.[90] The Roberts court added three appointees during the Trump administration, making the court a conservative 6–3 supermajority. Conservative judges are notorious for their anti-Indian positions, though Trump appointee Neil Gorsuch, known to have a better grasp of and track record on tribal issues, is generally seen as pro-Indian. Still, Indian country had plenty of reason to fear the outcome of *Brackeen*.

The *Brackeen v. Haaland* decision was handed down in June 2023 among a slew of civil rights decisions, including a free speech and gay rights case (*303 Creative LLC et al. v. Aubrey Elenis et al.*), an anti-affirmative action case involving college admissions (*Students for Fair Admissions v. Harvard University* and *Students for Fair Admissions v. University of North Carolina*), the overturning of President Biden's student debt forgiveness plan, and another Indian rights case in which the Supreme Court eroded water rights for the Navajo Nation (*Arizona et al. v. Navajo Nation*). All the cases ended in predictably negative outcomes given the conservative leanings of most of the justices. It was thus highly unexpected when the court issued a ruling in *Brackeen* that was widely celebrated as a win for Indian country. In a 7–2 ruling, the Supreme Court upheld ICWA, first on the basis that the plaintiffs had no legal standing. (Because petitioners did not include "state departments of family services," only federal defendants, judicial relief for alleged injuries was unavailable. Thus, the equal protection issue was dismissed based on a technicality.[91]) The court also rejected the anti-commandeering argument. Justice Amy Coney Barrett authored the opinion for the majority, with Justices Gorsuch and Kavanaugh issuing concurring opinions. Gorsuch contextualized the case with a lengthy historicizing of *Brackeen* within the context of a continuum of abusive federal Indian policy that necessitated the passage of ICWA in the first place. Kavanaugh, on the other hand, wrote a brief two paragraph commentary focusing on equal protection, emphasizing race—not the political status—of Indian adoptions, anticipating a future case where the issue is raised appropriately:

> In my view, the equal protection issue is serious. Under the Act, a child in foster care or adoption proceedings may in some cases be denied a particular placement because of the child's race—even if the placement is otherwise determined to be in the child's best interests. And a prospective foster or adoptive parent may in some cases be denied the opportunity to foster or adopt a child because of the prospective parent's race. Those scenarios raise significant questions under bedrock equal protection principles and this Court's precedents. . . . Courts, including ultimately this Court, will be able to address the equal protection issue when it is properly raised by a plaintiff with standing.[92]

The *Brackeen* victory, therefore, while staving off for now a devastating equal protection ruling, leaves the door open for potential future challenges that push for framing Indian rights and sovereignty as race-based law.

There is no reason to believe that those committed to derailing tribal sovereignty will stop their crusade after the *Brackeen* defeat. Once again Gibson, Dunn, and Crutcher, the corporate law firm who took on the *Brackeen* case pro bono, is complicit in the anti-tribal sovereignty movement. While Gibson, Dunn was litigating *Brackeen*, it also began representing a nontribal gaming entity's challenge of Indian gaming in Washington State. Seeking to expand its cardroom operations to include sports betting, Maverick Gaming—paradoxically owned by a member of Washington's Shoalwater Bay Tribe and professional poker player Eric Perssons—said that the state's law allowing sports betting only in tribal casinos constitutes a "discriminatory tribal gaming monopoly."[93] Shoalwater Bay Tribe filed for a motion to dismiss, which was granted in February 2023; Perssons made it clear he intended to file an appeal, and the case is currently making its way through the appellate court system. *Maverick Gaming v. United States* is fundamentally a challenge to the Indian Gaming Regulatory Act, according to a story in Indian Country Today. The arguments in *Brackeen* and *Maverick Gaming* are nearly identical, relying on claims of equal protection violation. "They did tweak it a little bit. It's not exactly word for word the whole way through, but it's pretty darn close," a source said.[94]

\\\\\\\\\\\\\\\\\\\\\\\\\

While the United States is unquestionably a colonial construction that has always been contested and resisted by American Indian and Alaska Native peoples, Native identity cannot be meaningfully separated from the US colonial foundation because there is no one not shaped by it. Indigeneity is irreducibly defined by relationships to place and people, and inescapably mediated by relations of power and processes not of our choosing. We can discursively reject the oppressive and nonconsensual nature of those processes, we can do cultural reclamation work, we can form intercultural, intertribal, and international relations with each other within and beyond state boundaries, and we can work toward decolonial futures however we may imagine them. Yet indigeneity is also shaped by the relationships our ancestors forged with the US state and its colonial predecessors in treaties, agreements, and other interactions. To dismiss, as some do, these legal and structural realities as perpetuating colonialism or not necessary to legitimate Native identity is shortsighted and rejects the agonizing decisions our ancestors made to ensure the existence of future generations.

There must be a baseline by which we determine, name, and inhabit the paradoxical relationships we now find ourselves in with the US. In the language we inherited from our English colonizers, we call it tribal nationhood and sovereignty, framed as they are by legal structures not our own. Whether we have clearly documented tribal lineages and enrollment within a federally recognized tribe to which our Native identities are legally tied or not, we should care about these processes and relationships because, without them, there are no Indians that the state is bound to recognize at all. There would be no tribal land bases or treaty rights the state is legally bound to protect. Without those legal realities, colonial though they may be, American Indian people are just part of the multicultural mass that the US prides itself on. Without legally defined Indians, the state evades accountability to the Original People of this land.

CHAPTER THREE

WHO'S RUNNING THE SHOW?

*Indians in Hollywood and the Birth
of Native American Ethnic Fraud*

THE NIGHT SACHEEN LITTLEFEATHER stood up to decline the Oscar on behalf of Marlon Brando, history was made on several fronts. Not only had the Academy Awards never been used as platform for protest, but it was apparently the first time a Native American woman had graced the stage at an Oscars ceremony. Most important was the message: Hollywood had a deplorable history when it came to the treatment and representation of American Indians, and things had to change. It was no small irony that the act of protest on these grounds by Sacheen Littlefeather, who lied to millions of people on live TV about being Apache, was a direct perpetration of what she was, at least in part, protesting: the lack of accurate Native representation in the film industry. The colossal hypocrisy aside, the message was necessary and timely, as she pointed out, as Native people at that moment were engaged in an armed struggle with the federal government over demands for their basic human rights, treaty-based tribal rights, and fair treatment. Fair treatment as implied in her speech that night addressed a suite of concerns that Native actors in the industry were well acquainted with. At the top of the list were racist stereotypes, pay equity, and Native roles going to Native people. It was common in those days for non-Indians to play Indians, especially in lead roles, and as I show in this chapter, pretendianism as we know it today has its origins in the movie business. Some progress has undeniably been made, with the deliberate rejection of problematic stereotypes and greater Native presence and control, but problems persist when it comes to questions of identity and authenticity. Despite progress in the quality of representation, the industry continues to be plagued by a lack of standards and transparency for determining the authenticity of those who identity as Native, for what determines being authentically Indigenous. The consequences have been the creation of an industry infrastructure of gatekeepers who lack the appropriate knowledge and skills, individuals who wrongly claim Native identities, and others who knowingly cover for them. I begin with a historical overview of American Indian representation in entertainment at a critical moment in turn-of-the-century America to show how industrial capitalism led to the commodification of Indianness and new motivations for spurious claims to it. The impulse toward ethnic fraud embedded in the film industry has since carried through to all aspects of arts and entertainment.

SHOW INDIANS, HOLLYWOOD INDIANS, AND THE COMMODIFICATION OF INDIANNESS

The study of Native American representation in film and entertainment is fairly extensive; my intent is not to give a broad historical analysis but to investigate how claims to Indigenous identity in the film and entertainment industries and related cultural arts spaces are registered and negotiated. Nevertheless, peering into the history of American Indians in the entertainment world reveals the ways Native identities were both leveraged and contrived in the rapidly changing political and cultural economies of Indian country beginning in the late nineteenth century, a time when the US was bearing down heavily on tribes, especially in the West. As the military balance of power became weighted toward the US, the imposition of land cession treaties and creation of reservations became more aggressive until 1871, when Congress ended treaty-making as federal Indian policy. By 1879, the first Indian boarding school, Carlisle Indian Industrial School, had opened as the US began implementing an approach designed to assimilate Indians into the American body politic. Settler colonial domination continued unabated throughout the end of the century and early into the next, with a long line of laws and Supreme Court decisions designed to strangle Indians into submission. One of the more corrosive actions was the passage of the Code of Indian

Offenses, aka the Religious Crimes Code, targeting and criminalizing Native spiritual practices in 1883. In 1887, the Dawes Act broke up community-held tribal lands through allotment, leading to a US land grab of ninety million acres of treaty-reserved lands and the mandating of the boarding school system. In 1890, the massacre at Wounded Knee took place, and with it, the effective end of Indian armed resistance against the now superior US military. Continental western expansion was complete, and Indian nations were brutally contained. US power over the land and lives of Indigenous people was consolidated, ending the free and independent existence of Indian life as it had been known for thousands of years.

Native American assimilation depended on the fostering of individual identities devoid of their tribal cultures—what was meant by "Kill the Indian to save the man," the de facto defining strategy of the boarding schools. Another major component of assimilation was the merging of Native people into the American capitalist economy. The stated purpose of land allotment, after all, was to teach the values of selfishness through private ownership. Land conceived as private property was dichotomous to the Indigenous view of land as kin, so it was a seismic shift in perspective and behavior. The boarding schools with their civilizing mission were in essence incubators for indoctrination into the logics of US capitalism, or as Alice Littlefield puts it, "Proletarianization better characterizes the efforts of federal Indian schools than assimilation."[1] Littlefield contends that between 1880 and 1930 the federal boarding school system responded to US economic conditions, undergoing insatiable demands for low-wage labor met largely through European, Asian, and Mexican immigrants,[2] and the schools became ever more subordinate to this process. This was accomplished especially through focused vocational training, which taught students how to sell their labor in a marketized social system. Such training for children who had been raised in tribal communities structured by non-capitalist land-based economies could only be achieved through language eradication, Christian conversion, and other Eurocentric disciplinary tactics, such as replacing gender-equitable societies with patriarchy and orientation to labor governed by clock time.[3] One example of the targeted disciplining of students into the capitalist economy was the "outing program." The program trained Indian youth to be of service to white families by sending them to work without pay as farmhands and domestic servants; it was ultimately little more than a source of free child labor to those families.[4] Armed with skills, they would be fit for employment after leaving school, converted into productive workers in service to the US monopoly capitalist regime, which was by then well established.[5]

Another avenue for Indians to enter the settler wage economy was through Wild West shows and the performing of Indian culture for white audiences. But the shows posed inherent contradictions between the US's imperative to instill the values of capitalism and the goal of cultural eradication. In 1883, as the so-called era of the Indian wars was waning, new but complicated opportunities arose for Indian veteran warriors with the birth of the Wild West shows. *Buffalo Bill's Wild West* and the many other shows that followed recruited veterans of the Plains Wars into their traveling shows, which reenacted famous battles and other features of western life, such as Indian dances and other expressions of traditional culture. Drawing on a fascination with Indian warrior prowess depicted in the dime novels and western melodramas of the 1860s,[6] the Wild West shows both contributed to and exploited the growing romanticization of horseback-riding, buckskin-clad, and feather-adorned Plains Indians. Wildly popular in the US, the shows also traveled throughout Europe, providing Show Indians the opportunity to see the world and earn a good living. Their employment in the shows was paradoxically a way for them to continue practicing elements of their cultures that were outlawed in their reservation communities by the Religious Crimes Code.

The era of the Wild West shows was part of a centuries-long pattern of cultural imperialism[7] that exploited Indigenous peoples in a range of ways that appealed to the white settler and foreign gaze, describing what Robert Berkhofer famously called the "white man's Indian" in the titular 1978 book. Civic expressions of Indian play, as Deloria described it, was only one aspect of a larger pattern of exploiting American Indian cultures for various purposes. Researchers

Carter Jones Meyer and Diana Royer point out how non-Native representations of Indians have changed since the earliest colonial times in ways that were always self-serving, becoming today's blatant commercialization. Some of the most common depictions of Native people were as subjects in literature dating at least to the seventeenth century. The Indian was always a representation for America itself, and with the rise of industrial capitalism[8] in the nineteenth century came the deploying of Native culture for explicitly commercial purposes. To illustrate, in his study on Native Americans in advertising and marketing, William M. O'Barr locates the carved wooden cigar store Indian as one of the earliest Native American images—as early as the 1700s.[9] By the late 1800s, Indians appeared in print ads in the form of trade cards, similar to baseball cards, inserted in a wide variety of products like cigarettes and coffee or as stand-alone advertising. It's also in this era we see Indians being recruited to sell products in traveling medicine shows. Studies on turn-of-the-century industrial modernity describe a growing sense of anxiety and malaise resulting from urban industrial life, making people, especially women, "susceptible to a troublesome variety of physical and psychic woes associated with civilized leisure," as Kevin Armitage writes. The cure was closer contact with nature, aided by a growing array of patented medicines that often made false claims, in what Stuart Hall Holbrook called the "golden age of quackery."[10] Indians as "children of nature," the perfect symbol of health and vitality, were regularly invoked in the packaging and advertising of these remedies. The Kickapoo Medicine Company, for example, hawked Indian Sagwa, Kickapoo Indian Oil, Indian Worm Killer, and Genuine Kickapoo Cough Syrup "at elaborate medicine shows that featured singing, dancing, acrobatics, carnival skits . . . and included among its performers a number of real Indians, whose tribal identities were all subsumed under the 'Kickapoo' banner." Armitage notes that in the 1880s as many as seventy-five Kickapoo shows might be touring the country at once.[11]

Performing in live venues provided a means of economic self-sufficiency for Indians, but the performance of culture conflicted with the federal government's assimilationist agenda. Early on, Indian Affairs commissioners staunchly opposed Indians' employment in the

Wild West shows, viewing it as incompatible with the federal government's civilizing mission, but they were also motivated to protect the
Indians from unscrupulous employers. The Office of Indian Affairs
carefully oversaw the business of "Buffalo Bill" Cody's Show Indians,
seeking contractual assurances of their protection from "immoral in-
fluences and surroundings." To discourage them from working in the
shows, allotments and annuities were sometimes withheld.[12] Indians
worked in the shows anyway, sometimes without federal approval.[13]
The pay, twenty-five to ninety dollars a month, was good, and as L. G.
Moses writes, "Few Indians who took out allotments and farmed the
land or ran livestock could boast comparable incomes."[14] Unable to
completely control the situation, government anxiety over the Show
Indians eventually subsided, and Indians playing themselves came to
be seen as an acceptable vocation. Meanwhile, with the birth of film,
Indian themes factored prominently and overlapped with the Wild
West shows. In fact, "Buffalo Bill" Cody made some of the earliest silent films in the late 1890s, called "shorts,"[15] seamlessly linking Wild
West shows with the budding film industry and facilitating a career
transition for many Show Indians into the movie business. Show Indians became Movie Indians.

With paternalistic policies of the federal government pushing Indians to assimilate into the dominant society, for Indian people, the
Wild West shows were the path of least resistance into capitalism and
a political economic system that was foreign to them.[16] If capitalism
is the "commodification of everything,"[17] including labor, and if some
forms of labor are dependent upon the exploitation of personal identity, as was arguably the case with Show Indians, then it's reasonable
to see the late nineteenth century as the beginning of the commodification of Indianness. Indianness becomes a product that could be
leveraged for profit on the open market, constituting the start of a
process that blurs the lines between fantasy and reality. The study of
film, entertainment, and media in American Indian studies largely at-
tends to issues of representation—changes over time, the perpetuation
of stereotypes and misrepresentation, Indigenous agency and power,
and cultural sovereignty. Throughout the twentieth century, visual
representation through film and advertising had outsized influence

on shaping the perceptions of non-Native populations about American Indians. Seneca film scholar Michelle Raheja observes that early Hollywood cinema included more Native Americans than later eras, and that while they are hyper-visible in commercial spaces like advertising, they are virtually "invisible when it comes to most everything else of substance."[18] What most people understand about Indians they have learned from the films and ads they grew up consuming— and the limited and skewed historical narratives they were taught in school. But in the early days of film, in turn-of-the-century America, there was little reason to question the identities of Show Indians or early Movie Indians.

Relatively little attention has been paid to the political economy of Native Americans in the film industry, but the history of the early film industry offers valuable insights into the motivations behind Native identity fraud, especially when viewed within the context of the changes imposed on Indians with their conscription into the American economy in the late nineteenth century.[19] The pushing of Indians into the cash economy through the financial incentivizing of labor overlapped with a systematic stripping of their identities and social dynamics within popular culture that increasingly romanticized them through stereotypical misrepresentations. As we've seen, playing Indian has always been a part of the American social imagination, but there is a point at which the impulse to play Indian morphs into the impulse to become Indian, and it occurs at the intersection of all these processes. When people played Indian for political reasons, like during the Boston Tea Party, or through fraternal organizations and other social clubs as Philip Deloria described, it was a temporary performance. At the end of the day, the costumes came off and they returned to their normal lives as white settlers. Prior to the twentieth century, Indians suffered consequences for being Indian; there was no benefit for white people to pretend to be Indian in daily life. Things changed, however, when Indians were paid for performing Indianness in various entertainment spaces. Although life remained excruciatingly difficult for Native people, the survivors of the Indian wars suddenly had not only the opportunity to continue expressing their cultures, which had been systematically suppressed on the reservations, but there was also economic incentive. The precarity of their existence puts Indians in the bizarre position of producing mimetic representations of themselves through social and political domination and economic imperative. The floodgates were thrown open to a new era of professionalized Indigenous performance.

BECOMING INDIAN AND PERFORMING INDIGENEITY

The Show Indians are well-documented, with all of them coming from tribal cultures. They were recruited from reservation communities or from the Miller 101 Ranch in Oklahoma, which became a kind of clearinghouse for Indian performers.[20] There was little opportunity to fake an Indian identity and no evidence of it happening in the Wild West shows.[21] However, we begin to see the emergence of Native American fraud in the early days of film. Historians highlight the strange tale of Chief Buffalo Child Long Lance. Long Lance, a figure known mostly within scholarly circles, is now remembered as an imposter who fabricated an Indian persona, which he used to build a successful career as a writer, actor, and public advocate for Indian rights. After living in Canada and adopting a Blackfoot identity, he became a journalist, writing and lecturing widely about American Indian issues. In 1928, he published an autobiography, *The Autobiography of a Blackfoot Indian Chief*, which quickly became an international bestseller. Achieving celebrity status, he was accepted into New York's elite social scene as high society's first Indian. The following year, he took a role in *The Silent Enemy*, a film released in 1930 to critical acclaim.

But Long Lance had a lot to hide. He was born Sylvester Long in 1890 in North Carolina. His family was of a mixed-race background; most scholars characterize him as triracial Black, white, and Indian. Deeper research into his racial ancestry shows his ethnic background to be much more unclear. Historian Donald B. Smith, likely the foremost expert on Long, in a 1982 biography reports Long's mother descended from an enslaved Indian of Croatan origin and her white owner, while his father, Joe Long, was of possible Catawba or Cherokee extraction.[22] Smith notes that Joe Long was adopted, and his obituary stated he was a "member of the Catawba tribe," but he believed his father was white and his mother a Cherokee slave, which Smith suggests meant she was Black.[23] It is unclear where the Black heritage, if any, enters either lineage, but Smith says that while both denied Black ancestry, because they could not prove Indian ancestry they were classified as "colored." Long Lance, like the rest of his family, was perceived by many to be Black despite his persistent claims to be Indian. After a stint in the circus as a teenager, Long tried to enroll at the Carlisle Indian school at the age of nineteen; with the support of his parents, he lied about his age on the application, which cut off enrollment at eighteen, and claimed to be half Cherokee. It was the beginning of Long's remaking himself into an Indian, and the start of a long list of prevarications in which he portrayed himself as the son of a Blackfoot Indian chief (his father was actually a school janitor in North Carolina). After Long's identity was called into question by *Silent Enemy* star Chauncy Yellow Robe and a scandal unfolded, Long was presumed Black by New York's prejudiced elite, who rejected him, horrified that they'd entertained a Black man. Long's life ended tragically in 1932, in an apparent suicide.

Long's legacy of ethnic fraud is one of two high-profile cases of Indian impersonation after Indianness had become a marketized commodity.[24] For the Show Indians performing Indianness was one thing; as Indians they were conscripted into a foreign economic system with little choice, and leveraging their Indian identities as a commodity to conform to federal pressure was a strategic assertion of agency, as Linda McNenly and others have noted. The same might also be said for Long Lance, a Black-presenting mixed-race person from the Deep South who also had limited options. This is how some scholars have explained Long's inventing of Indian identity. But the difference between Show Indians capitalizing on their Indianness for economic reasons and Long Lance is the use of deception to fraudulently leverage an Indian identity for personal and financial gain. It was the beginning of a pattern that started in the early days of the Hollywood film business and continues today.

Another case of Native fraud in the early film business is the story of James Young Deer. Young Deer slightly predated Long Lance, but the story was markedly different as his fraud was not exposed until long after he died. While Long Lance was working on his journalism career as the fictitious son of a Blackfoot chief, Young Deer had already become the first supposed Native American film producer and director on the heels of a successful acting career. Born James Young Johnson, Young Deer was the general manager for Pathé Frères West Coast Studio from 1911 to 1914, having worked alongside film legends D. W. Griffith, Fred J. Balshofer, and Mack Sennett. According to film scholar Angela Aleiss, "As one of Hollywood's pioneer filmmakers, Young Deer oversaw the production of more than one hundred one-reel silent Westerns for Pathé, the world's largest production company with an American studio in Edendale in Los Angeles." Born in Washington, DC, to "mulatto" parents in 1878, Young Deer reinvented himself as a full-blooded Winnebago Indian after a stint in the US Navy during the Spanish-American War that ended with a medical discharge in 1901. By 1906 he had met and married Lillian Red Wing St. Cyr, who was from a prominent Winnebago family, and together they entered show business performing as Indians in theater productions such as "Pioneer Days: A Spectacle Drama of Western Life" in New York City. Few suspected Young Deer's sham identity while he was alive, and it wasn't until recent years that the deceit was uncovered. Genealogical research by a descendant relative, coincidentally unaware of his connection to Young Deer, traced Young Deer's paternal family origins to a Delaware community known as the Moors of Delaware, a little known triracial community in the homelands of the Nanticoke Indians. Ironically, Young Deer could have had some Nanticoke ancestry without knowing it. His career began to decline after being linked to a sex trafficking ring in 1913, and in time, his marriage to St. Cyr unraveled. In the end he was remembered by the St. Cyr family with bitterness—and the sense that he contrived an American Indian identity because it was profitable.[25]

In her illuminating book *Picturing Indians: Native Americans in Film, 1941–1960*, Liza Black studied Native people in film to examine the intersections of history, film industry labor practices, and representation. Her research reveals how Hollywood created a look that manufactured the Movie Indian in a fantasy world, where Indians couldn't be seen as they actually were. With the right makeup, wardrobe, props, and speech, anyone—white, Indian, or anything else—could be transformed into the image film creators wanted to project that fit a preconceived if wildly inaccurate representation of "the Indian." These projections were paradoxically bound up with ideas about and demands for authenticity, but only a kind of authenticity that could fit within an already preconceived schema. Black concludes about filmmakers' brand of Native authenticity:

> Although filmmakers had the power to access a variety of resources on Native history and culture, they obstructed their own efforts to harness Indian authenticity by adhering to stereotyped notions of what was and was not Indian. When they hired Indians who held and shared knowledge studios found valuable, which was extremely rare, the filmmakers held Native power in check by limiting their creative control to minute aspects of the filmmaking process. According to Hollywood's stereotypes, other Indians lacked the knowledge Hollywood wanted but were willing and able to provide them with an ersatz Indian culture. Apaches thus borrowed from the Boy Scouts. Diné copied Indian dances from movies. Filmmakers were looking for something they believed existed but could not locate in actual Indians . . . Instead, filmmakers created films they believed the American public would understand with ease, which meant story lines focused on whites and Indians who looked and acted like Indian characters already familiar to movie audiences.[26]

The concept of authenticity rests on an assumption of cultural stasis, that "authentic" Native cultures and people are pure and unchanging. Deviations from an imagined cultural purity marks inauthenticity, so Hollywood's striving for an elusive authenticity doesn't allow Native people to be who they really are, thus perpetuating inaccurate representations. Michelle Raheja uses the term "redfacing" to describe the "process and politics of playing Indian."[27] Liza Black found that film production teams assumed that twentieth century Indians were mere shells of their former selves, never able to measure up to the fantasies of who they thought Indians were or should be, so even Indians had to be redfaced. In an environment where Indians can't be seen for who they are, anyone can stand in and assume a contrived Indian identity and with jobs to be had and money to be made, they increasingly did. Black's research found that in the early days film studios tended to hire Native American people for Indian roles, but by midcentury, while they claimed they preferred Indians actors, they hired more non-Indians to play Indian characters due to changing labor practices that favored unskilled, non-union workers.[28]

Actors had plenty of reason to present themselves as Indians, and Black believes that ethnic fraud may have been common in Hollywood.[29] She names numerous examples of actors who claimed to be Indian but weren't. None was more notorious than Iron Eyes Cody. Cody built an entire film career playing Indian characters from 1927 to his last film in 1990. He seemed happy to have been typecast as an Indian in the multitude of small film and television roles he played, but he rocketed to fame in 1971 with the famous "Crying Indian" commercial created for the Keep America Beautiful, Inc., anti-littering campaign. Like Long Lance and Young Deer, Cody didn't just play Indian in film, he constructed an Indian guise that he maintained in his daily life. He'd concocted an elaborate story about being Cherokee, which included descent from a great-great-grandfather who had been driven out of the Southeast to western Arkansas on the Trail of Tears, as he recounted in a 1982 autobiography.[30] In great detail he shared that his family moved farther west into Oklahoma, that they had been well-to-do Cherokees, and that he had a grandfather who fought for the Confederates during the Civil War. He described this grandfather as a guerrilla fighter with the Quantrill Raiders, and as a "professional killer" after the war, he had taken up a life of crime as a highwayman, holding up stagecoaches and robbing banks. Cody claimed that his father was an expert horseman with Buffalo Bill but also a nasty and hopeless drunk, that he was the only "real" child out of nine, all the rest of whom were adopted, and that his mother was a "typical Cree Indian." All this detail appears in the first pages of the book, as if Cody is trying to establish himself as unquestionably Indian from the very start.

Cody wore the costumes and wig in his daily life as the characters he played became his identity. He married the daughter of the prominent Seneca archeologist and a founder of the Society of American Indians, Arthur C. Parker, and adopted two Native children. Cody ingratiated himself with the Hollywood Indian community, supporting their causes and donating money, and they in turn loved and supported him till the end of his life in 1999. It seems to have been an open secret among Hollywood Indians that Cody was not actually an Indian, but for them, that was irrelevant because he'd done so much good for them. Cody's cover was not blown until 1996, when Angela Aleiss published a story in the New Orleans *Times-Picayune* after tracking down Cody's half sister, May Abshire. Abshire disclosed that Cody, born Espera Oscar DeCorti in Louisiana's Vermillion Parish, was one of four children of Sicilian immigrants, proven by baptismal records and ship passenger lists. The parents were part of a large wave of Sicilian immigration to the New Orleans area between the 1870s and the 1920s. Cody's father, Antonio DeCorti, ran afoul of the local mafia and fled to Texas, where the family eventually joined him. In time the family splintered, and Cody and his two brothers stayed in Texas but soon made their way to California, changed their names from Corti to Cody, and Iron Eyes began his acting career. His mother, Francesca, remarried Alton Abshire when Cody was still a boy.[31]

As the film industry evolved in the twentieth century, the Movie Indian became the epitome of the white man's Indian, blurring the lines between reality and fantasy that audiences already confused about Indians couldn't perceive. The invention of the Movie Indian helps us understand how Native identity fraud became normalized in the early twentieth century through the commodification and performing of indigeneity. Performing indigeneity for money (and fame) incentivized the donning of false American Indian identities and, in the second half of the century, was exacerbated by the growing ethnic renewal movement, the new census rules that allowed self-identification, and growing urban pan-Indianism. By the 1960s, the stigma previously associated with being Indian was waning, and with the emergence of the hippie counterculture, being Indian was fashionable. Claiming Native American heritage, now vested with cultural capital, was not limited to what could be monetarily gained as it became tied to other less tangible, more affective psychological benefits. So, while for some it presented a newfound freedom to reclaim a legitimate birthright denied to their ancestors, for others, it was the taking of liberties based on little more than speculation, family rumor, or pure imagination, driven by a sense of entitlement to claim whatever one wanted.

Recent scholarship has theorized Indigenous performativity in varying, sometimes conflicting and troubling ways. Indigenous performance can take many forms, deployed for many reasons. As we see with the Wild West shows, they began as performances designed strictly for white audiences, geared to reinforce American mythologies of conquest, the "winning of the West." The role of Indians, cast as noble savages, was to prove the superiority of everything the Eurocentric United States stood for. Industrialism and modernity (i.e., colonialism) wins, primitivism loses, and it's clear who is who in that equation. And thus, incidentally, who deserves the land. Manifest destiny is achieved to the delight of white settler audiences and Indians, no longer a threat to the colonial project, are romanticized. Early filmic representations sympathetically lamented the inevitability of the "Red Man's" disappearance, but by the 1940s, Indians once again are marauding savages. The performances catered to the white settler gaze and Native people, hired for a job, performed their tragic roles dutifully. Rejecting victimizing narratives, scholars lean into perspectives that instead emphasize Native agency, where actors leveraged what limited power they had at any given time to their own advantage, be it through the earning of decent wages or the ability to practice elements of their culture.

The performance of indigeneity, however, always exists within the context of history, place, and circumstance, and we can see this reflected in the writing of Indigenous researchers globally. South African professor of development studies Morgan Ndlovu reminds us, for example, that the concept of indigeneity is a colonial construct forged through domination and oppression as European modernity was imposed on original peoples without their consent. The most potent strategy of colonization, he contends, is the colonization of the Indigenous mind through epistemicide, the killing of Indigenous knowledge and ways of knowing. "Formal schooling and [in] other subtle ways . . . if one is not looking carefully, appear to affirm the humanity of the colonized subject, while actually performing the opposite," Ndlovu writes.[32] The modern/colonial education system has always been "predicated on producing a consenting subject to modernity/coloniality."[33] When Indigenous people perform Indigeneity (here he refers to Zulu and Maasai tourist cultural villages), even when seen as an act of agency, it can unintentionally produce "an indigenous subject in a way that suits the colonizer's gaze at the expense of the interests of the colonized subject."[34]

In addition to the risk of reinforcing colonial logics and structures, a myriad of other unintended consequences can and have resulted from performing Indigeneity. In the context of Aotearoa/New Zealand, Māori scholar Brendan Hokowhitu observed how public performances of the haka (a type of dance accompanied by a chant) by the All Blacks national rugby team has been appropriated by transnational corporations in marketing schemes and in national culture. Hokowhitu argues that when the global sports clothing company Adidas took over primary sponsorship of the team, not only did it use the image of haka performances as corporate branding, it "signified a mass wave of marketing based on selling the exoticism of 'traditional' Māori masculine culture."[35] The "Ka Mate" haka has since become the most maligned and abused of all haka, commodified by other corporations including Fiat and Lego, and appropriated by American football teams. It has become what Hokowhitu calls a "masculine national anthem, performed religiously . . . at significant national and local events, such as funerals."[36] Reflecting Ndlovu's view on the colonizing of Indigenous cultures, Hokowhitu maintains that the commodification of the haka is an example of how Māori culture and knowledge became synthesized into New Zealand's dominant culture, with the subversive nature of the haka becoming "assimilated into service of imperialism itself" and the making of the Indigenous person into the postcolonial citizen.[37]

Discussions of Indigenous performance inevitably raise academic questions about the nature of indigeneity and critiques of essentialism. What constitutes indigeneity, who says it, who gets to claim it, and who legitimately gets to perform it? In their 2014 edited volume *Performing Indigeneity: Global Histories and Contemporary Experiences*, Graham and Penny argue for an understanding that avoids reducing indigeneity into rigid, essentialist categorization, deferring instead to a conception of indigeneity as an emergent process, or a "bundle of generative possibilities."[38] Sensibly, they couple Indigenous performativity with cultural sovereignty, but in eschewing more solid definitions of indigeneity linked to political sovereignty they fail to address the co-optation of indigeneity by non-Indigenous people for their own often dubious purposes.[39] For example, an essay on German Indian hobbyists characterizes the country's Indian hobbyism as "surrogate indigeneity." Germans have been fascinated with American Indian culture, fetishizing Plains horse cultures in particular since their prolonged contact with Indians in the touring Wild West shows, and before that, in popular literature. For decades Germans have evolved an elaborate subculture of playing Indian (some prefer to call it "practical ethnology"), organized in clubs that number in the hundreds throughout the country. German hobbyists devote themselves to studying the traditional cultures of predominantly Plains Indians, painstakingly learning how to reproduce authentic precolonial buckskin clothing, weapons, and other accoutrements of Plains Indian life, and performing in full costume at weekend and week-long encampments and powwows that can include spiritual ceremonies and attract huge crowds.[40] Penny, who contends that the German affinity for American Indians grew out of a view of their own history as conquered tribal peoples, wrote, "By the 1950s many hobbyists saw themselves engaged in an effort at preservation, an attempt to locate the traces of specific American Indian cultures both for their own edification and, ultimately, for the use of the survivors of ethnocide in North America."[41]

Penny strenuously argues that rather than critically dismissing German hobbyism as neocolonial, "we" should be willing to see hobbyism as an alternative form of knowledge production—"one that stands outside the academy and is based on often-stringent discursive readings of texts and interviews that are later circulated through oral traditions in this German/European subculture rather than through academic publications or journalistic essays."[42] It's unclear what "we" he is referring to, but presumably, he is talking about academics in general. In the chapter he goes to great lengths to emphasize instances where American Indian people have visited and given their blessings to the German hobbyists. Little attention, however, is given to critical American Indian perspectives, and in the one short paragraph addressing it, one of the few cited sources is Ward Churchill, who has long faced accusations of fraud. When the essay was published in 2014, the issue of Native American cultural appropriation and ethnic fraud was well-known, and it seems irresponsible to have not analyzed more fully the German hobbyist scene in the context of the literature on cultural appropriation. It's not unreasonable to ask certain pointed questions: How many of today's American Indian people are willing to consider German hobbyists (some would use the term impersonators) as repositories for authentic material culture? What does "authentic" mean and who has the authority to determine it? Doesn't the fetishizing of pre-1900 Plains Indian cultures reinforce romanticized images of Indians, restricting them to a bygone past? What does the performing of Plains Indianness and religion mean outside the context of Plains cultures and the land itself?

As Penny points out, while the German hobbyists see themselves as doing something more serious than just playing Indian, they also are not trying to pass themselves off as Indians. I reject Penny's framing of German Indian hobbyism as surrogate indigeneity. Their brand of performing indigeneity simply falls into the category of playing Indian, but it does remind us that Indigenous performativity is a central aspect to both playing Indian and becoming Indian. For those who traffic in identity fraud, a convincing performance is key. As we saw with Sacheen Littlefeather, the generative moment of her fraud at the Academy Awards was constituted by the words "I'm Apache" in conjunction with her appearance, clearly intended to send the message of Indigenous identity. It was the buckskin outfit and her adaptable physical features that were intended to convince the public that she was an Indian, just as she understood when she began her modeling career that she could successfully exploit an increasingly popular "Indian" look. This is the same kind of Indigenous performativity Paul Olivas/Semu Huaute relied on to fraudulently convince people he was an Indian medicine man and later the last full-blood Chumash. As we'll examine in the following chapter, he began as a performer with the Southern California Laguna Pueblo Indian dance group in the 1950s, as did the faux medicine man Rolling Thunder, who effectively adapted his appearance to cast himself as a Cherokee medicine man. Iron Eyes Cody went overboard with his performativity, but it didn't seem to hurt him.

Entertainers who fake an American Indian identity have always known how to construct a convincing image; it's not difficult, and it's easier for those with an ethnically ambiguous look. It's why James Young Deer, Long Lance, and Iron Eyes Cody could pull off their sham identities for as long as they did. The same can be said for the superstar entertainer Cher, who in the late 1960s and early 1970s adopted an appearance seemingly intended to be Native American at a time when Indians were in vogue, accentuated by her straight, waist-length black hair, strong facial features, Southern California tan, and Indian-inspired fashion and jewelry. She doubled down on the image in 1973 with her hit song "Half-Breed," featured in a painfully campy performance on *The Sonny & Cher Comedy Hour* in which she sat on a horse in a skimpy, Indianesque outfit and a massively long feather headdress. The blatant sexualizing of what would or could have been a proud cultural representation indicates a lack of connection to culture, and resembles the way Sacheen sexualized her supposed Native American heritage with her *Playboy* spread. Had there been a tribal community either Cher or Sacheen were accountable to, it's hard to imagine them thinking they could get away with what tribal communities would have considered highly disrespectful displays. One website authoritatively stated that it wasn't until 1973 that Cher's biography started describing her as one-sixteenth Cherokee.[43] Cher, born Cherilyn Sarkisian, was born to an Armenian father and a mother of western European heritage and from whom Cher claimed her alleged Cherokee heritage, despite Cherokee genealogists rejecting her claims. Inheriting her ethnic look from her Armenian side made it easy for Cher to attempt to convince an unknowing public of her supposed Cherokeeness.

Buffy Sainte-Marie similarly leveraged an ethnically ambiguous physical appearance to pass herself off as Indigenous. Buffy is alleged to have invented a story about being adopted at birth, and her lack of knowledge about her birth family became the basis for her claims to Cree heritage. From there the story shifted and changed over time, eventually exposing the contradictions that would lead to an in-depth investigation in 2023 that would then unravel what was depicted as a fabric of lies she had woven over sixty years. It's interesting to note that she began constructing her Indian identity story about the same time Semu did, in the early 1960s, when the general public knew nothing about American Indians other than Movie Indian stereotypes, making them arguably much easier to fool, and around the same age Sacheen did, right after high school. The stories of the high-profile frauds highlighted in this chapter and others, reveal similar patterns. Ethnic fraud is well-constructed deceit, but like any elaborate lie, over time it becomes difficult to keep track of the details and the inconsistencies begin to show. The truth always comes out, and superficial performances of indigeneity may be convincing for a time, but in the long run, they are fragile and unreliable. Buffy embellished her image as an Indigenous woman over the years, using makeup, costuming, and other accoutrements to accentuate her non-white look; her performance would have been much less believable had she been blonde, blue-eyed, and fairer skinned. The bottom line is, it's impossible to tell Native people on looks alone, or based on non-verifiable stories.

Performing indigeneity in all its forms, whether for the purposes of legitimate cultural representation or as a means of pretense, is bound up with complicated questions about meaning, authenticity, authority, aesthetics, historical context, and place. We've seen what happens when people assert performances of indigeneity outside the bounds of legitimate cultural belonging, absent mechanisms for accountability and assurances that jobs and resources meant for American Indian people go to actual American Indian people. The result is the inequitable distribution of resources, and people including children, are devastated when they find out they have been betrayed by people they have looked up to their entire lives, to say nothing of the damage done to families through the lies frauds tell. Pretendianism is gaslighting of another sort, causing psychological harm to those who have already endured centuries of harm. History shows that the film industry is the breeding ground for Native American ethnic fraud, and it has extended to all realms of entertainment. The problem was so pervasive that it led to the first formal organizations for Indian actors, but over time, similar organizations meant to protect Indian actors became infiltrated by impersonators, marking the consistent inability of these groups to establish a coherent system of accountability to root out Indian ethnic fraud. This lack of accountability haunts Native Hollywood today and is what led to the academy's canonization of Sacheen Littlefeather at the end of her life in 2022, despite lingering doubts about her identity.

INDIGENOUS ADVOCACY IN HOLLYWOOD

"Natives have been fighting for centuries to preserve our lands and cultures and we are still working to reclaim our identities. Our identity is our birthright. There is no need to cast non-Native performers and actresses in Native roles . . . The practice of whitewashing is unnecessary, unacceptable and discriminatory. It promotes . . . erasure . . . Natives are often typecast in stereotypical roles or removed from the narrative entirely."[44] This sounds as if it might date back to 1926, but in fact, it was written in 2017 as an open letter by Anishinaabe actor Adam Beach, published in the online entertainment industry rag *Deadline*. Beach, one of Hollywood's most celebrated American Indian actors today, released the letter for the express purpose of addressing the casting of non-Native people in Native roles. "This is not 1950 anymore," he passionately asserts, saying that considering the epidemic of missing and murdered Indigenous women, it's especially troubling to see Native roles go to non-Native women. He goes on to explain that claiming to be Native American without proof is fraud, and that even for those who don't have proof, there are other markers of indigeneity like kinship and community bonds. Beach takes a committed stand: "Hollywood profits off of telling our stories, using us as backdrops in their white savior narratives, sending the message to our people that we are disposable. The least Hollywood could do is cast Natives who are actually connected to their tribe."

By 1926, the problem of non-Native actors misrepresenting themselves as Indians and competing with Indians for roles was so common it motivated the creation of the first Indian advocacy group in the film industry, the War Paint Club. Akins and Bauer in 2021 write that by 1928 a special census counted seven hundred Indians in Los Angeles, and that by the 1930s, an intertribal culture had emerged in the city, with organizations like American Indian Progressive Association, Wigwam Club, California Indian Land Rights Association, and National Justice to the American Indian.[45] The War Paint Club, organized specifically to address issues in the film industry, fits within this milieu. Started in 1926 by the legendary Lakota activist, author, tribal leader, and actor Luther Standing Bear and others, the organization came together to promote fair pay, better working conditions, and respectful representations. Assurance that Indians received Indian roles was also at the top of the organization's priorities.[46] There was a thriving community of Indian actors in LA by then, but because of a belief that Indians were incapable of serious acting, they earned only bit parts while leading roles inevitably went to non-Indians. Spotlighting the problem of competition for roles, in 1926 for example, popular Western star William S. Hart and friend to Indian actors reported that "since the motion pictures have become controlled by business interests they do not go in for the real things so much. They use Mexicans for Indians and there are a great many Mexicans in this country."[47]

By 1936, the War Paint Club had given way to the Indian Actors Association (IAA). It's evident that after ten years, little progress had been made in assuring roles went to Indians. At that point, the IAA was needed because of the "practice among some studios of engaging pseudo-Indians for leading roles and the need to 'try to displace the Syrians, Swedes, Aryans, and Latins who [were] being manufactured into Indians by sun-tan oil and braided wigs.'"[48]

Another problem was that the lack of Indian hiring pit Indians against each other. Bill Hazlett, a Blackfoot Indian and a founder of the IAA, wrote:

> When [the studios] were casting *The Last of the Mohicans* [George B. Seitz, 1936], some of us noticed that Indians were underbidding each other just so they could get work. We knew it was wrong, we didn't like it but we also knew that the only way we could change things was by organizing. So [a group of Indian actors] helped start the association. Our objectives were to stop the movie producers from encouraging and allowing this price cutting and to replace non-Indians in acting jobs with Indians.[49]

The IAA became affiliated with the Screen Actors Guild (SAG), and with a closed shop clause that guaranteed jobs went to union members, a more equitable wage structure was instituted.[50] Despite the activism of the IAA, by the 1950s, when the hiring of Indian actors peaked, as Liza Black argues, only a handful of Indians were SAG members,[51] and the practice of hiring non-Indians stubbornly persisted. The lack of Indians in SAG may be at least partially attributable to the passage of the Taft-Hartley Act in 1947, which outlawed the union practice of closed shops. If fair wages were no longer guaranteed through requiring employers to hire union members only, there may have been little motivation for Native actors to maintain union membership.

By the mid-1960s, little progress had been made; impersonators had thoroughly infiltrated Native Hollywood, sabotaging Native efforts to protect roles for Native actors. Jay Silverheels, born Harold Jay Smith, of indisputable Mohawk heritage, one of the few Indian actors to make it big in Hollywood, "worked against the hiring of white actors for Indian roles in the 1960s by forming the Indian Actors Workshop."[52] Silverheels wrote in 1970, "We're trying to provide for Indians an opportunity for education in theater arts that they would not have otherwise . . . [but] our main purpose is not only to create skills but to establish an Indian repertory theatre, to take from the past and the present and to create something that is definitely Indian.

We hope to be the voice of the Indian and the problems he faces and be a showcase for Indian talent."[53]

In 1973, as film studies scholars were becoming more critical in the way they were analyzing Native American representation in film, John A. Price tracked cinema's gradual improvement in Native representation, but noted the ongoing problem of Indian actors not appearing in Native roles. He documented Jay Silverheels's work in founding the Indian Actors Guild in 1966 to help Indians develop their acting skills and the Indian Actors Workshop, which operated out of the Los Angeles Indian Center, "with the help of other Indians such as Buffy Sainte-Marie, Iron Eyes Cody, and Rodd Redwing," all of whom have had dubious claims to Native American heritage.[54]

Clearly, by the mid-1960s, it was either impossible to tell the imposters from legitimate Native people, or it was too politically fraught to call out fraud, or there was some other complex set of dynamics in Native Hollywood that was encouraging people to falsely present themselves as Indians, such as fear of losing jobs. By then, Indian-claiming had become normalized. We really shouldn't be surprised that pretendianism as we know it today has its roots in the California-based entertainment industry, where Indigenous performativity had been rewarded since the turn of the century and individuals, Indian and non-Indian, had built entire careers on it. The social rupture created by the convergence of Indian identity commodification, census self-identification, and urban pan-Indianism became the foundation for systemic Native American ethnic fraud, and by 1973, when Sacheen Littlefeather took the stage at the Oscars, the conditions were ripe for the perpetuation of her mythological performance. It begs certain questions: Could anything have been done to prevent the kind of identity hoaxes perpetrated by Littlefeather, Iron Eyes Cody, Buffy Sainte-Marie, and so many others? Why were the efforts of American Indian actors to block non-Indians from taking Native roles so unsuccessful? What are the mechanisms in Native Hollywood today that allow non-Natives who claim to be Native to continue taking roles from Native actors?

The 1970s and '80s saw the emergence of a new era of Native filmmaking, and with it, Native organizing in the film industry became more sophisticated with the formation of new alliances and Native film festivals.[55] Critical to the success of Native film was support from a few high-profile allies, such as actor and director Robert Redford, who had long been an advocate for Native American causes. The first Native film festival was started by Fort Peck Sioux Michael L. Smith, with the help of Will Sampson (the unforgettable Chief Bromden in the 1975 blockbuster *One Flew over the Cuckoo's Nest*) and Coast Salish actor Chief Dan George (*The Outlaw Josie Wales* and *Little Big Man*). The American Indian Film Festival, first held in Seattle in 1975, moved to San Francisco, where it became the American Indian Film Institute in 1979.[56] In 1982, "The American Indian Image on Film: The Southwest" was the first conference to be held on a college campus—the University of New Mexico—and featured presentations by writers, scholars, and filmmakers, including Redford. Just the year before, Redford had established the Sundance Institute at his Sundance ski resort in Utah that was devoted to independent filmmaking.[57] In 1983, the American Indian Film Registry for the Performing Arts was founded by Will Sampson and others to promote the employment of tribally enrolled Native Americans in the film business.[58] An advisory board included Hollywood notables like Burt Reynolds, Hoyt Axton, Ralph Bellamy, Max Gail, Dennis Weaver, and Jonathan Winters. Members were offered casting assistance, industry seminars, acting workshops, and other benefits. Due to a lack of financial support, the registry folded in 1994, but it was instrumental in advancing the careers of some of today's most important Native actors, like Tantoo Cardinal and Wes Studi.[59]

The year 1994 marks an interesting turning point for Native film advocacy in the industry. It was the year Robert Redford's Sundance Film Festival added a Native American program category and established the Native Lab as part of what is today known as the Native American and Indigenous Program, or just the Indigenous Program, dedicated to the cultivation and mentoring of Indigenous storytellers. It all began in 1985, when Redford took over the floundering US Film Festival, which became Sundance by 1990, and quickly earned a reputation as the most prestigious film festival this side of Cannes.[60] It is by far the most significant Native American advocacy initiative in the industry; many of today's most celebrated Native American and Indigenous filmmakers participated in the Native Lab, the Indigenous Program, or another Sundance fellowship or grant program, or launched their films at the festival. The list includes Chris Eyre's *Smoke Signals* (1998), Sherman Alexie's *The Business of Fancydancing* (2002), Taika Waititi's *Two Cars, One Night* (2003), and Sterlin Harjo's *Four Sheets to the Wind* (2007).

Sundance has maintained its position as ground zero for aspiring Native filmmakers, and out of that has surfaced an infrastructure composed of power brokers with the ability to influence Native Hollywood. The film industry has long been governed by the old axiom, "It's not what you know, it's who you know," and it's no less true for Indians. In the center of Native Hollywood's sphere of influence is a small handful of individuals who have risen through the ranks and now function formally and informally as gatekeepers, shaping what and who gets visibility and advising the industry's larger power structure—most notably the Academy of Motion Picture Arts and Sciences—on Native issues. In this sphere, no one stands out more than Bird Runningwater and Heather Rae. The two have been closely aligned for over twenty years, beginning at the Sundance Institute in 2001.[61] Rae had been running the Native American Program since 1996 when Rae met and tagged Runningwater in 2001 to take her position at Sundance, a job he held for two decades. Runningwater had built an arts and culture program at the Ford Foundation, followed by a short stint at the Rockefeller Foundation.[62]

Of Cheyenne and Mescalero Apache heritage, born and raised on the Mescalero Apache Reservation, Runningwater is unquestionably Indigenous. His master's degree in public policy and experience at Ford must have made him a good fit for the Sundance Native Program, even without film experience, which presumably would come later. Rae had a short roster of film credits to her name when she arrived at Sundance, and over the years, she has built her resume as a producer and director.[63] Most of her films have Native American themes, a few of which are some of the more significant Native films and documentaries in the last twenty years, including *Trudell* (2005), *Frozen River* (2008), an episode of the Canadian TV series

Rise (2017), and the Emmy Award–winning *Dawnland* (2018). Rae is also a producer on the 2023 Amazon Prime original series *Outer Range*. For years, she consistently echoed claims to being Cherokee, without connecting to any of the three federally recognized Cherokee tribes or a family.

It's hard to pinpoint the beginning of the current pretendian controversy because, as we have seen, it started with the invasion of imposters in the film industry a century ago. The term *pretendian*, a portmanteau of the words *pretend* and *Indian*, is a more recent invention. But writers have used the term "pretend Indians" since at least 1981, with the publication of the anthology *The Pretend Indians: Images of Native Americans in the Movies*, only the second book of its kind at the time to interrogate American Indian imagery in film.[64] Philip Deloria used the term in 1999: "Pretendians build lives and careers on ethnic fraud."[65] The pretendian moniker gained steam in the 2010s as Indigenous people in the US and Canada grappled with the proliferation of fraud in academia and publishing. Meanwhile, the battles against oppressive government action and corporate exploitation continued in Indian country, and 2016 marked an inflection point, when the Standing Rock struggle against the Dakota Access Pipeline exploded with its nine-month-long protest camp near the Standing Rock Sioux Reservation. Indians and their problems were becoming more visible again, building on the momentum from the Occupy Wall Street movement in 2011 and the Idle No More movement that erupted the following year. What made these protests different from those of the 1970s was their environmental focus, highlighting how Indigenous issues were not just Indian problems but concerns for everyone now. The new world of social media also made it impossible for the outside world to ignore the injustices that had never stopped in Indian country.

After Standing Rock, things were decidedly different in all corners of Indian country. In the months and years that followed came a stream of film productions, dozens of them documenting the historic event. Among the most prominent was Viceland's 2017 eight-part television docuseries *Rise* chronicling Indigenous resistance movements, including two episodes on Standing Rock. Viceland was a new US cable channel brand with Canadian partnerships; *Rise* was produced in partnership with VICE Canada and the Aboriginal People's Television Network (APTN). The series was received with much fanfare, and three of the episodes, including the Standing Rock episode *Sacred Waters*, premiered at Sundance in 2017.[66] One aspect of *Rise*'s acclaim was the series showrunner and director Michelle Latimer, who was celebrated as a female Indigenous filmmaker. Beginning her acting career in the early 2000s, Latimer moved to filmmaking a decade later and has since won numerous awards and accolades. In addition to the Sundance festival, her films have been screened at the Toronto International Film Festival, Berlin International, Rotterdam, Oberhausen, Cannes, the National Art Gallery of Canada, and MoMA.[67] *Rise* won the Canadian Screen Award for Best Documentary Program in 2018.[68]

Latimer, whose successful two-decade long career as an Indigenous filmmaker often linked to her claimed Algonquin and Métis heritage, came under scrutiny in August 2020; she had added Kitigan Zibi (Maniwaki) heritage to press materials for her latest film *Inconvenient Indian*. The press release was met with anger by Kitigan Zibi tribal members, who demanded that Latimer show proof of her connection to the community. Latimer responded that her claims were based on her father's families' oral history; a Canadian Broadcasting Corporation news report found a census record showing her grandfather of French Canadian ancestry but no direct link to Kitigan Zibi. Ironically, an independent genealogical investigation found in Latimer's family tree two Indigenous ancestors of undefined tribal origin dating back to the early seventeenth century in the general region of today's Kitigan Zibi, seemingly validating the family's Métis claims.[69] In December 2020, Latimer issued a public apology for her claims to Kitigan Zibi, but the controversy resulted in *Inconvenient Indian* being pulled from distribution and its debut at Sundance. She sued the CBC for libel but later dropped the suit, and in 2021, released a statement reaffirming her Algonquin and Métis ancestry.[70] Latimer's distant heritage, if true, may exonerate her from accusations that she fabricated a story about Indigenous heritage. But it does raise the question: At what point does one lose the ability to claim to *be* Indigenous when the Indigenous ancestors are so far in the past and there has been no retention of connection to a tribal community?

The Latimer controversy landed smack dab in the middle of larger public debates about pretendians within Canada. In 2016, the acclaimed author Joseph Boyden was accused of mispresenting himself as Indigenous, followed over the next few years by exposures of accomplished academics, a high-ranking federal health agency official, and a former judge. In the US a parallel process was underway, and things became especially heated with the circulation of the *Alleged Pretendians List* in the form of a spreadsheet started by journalist Jacqueline Keeler in early 2021. Access to the online spreadsheet required permission but the list of almost two hundred names nevertheless got around. The list homed in on those in academia, entertainment, and publishing. A minority of the names on the list included hard evidence of pretendianism, but there were many who were long thought to be frauds, while others seemed to be unfairly accused.[71] On the list were both Michelle Latimer and Heather Rae. There had been whispers from Native Hollywood insiders for some time about the veracity of Rae's Cherokee claims, and for a while it seemed strange that Latimer was so harshly taken down while Rae seemed to be given a pass.[72] Things changed, however, in March 2023, when a story broke from a group calling itself the Tribal Alliance Against Frauds (TAAF) alleging Rae had no verifiable Cherokee ancestry. The story, which first ran in the *New York Post*, was picked up in *The Guardian*, Indianz.com, and a number of conservative-leaning publications.

The timing could not have been worse for Rae. Within the previous year or so, a group called the Indigenous Alliance within the Academy of Motion Picture Arts and Sciences surfaced without fanfare or even a public-facing profile. It wasn't on anyone's radar until 2022, when the academy released its apology to Sacheen Littlefeather, at which point it became clear that the Indigenous Alliance was none other than Heather Rae and Bird Runningwater. The previous year the academy had celebrated the opening of its Academy Museum of Motion Pictures in Los Angeles and included an exhibit dedicated to Sacheen Littlefeather. It didn't seem unreasonable to assume that the Indigenous Alliance—that is, Rae and Runningwater—were the force behind the apology, the apology ceremony, and perhaps even the exhibit.[73] In hindsight, the optics were bad, prompting us to ask questions about who gets to make decisions about Native representation in the film industry and what is the criteria when Native claims are made? Only in Hollywood!

Things got stranger still after some troubling information about Bird Runningwater came to light. Runningwater wrote a master's thesis in 1996 about the problem of Native fraud in higher education, a view that bore no resemblance to the world within which he was now embedded. Recall that after the Sacheen Littlefeather scandal broke in October 2022, the response from the academy museum explicitly stated that "[w]ith the support of its Indigenous Alliance—an Academy member affinity group—the Academy recognizes self-identification."[74] Runningwater's thesis is titled *Exploring Ethnic Fraud: An Analysis of Verification Policies for American Indians in Higher Education.* Its abstract states:

> The determination of who is an Indian? [sic] Will constantly plague American society until tribal governments are honored, respected and allowed to continue acting as sovereign nations. This report addresses who is an Indian? For the purposes of higher education, and confronts the issue of ethnic fraud [sic].
>
> Institutions of higher education are currently usurping tribal authority by continuing self-identification processes. This report analyses who is an Indian? [sic], tribal sovereignty, verification policies and gives recommendations for addressing ethnic fraud and honoring the inherent sovereignty of tribal nations.[75]

The paper makes a very strong case for why colleges and universities should implement policies ensuring that documented Native Americans receive admission, scholarships, and benefits meant for Native students in higher education. It gives specific definitions of who is an Indian and even breaks down the definition of fraud into two discrete categories, ethnic fraud and ethno-political fraud:

> For this analysis, the term "ethnic fraud" will be defined as the act of purposefully and deceitfully claiming an ethnicity to which one does not belong in order to gain college admission and scholarships

designated specifically for American Indians as an ethnic group. The term "ethno-political fraud" will be defined as the act of purposefully and deceitfully claiming to be an American Indian when one is not a member of a federally recognized tribe, to receive benefits such as college admission and scholarships designated specifically for American Indians.[76]

Runningwater rightly argues that the definition of *Indian* should be regarded as a political designation in line with federal policy deferring to tribal sovereignty. It lays out policy recommendations designed to avoid fraud based on specific criteria but notes that could be overly burdensome in many contexts. There are reasons to argue why his view is too stringent and limiting, but for this discussion, what matters is that he appears to have made a complete about-face from his previous grad school perspective of grave concern about ethnic fraud. Or his views about ethnic fraud in higher education are completely different from his views about self-identification in the entertainment industry, implausible since the principle is still the same: people who claim to be Indian in any realm of life to receive material benefits wrongfully take what is meant for legitimate Indians. The obvious question is: Why the change of heart? It's not that personal or even scholarly viewpoints can't or shouldn't change, but in this instance, with pretendianism as rampant as ever, shouldn't we advocate for ways to rein it in, especially considering that the film industry is precisely where the practice of Native American identity fraud began? Shouldn't Native people in the industry have their interests represented by Native people as Native film professionals have vigorously contended for a century? Even with the uptick in Native film production and distribution in recent years, why has it been so difficult to achieve standards and protocols that establish any accountability for those claiming Native American identities?

Bird Runningwater left his post at Sundance, signing a first-look deal at Amazon Studios in 2021 to produce television and film projects for Amazon Prime Video.[77] He again followed in the footsteps of Heather Rae, who secured a first-look deal with Amazon in 2019.[78] Runningwater has thus set himself up in a gatekeeping role in Native

Hollywood, with the power to strongly influence who gets coveted Native roles in the industry. Yet self-identification continues to be the predominant industry standard. Sundance adheres to a policy of self-identification, while its values statement emphasizes its "Indigenous Program honors and upholds the inherent Sovereignty of Tribal Nations and Indigenous Peoples."[79] The Screen Actors Guild (SAG-AFTRA) also has a policy of self-identification.

PRETENDIANS IN OTHER ARTS

Theater and dance spaces are also, unsurprisingly, plagued by pretendianism. The American theater and dance community is small, almost entirely dependent on funding from granting agencies in the arts, such as the National Endowment for the Arts, the Doris Duke Foundation, and the Andrew W. Mellon Foundation. Funding is always competitive which is intensified when there are Native dance or theater companies competing with each other. When a company is led by a pretendian, it adds insult to injury. In 2020, as the wave of pretendian callouts was building and the pressure was on, a statement was issued by Rulan Tangen, founder, choreographer, and artistic director of the popular Dancing Earth company. With a thirty-year history in the dance world, Tangen has won numerous coveted fellowships, grants, residencies, and awards, the majority of them intended for American Indians. Tangen has modeled professionally for Native clothing designers, and acted in film roles playing Native characters.

Throughout her career, Tangen presented an image and narrative of herself as American Indian. As a Filipina, her appearance could be mistaken as American Indian. Her projected identity hinged on a *hunka* (Lakota adoption ceremony) relationship with an elderly Crow Creek woman who had passed away decades ago. For Tangen, performing indigeneity literally became an art form she excelled at. Her looks, combined with her Indigenous dance aesthetic, her adoption narrative, and the Indigenous dancers she surrounds herself with, are disorienting, especially in social circumstances where questioning someone's indigeneity goes against unspoken rules of etiquette. I know because this was my experience with her.

I spoke at a campus event a few years ago and was invited to participate in an unrelated public conversation with Tangen (Dancing Earth was performing on campus that week). In addition to the discussion, we socialized with a couple of faculty members over dinner. When I asked about her tribal background, as Native people do, she mentioned her Filipina heritage but emphasized her Lakota *hunka* connection. The mention of *hunka* was a red flag for me, but in the context of the professional situation, especially with non-Native folks, it would have been awkward to put her on the spot by questioning her heritage so, wanting to be a gracious guest, I let it go. Shortly after the event, I learned that Tangen had garnered huge sums of money from major foundations targeted for Native American artists based on her *hunka* Lakota story. A coordinated effort by Native American dance professionals to educate one of those foundations about Tangen and the issue of granting money for Native projects based on self-identification led to the penalizing not of Tangen but of those who brought up the issue.[80] Real harm had been caused over the years by Tangen's misrepresentation as Native American. I felt embarrassed and angry that I had unknowingly participated in a public program with someone who had harmed the careers of my colleagues.

Rulan Tangen's statement in 2020 came just short of a year later. Tangen's "personal statement of identity" is a long, rambling document that begins by saying her "mixed ancestral heritage is Kampampangan and Pangasinan from Luzon Island, known colonially as part of Pacific archipelago of the Philippines, and Norweigian/Irish [sic] lineage." While she disavows any claims to "bloodline, enrolled membership, or citizenship in any North American tribal nations or First Nations," she describes in detail her *hunka* Lakota relationship from over thirty years prior, using the terms "kinship," "extended familial connections," "claimed by specific Native families," and "chosen kin/adopted families" in what seems a doubling down of her claims to North American indigeneity. She even attempts to justify applying for Native American program grant funding. Tangen's identity statement joins those of others, notably Elizabeth Hoover (discussed in a later chapter) and Buffy Sainte-Marie, sharing commonalities in tone and structure—justifying shady claims of Native American heritage while appearing to dispel concerns about fraud.[81]

There are patterns in pretendians' performances and misrepresentations of themselves, and by now, you can probably identify some of them for yourself. A report by the University of Saskatchewan in 2022 responding to the crisis of Indigenous identity fraud outlines some of the patterns, or red flags. These can involve shifting Indigenous identities; conflicting facts and stories; vague claims that may include being Métis, which is French for "mixed" but also a term for specific tribal communities in Canada; claiming membership in Indigenous or pan-Indigenous organizations as proof of their Indigenous identity; reliance on past institutional recognition; repeated references to ceremony; family stories and family secrets; lateral genealogical claims; reliance on DNA; playing on stereotypes, such as alienation from culture and heritage, intergenerational trauma, family violence, addictions, racism, and poverty; grooming of elders; the adoption "passport" fantasy (the adoption story is a passport to indigeneity); Native names; and recent identification.[82] Efforts to address Indigenous identity fraud is more advanced in Canada than the United States owing at least in part to Canada's Truth and Reconciliation Commission, which has been underway for many years and produced several governmental reports. The University of Saskatchewan's report is the first institutionally-based one to seriously consider identity fraud. To their list of red flags, I would also add performativity, characterized by dramatic or subtle efforts to appear Indigenous, and frauds ingratiating themselves to Native communities through positive representations and deeds, making them unassailable to their core friends and fans. The danger with red flags is many of them are genuine attributes of actual Indigenous people, so taken alone, they are not always an accurate gauge. The presence of several of them in combination and the pretendians' lack of clear familial connections to a tribal community give the red flags credence.

Studies in Indian art and literature engage concepts referred to as visual and narrative sovereignty to highlight the importance of authentic representation in the performing, visual, and literary arts. It can refer to the authenticity of the representations themselves as well as creators, performers, and writers. Sovereignty in this sense is most associated with cultural sovereignty, which has been defined in a variety of ways. Beverly Singer relates it to "trusting in the older ways and adapting them to our lives in the present."[83] For legal scholar Robert Miller, cultural sovereignty is the right of an Indigenous people to determine for itself what "constitutes its traditional culture and how it will honor and practice that culture."[84] Cultural sovereignty may be tied to political sovereignty, meaning there are not always legal mechanisms to guarantee its protection. This may explain the implacability of Native fraud in performing arts and literature. The visual arts is an exception, however, where there is a mechanism to protect cultural sovereignty and contain fraud. The Indian Arts and Crafts Act (IACA), passed in 1990 as a truth-in-advertising law, creates guidelines for what can be considered authentic Indian art. Something can be sold as "Indian made" only if the artist is a member of a federally or state recognized tribe or is certified as an artisan of the tribe. Violations carry penalties up to a $250,000 fine or a five-year prison term, or both. If a business violates the IACA, it can face civil penalties or be prosecuted and fined up to $1 million.[85] IACA has not always been effectively enforced, but in recent years, the federal government has stepped up its efforts with multiple prosecutions.

The IACA is far from perfect as a vehicle for limiting fraud in the Indian art world, and it has been widely criticized, mostly for being too restrictive for how "Indian" is defined. Some have argued that the IACA should be extended to include writers, and there may be a worthy case for how it or other mechanisms can be enabled to safeguard the cultural sovereignty within the performing arts world, including theater and film. What's clear is that what exists now—nothing—is not working. There is a pressing need for systemic change within the structures that currently govern the American Indian performing arts. The existing state of affairs has proven ineffective; it is essential for influential figures to step up and pave the way for a more functional and fair system. Individuals like Bird Runningwater, who has held prominent positions in the Academy of Motion Picture Arts and Sciences, Sundance, SAG-AFTRA's Native American Committee, and elsewhere, acknowledge the urgency of the situation. It is time for them to relinquish their gatekeeping keys and make room for others to lead creative organizations with integrity, inclusivity, and transparency. Self-identification as a foundation for identity in arts and entertainment must also be rejected. The current stagnation cannot continue; decisive action and a new viable plan are needed to serve the best interests of American Indian performing arts professionals. The call for change is not just timely; it is a responsibility that has been deferred for too long.

CHAPTER FOUR

INDIANS, HIPPIES, AND SHAMANS, OH MY!

California and the Birth of Neo-Indianism

B Y THE MID-TWENTIETH CENTURY, the racializing of American Indians through the language of blood quantum had become how average Americans understood who was Indian. For non-Native Americans with little to no understanding about tribes as functioning governments, determining who was an Indian was a matter of how much "Indian blood" one had, not as citizens of, or proximity to, tribal nations with a political relationship to the United States. The growing ethnic pride movement, on one hand, made it less dangerous and stigmatizing for those who previously hid their Indianness out of sheer survival, while on the other hand, Indianness was now chic, a way to disassociate from whiteness or other ethnicities, to distance oneself from the US' violent history of colonization and genocide, and sometimes, to cash in on Indian land claims and other material benefits. After all, the ground for ethnic fraud had already been well cultivated in the early years of the film business. By mid-century, census-based racial self-identification and the emphasis on Indianness as cultural expression made it easy for Americans to ignore Indianness as a matter of tribal national belonging and sovereignty. This was especially true in urban areas, and California stands out with its explosive growth of newly self-identified Indians. With the foundation having been laid for ethnic fraud in Hollywood's film industry, California is a focal point, and for all intents and purposes, is the origin of the contemporary pretendian phenomenon. The cultural capital accrued through claims to Indianness has, unsurprisingly, manifested in Indian identity claims levied for professional gain, but also for intangible affective and psychological benefits. In this chapter, I build on the argument that California is the birthplace of modern pretendianism utilizing a concept referred to as neo-Indianism as a gateway to a deeper discussion that raises critical questions about what constitutes legitimate claims to Indianness and indigeneity.

NEO-INDIAN EMERGENCE IN CALIFORNIA

In June 2019, the *Los Angeles Times* published an exposé revealing that companies had secured over $300 million in government contracts based on wrongful claims to Cherokee heritage since 2000. The authors looked at fourteen companies, twelve of which cited ties to three fraudulent Cherokee tribes—the Northern Cherokee Nation, the Western Cherokee Nation of Arkansas and Missouri, and the Northern Cherokee Nation of the Old Louisiana Territory, all in Missouri, where there are no federal or state recognized tribes. Although research found no legitimate documentation of Native American ancestry for any of the companies' owners, they obtained multimillion dollar contracts under federal, state, and municipal programs for minority businesses spanning eighteen states, and they were all registered as Native American–owned businesses with the federal Small Business Administration. One of the article's authors, Adam Elmahrek, explained in a video embedded within the online article that the investigation started with a tip the newspaper received that William Wages, brother-in-law of House Minority Leader and later ousted Speaker of the House Kevin McCarthy (R-Bakersfield), was the owner of one of the twelve companies with fraudulent Cherokee claims.[1]

Later that year, the *Los Angeles Times* published another story exposing Native American identity fraud in Southern California.[2] By following the money, the article probed the Chumash identity claims of Mati Waiya, CEO and president of the Malibu-based Wishtoyo Chumash Foundation. The article underscored that the nonprofit had raised more than $12 million since 2015 after engaging in legal battles to protect Chumash cultural sites and waterways from polluting development projects, highlighting that it employed several family

members, all of whom claimed to be Chumash. There is only one federally recognized Chumash tribe, the Santa Ynez Band of Chumash
Indians, with a reservation in inland Santa Barbara County. But there
are several non-federally recognized Chumash groups in the coastal
region with varying degrees of legitimacy.[3] Mati Waiya, whose birth
name is Frank Rocha, is a controversial figure, stemming primarily
from his Chumash claims. Waiya/Rocha is known for his unusual
appearance, sporting a bone piercing through his nose and dressing
in elaborate coastal Indian regalia as a "ceremonial leader." This has
sometimes led to accusations of inauthenticity and performative behavior by Chumash and other Southern California Indian people.
Waiya is backed by current and past members of Wishtoyo Chumash
Foundation's board of directors, including actors Beau Bridges and
Max Gail, University of California, Los Angeles, law professor Carole
Goldberg, and LA County Superior Court judge Deborah Sanchez.
Wishtoyo has been funded by the Leonardo DiCaprio Foundation,
the Baltoro Family Trust (Yvon Chouinard Family Trustees), Edison
International, California Department of Fish and Wildlife, Marisla
Foundation (created by heirs to the Getty oil fortune), San Manuel
Band of Mission Indians, Resources Legacy Fund, Center for Bio-
logical Diversity, among others.[4] The *Los Angeles Times* examined
Waiya's genealogy with the help of an expert on Chumash ethnohistory and genealogy, Dr. John Johnson. Johnson recalled that Waiya's
cousin had contacted him in the late 1990s for help establishing the
family's Indigenous lineage and "were disappointed that we didn't find
any Chumash ancestry." When asked about the newspaper's findings,
Waiya responded that his detractors "[are] submissive to a genocidal,
colonial thinking that's destroyed our people. . . . We don't have to
prove this. . . . They're not the Chumash police or the Chumash God"
and that they could "take us to court." His supporters, including law
professor Goldberg, were dismissive of the lack of documentation for
Waiya's Chumash claims.

The case of Mati Waiya and his contested Chumash identity opens
the door to a bigger conversation about California as a site where
American Indian identity issues have played out in particularly disturbing ways. With the largest population of Native Americans in the US,

California has more tribes, federally recognized and non-recognized, than any other state.[5] The state also has the unfortunate distinction of being the epicenter of both modern pretendianism and tribal disenrollment. The broader history of California is the context for the troubling Native identity issues we see today. The violent foundation laid by the Spanish through the cruelties of the mission system in the latter eighteenth century continued through three colonial periods, including the brief secularized Mexican era, and intensified in the American period. From the inception of the mission system, settlers of early California declared their commitment to the extermination of Indigenous populations, as proclaimed in the first state-of-the-state address given by Governor Peter Burnett in 1851.[6] Even after California Indian populations were decimated by disease and the genocidal gold rush, a sweeping state law misleadingly named the Act for the Government and Protection of Indians, which had passed in 1850, confined California Indians to indentured servitude to white settlers and led to twenty-seven other laws funding militia-driven killing sprees ("expeditions against the Indians") from 1851 to 1859, at a cost of $1.3 million.[7] The law preceded the federal policy of assimilation through the boarding school system and land allotment, constituting a sustained genocidal attack on California Indian communities at the state and federal level over a period of at least eighty years. Land theft was normalized through the suppression of eighteen treaties federal agents negotiated with California tribes between 1851 and 1852. The treaties were never ratified by the Senate and were subsequently concealed for decades.

Violence against Indigenous people is woven into the cultural DNA of California, and though much of the operationalized violence via policy has been left in the past, its legacy lingers in the present. Its impacts can be seen in multiple ways, from the miniscule size of reservations, often called "rancherias," to the number of tribes that were terminated in the 1950s and remain federally unrecognized. As the dust settles from centuries of colonial violence, tribal communities find themselves in various stages of cultural recuperation. Some are more intact than others, and a few cling to not much more than remnants of their precontact existence. Especially hard-hit were the tribes in the most populous areas of the Los Angeles and San Francisco basins. In these areas, where Indigenous lands have been transformed into some of the world's most valuable real estate, there are no federally recognized tribes. In the areas of Orange County, Los Angeles, Santa Barbara, and San Luis Obispo, several bands of Chumash, Tongva/Gabriellino, Tataviam, and Acjachemen/Juaneño still assert their tribal existence, as do several bands of Ohlone and Costanoan people in the broader San Francisco Bay Area. Some have vied and failed to meet the criterion of the federal acknowledgment process. Many of these groups began reemerging in the mid-twentieth century and continue to pop up in this century, leading to the term *pop-up tribes*, sometimes used to describe neo-Indian groups. While these tribes and individuals still exist, California is an ethnically cleansed landscape where systematic erasure has rendered them largely invisible. By the early twentieth century, the general public assumed that there were no California Indians left, leaving a void of perceivable authentic indigeneity. All the public knew were the portrayals Hollywood's fantasy-driven film industry showed them—Indians who were always tragically vanishing, almost always depicted as buckskin-clad Plains Indians, and typically played by impersonators. Into this liminal space would step actual Native people, those who believed they might have California Indian or other Native American heritage, and imposters.[8] Telling them apart is the challenge contemporary pretendianism presents, and arguably, nowhere is the problem more acute than in California.

California has long been a place people have come to seek their fortunes and reimagine themselves. For some, it is a place to find themselves, and for others, it is a place to hide. Beyond the weather, it's the unique brand of bohemian exoticism that draws people in. Studies on bohemian culture offer some useful insights. A rich literature traces modern bohemianism's emergence initially to mid-nineteenth-century France from where it travels to the United States, with roots in New York and California. American bohemianism is often associated with the literature of Edgar Allan Poe, Mark Twain, Walt Whitman, Jack London, and Henry Miller, as well as a host of artists and intellectuals who embraced social nonconformity through a rejection of mainstream bourgeoisie values. In post–World War II era America bohemianism is most recognizable in the Beat generation, the precursor of the hippie counterculture. Studies on bohemianism tend to emphasize the primacy of cities, where radical and eclectic ideas were shared through newspapers, literary periodicals, coffeehouses, bars, cafés, bookstores, and art galleries.[9] More recent scholarship, however, shows California's brand of bohemian culture evolving differently from New York's, especially in Southern California. Here, bohemianism became more culturally and geographically diverse as it migrated to beach landscapes, forming ties to the budding surfing subculture of the 1920s.[10] Numerous bohemian and counterculture enclaves dotted the Los Angeles area from the late nineteenth century, centered in Arroyo Seco, Echo Park/Silverlake, Laurel Canyon, and Laguna Beach.[11] Several were—and still are—located within the historic Chumash areas of Malibu, Topanga Canyon, Santa Barbara,[12] and San Luis Obispo.

The Beat generation was predominantly a white literary and art movement that drew inspiration (some might say culturally appropriated) from Black culture, jazz music in particular. Like the earlier bohemian culture, the Beat movement traces its origins to New York and later established connections in San Francisco. Pushing the American cultural envelope, the Beats sought freedom from oppressive conventional social mores that could be found not only in relaxed censorship laws but in sexual liberation, drug use, and other unconventional thinking and behavior. Many Beats veered into the realm of religion and spirituality in their quest for a more authentic and liberated American identity. Although the literature on Beat religion and spirituality is sparse, Beat writers like Jack Kerouac, Diane DiPrima, Allen Ginsberg, and Gary Snyder were well-known for their contemplations on Christianity, Buddhism, and other religious traditions,[13] including Native American spirituality and culture. Kerouac, for instance, invoked Indians in the countercultural classics *On the Road* and *The Dharma Bums* as foils against crass American modernity but also in ways that just reconfigured the old tropes of noble savages and reinforced American settler discovery mythologies of rugged individualism, freedom, and rebellion.[14] The poet Gary Snyder, who had a degree in anthropology and was deeply influenced by the study of Northwest tribal cultures, became a prominent environmentalist, bridging the Beat generation and later the back-to-the-land movement. Alternative and new religious movements had long taken root in the US, with numerous branches leaning toward mysticism, metaphysics, and the occult. In the 1950s, American Indian spirituality and politics would encounter metaphysical practitioners in strange and unpredictable ways.

Meanwhile, in Indian country, tribes were still adapting to the governance structures of the Indian Reorganization Act (IRA) of 1934, and with decades of assimilation and cultural breakdown, many reservation communities became fractured. Tribal tensions were exacerbated in some places by growing environmental problems caused by dam building, mining, and other extractive and polluting processes, and by 1953, termination. It was also a time of concerted efforts to restore traditions, as Indians worked to reverse the cultural erosion caused by missionaries and the federal government. The Religious Crimes Code criminalizing Indian spiritual practices and church-run boarding schools did its work to ensure Indian children were cut off from their spiritual traditions. The religious ban would not be formally repudiated until the American Indian Religious Freedom Act of 1978.[15] In the mid-twentieth century, Indian religious suppression was not as severe as it had been, but the damage from the combined heavy-handed tactics of the federal government and churches had been done. From the 1940s to the 1960s, an emerging tribal traditionalist movement began calling for reconciliation between Native religions and Christianity and intertribal unity.[16] Over several decades, their well-intentioned efforts were met with limited success, but the questionable actions of one group of "traditionalists" would lead to unintended consequences that Native people live with today.

PROTO-NEW AGEISM MEETS THE NEO-CHUMASH

Brian Haley, a cultural anthropologist at the State University of New York at Oneonta, studies ethnogenesis—how identity shift occurs in cultures. He has been studying Chumash identity shift since the

1990s, publishing extensively on the intricate interweaving of Spanish, Mexican, American, and Chumash histories and how it surfaces as Chumash identity today. Tracking the rise of newly self-identifying Chumash, or what he calls neo-Chumash, Haley cites the patterns of Spanish incursions into today's California and the detailed record-keeping of the missions, the Spanish military, and Mexican government. These historical records, combined with later American data gathering and related research, are the foundation for understanding the changing Chumash world. Haley (and occasional coauthor Larry Wilcoxon) are controversial among neo-Chumash and his work has been challenged by scholars who align themselves with non-federally recognized, self-identified Chumash groups.[17] His work parallels, and sometimes intersects with, that of John Johnson, the Chumash genealogy expert hired by Mati Waiya/Frank Rocha's family to trace Chumash ancestry, only to be rejected when no Chumash ancestry was found. Despite the controversies and disagreements his work has sparked, Haley's extensive research offers important clues for addressing questions about American Indian identity, particularly since the twentieth century, and cannot be dismissed.

The most relevant strands of Haley's research for this discussion take us to the mid-1950s, with the unlikely convergence of Hopi traditionalists and metaphysical spiritualist practitioners. This trajectory leads straight to New Age cultural appropriation of American Indian spirituality, which implants itself in California's counterculture by the mid-1960s; it is directly connected to today's neo-Chumash communities. It occurs in tandem with race-shifting produced by census self-identification and urban Indian reclaiming and pan-Indianism, as discussed in chapter 2.

Haley tells the story of Craig Carpenter, a white man from Michigan who traversed through a variety of esoteric, pre-New Age terrains during his life beginning in the late 1940s, adopting an Indian identity along the way. Carpenter's life is contextualized by mental instability in college, suffering a breakdown that one relative described as resembling schizophrenia. After dropping out of college, Carpenter began a spiritual quest, journeying to California in 1947 in search of a mystical race of beings said to be living inside Mount

Shasta. It was known by different names, such as the Great White Brotherhood and the Ascended Masters within the I AM movement; teachings were disseminated through books as "channeled" information from an entity called Saint Germain as early as 1934, with roots in Theosophist and Rosicrucian thought.[18]

Failing to find the masters, Carpenter stayed in California for a few years before encountering Faithism in the Southwest and a Los Angeles–based group called the Essenes of Kosmon.[19] After receiving a message from a spirit voice to find the Hopi people and learn of their troubles, Carpenter finally succeeded in connecting with a group of Hopis he believed he was divinely guided to in 1955. He arrived on the Hopi reservation, or Hopiland, during a time of political upheaval—referred to misleadingly as a split between progressives and traditionalists—where he connected with the leaders of what's been called the Hopi traditionalist movement.[20] Led by Thomas Banyacya, Dan Katchongva, David Monongye, and others, the Hopi traditionalist faction reflected disagreements among Hopis springing from the Hopi formation of an IRA tribal council, influenced by the Bureau of Indian Affairs (BIA). Haley writes:

> Their "traditional" teachings were new interpretations of portions of the Hopi emergence myth, and many key figures lacked traditional qualifications for authority or leadership. Their centerpiece was that signs pointed to the imminent prophesied return of the Pahanna, or White Brother, and a cleansing of evil called Purification Day, which was a prelude to the fifth world. The movement emerged in reaction to increasing federal interaction and a rejuvenated tribal council. Around 1946 or 1947, talk in Second Mesa kivas equated the atomic bomb with the story of a gourd of ashes that brought destruction when it was cast on the ground. These discussions transformed the ash-gourd from a magical Hopi weapon used to defeat an enemy to one used by the United States to cause general destruction. This new interpretation unified opposition to a tribal council perceived as serving federal interests. A meeting in 1948 yielded a plan and organization that observers identify as the beginning of the Traditionalist movement.[21]

What began as an intratribal dispute would become fodder for the budding New Age movement, which widely circulated the newly reconceived Hopi prophecies, with Thomas Banyacya as a front man, laying the foundation for the exploitation of and by other Native American medicine men, "shamans," and charlatans. Carpenter, as the messenger of the Hopi traditionalists, was one of a milieu of other proto-New Agers who entered the Hopis' orbit in the 1950s and '60s as they universalized their message, "refashion[ing] themselves . . . [as] spiritual authorities occupying a sacred center."[22] By 1958, Carpenter's involvement with the Faithists at the Kosmon Essene Library in Montrose, Colorado, became a pipeline for spreading the Hopis' message; he volunteered his time in exchange for the opportunity to print and disseminate Hopi Traditionalist propaganda (to use Haley's term) to organizations consisting predominantly of war resisters, spiritualists, and members of other religious groups. Carpenter's involvement with Hopi traditionalists led him to the League of North American Indians (LONAI), one of many pan-Indian organizations that emerged in the twentieth century. LONAI has been largely overlooked in the literature on pan- and intertribal Indian organizations, but Haley's work shows that it played a significant role in the emerging neo-Indian phenomenon. Founded in 1935, a year after the passing of the IRA, the league supported treaty-based Indian land rights, intertribal unity, and Native religious practices and espoused a belief in a fringe nineteenth-century text called the *Walam Olum*, which allegedly told the Lenape origin story.[23] As the traditionalist movement spread through other tribal communities, LONAI sided with traditionalists, opposing the IRA tribal councils. The league lasted thirty-five years and became defunct by 1970 for a variety of reasons, not the least of which involved controversies stemming from the questionable, at times blatantly bogus, Native claims of many in its leadership.[24] It was during his LONAI years that Carpenter transformed himself into a Mohawk, despite having no genealogical evidence to support his claims.

One neo-Indian that LONAI attracted in its later years was John Pope, who became known as the "medicine man" Rolling Thunder. According to Steven Crum, Pope claimed to be a legal advisor to Western Shoshone traditionalists, although there is no record of his having a law or even a college degree. In the 1970s, he was most famous for his association with the Grateful Dead and other hippie era rock bands. He claimed to be Cherokee but had no ties to any of the three federally recognized Cherokee tribes.[25] John Pope/Rolling Thunder was friends with another LONAI neo-Indian named Paul Olivas, also known as Semu Huaute, the infamous Chumash sha-man. Olivas's story brings us back to Southern California as a key location for the origins of modern pretendianism, its relationship to neo-Chumash identity, and neo-Chumash/neo-Indian entanglements with New Age appropriation of Native spirituality. It is Olivas/Semu who connects the dots between all three, setting the stage for future generations of neo-Chumash, other neo-Indians, and other Native American ethnic frauds.

Brian Haley's continuing odyssey into the neo-Chumash phe-nomenon takes a deep dive into Olivas/Semu's history.[26] Semu's rise to acclaim as a Chumash medicine man began in the 1960s. Born in 1911, he was known as Grandfather Semu at the time of his death in 2004—a famous medicine man who, like his friend Rolling Thunder, was connected to rock stars, founded a commune, and as an aspir-ing actor, was involved in the Hollywood scene. He made numerous claims that proved fictional. Among his more outrageous claims was that he was the last surviving member and full-blood of the Chumash tribe,[27] that he had a steel plate in his head after being wounded in World War II (in fact, he enlisted but never left California except for a brief hospitalization in Seattle), and that his father had been sold into slavery by the Catholic Church on a Spanish land grant near Monterey in 1878.[28] Haley traces Olivas's transformation into Semu with painstaking documentation of Olivas's family lineage going back four centuries. The genealogical analysis finds the majority of Paul Olivas's ancestors were Spanish colonists, Californios (descendants of Spanish and Mexican colonists born in California before the Amer-ican period who were ethnically mixed Europeans, Sub-Saharan Af-ricans, Africans, and Indigenous people of Mexico), and Mexicans. It identifies one Chumash ancestor, a great-great-great-grandmother born in approximately 1760 and an ancestor named Monica Mora (born circa 1835) who was thought to be Cahuilla by an unsubstantiated claim.[29] Mora is the last Indian listed in Olivas's genealogy. Olivas lived with his family in Ventura for the first seven years of his life but was raised mostly in Pomona with extended family who worked in the citrus fields and packing houses. The family knew there was California Indian heritage in the family tree, but they were not explicitly identified with it. He did not begin identifying as Indian until around 1930. Haley speculates it may have been the influence of his first wife, who had some California Indian ancestry. He began a short-lived boxing career under the stage name Chief Semu Huaute,[30] and while Social Security and draft records show him referring to himself as Indian during the 1930s and '40s, no tribal affiliation is mentioned. In 1945, Olivas was medically discharged from the US Naval Reserve after a hospitalization in Oakland and Seattle for more than two months with psychoneurosis anxiety; he struggled with alcoholism until about 1950.

The passage of the Indian Claims Commission Act in 1946 fueled an ongoing effort to rectify Indian land claims in California through payments to those who could prove descendancy from an Indian ancestor at the time of statehood.[31] It marks a time of renewed interest in reclaiming Indian heritage that had often been left in the past, which Haley sees as the "beginning of neo-Indianism."[32] Olivas's ancestor Monica Mora qualified him for the Claims Commission's judgment roll, and by 1954, he had begun a career as a woodcarving artist under a California Indian identity. He had also began attracting media attention, which allowed him to hone a story about his Indianness peppered with a mix of truth and fiction. Around 1955 or 1956, Olivas met Craig Carpenter, who was living in Southern California, and became involved with LONAI, helping to spread the message of the Hopi traditionalists. At this time, Semu began adopting an appearance that drew on primitivist and stereotypical depictions of Indians, bolstering his Native American image. By the late 1950s, he had met a community of Laguna Pueblo Indians relocated to Barstow, California, to do railroad work. The Laguna Indians often performed their traditional dances around Southern California. Semu joined their dance group and began referring to himself as the medicine man of the Barstow Laguna tribe, further cementing his con-trived "traditional" Indian persona. By the 1960s, Semu was referring to himself variously as Pomona Indian, California Indian, Cahuilla, Soboba, Laguna, and eventually, Chumash.[33] He became involved in the Native American Church peyote culture, and in 1967, he con-nected with LSD guru Timothy Leary, for whom Semu conducted an LSD- and peyote-fueled wedding in Joshua Tree.

One of the things Semu was most known for in California's coun-terculture was the establishment of a commune known as the Red Wind Ranch, Red Wind Foundation, Red Wind Nation, Red Wind Oyate, and Red Wind Medicine Camp. The community, started in 1973, was located on 200 acres outside San Luis Obispo, purchased with a $10,000 down payment from the Franciscan Order of the Catholic Church. Land payments were aided by a series of fundrais-ing concerts performed by the Eagles, Jackson Browne, Neil Young, and Jerry Garcia and the Grateful Dead.[34] Red Wind also received grants from the federal Department of Health, Education, and Welfare for $42,000 and from the local Economic Opportunity Commission for $20,000. In 1975, there were fifty people on the commune.[35] Red Wind was steeped in controversy from the beginning. A 1973 news story from the earliest days of Red Wind's San Luis Obispo County location reported an exchange of gunfire that led to a fire, destroying most of their supplies. Semu claimed to be under sniper fire, but the story also describes sheriffs' concerns about militant violence, citing recent Indian militancy in other parts of the country, most notably at Wounded Knee.[36]

Other Red Wind controversies involved allegations of sexual ex-ploitation. One visitor to Red Wind in September 1980 told a dis-turbing but eye-opening story in an interview with me.[37] I will call him George. George, a Native man from a Southern California tribe, was living on the reservation of a tribe in another part of the state. He talked about it being a time when Native people were practic-ing the cultures of other Native people's tribes, and the Lakota Sun Dances and sweat lodges "became the new pan-Indianism, and it all started with Semu. I remember people in the American Indian Move-ment and at D-Q [University], they would talk about Red Wind. They would talk about supporting the land and have security over there. They called it the Western Gate." He elaborated:

> I went there with a group of people to help build a sweat lodge. I was told to watch out because Red Wind was possessed by an evil spirit, and I asked: What kind of evil spirit? and was told "the spirit of lust." It was right after Semu left Red Wind. From what I heard of it, I thought it would be this spiritual camp with Native people. But what I found is it was almost all white and Chicano women, mostly white women. The men, some were Native, some were not. A lot of them had just been released from prison. Semu was doing work at prisons and at the time was considered very respectable and he would allow these people when they got released to live at Red Wind.
>
> They had this meeting place, a communal hogan [traditional Navajo dwelling]. I was told by some of the guys about some of the rules at Red Wind. It pretty much centered on how women and men interacted, and it sounded more like a hookup than anything else. There was this dance the women did, called the "wolf dance." The women were spinning around and it looked more like the Dance of the Seven Veils while the men drummed. The men warned me that if the woman offered you coffee you could go sleep with her but leave before she cooks because if she cooks and you eat her food she can lay a claim on you.[38]

I asked: Why was Semu not there? George replied that there had been accusations of Semu sexually abusing a minor and having to flee as a result of the allegations. George went so far as to call Red Wind a "sex cult," based on his observations. He continued: "Semu and Rolling Thunder had a thing between their two groups, Red Wind and Meta Tantay out in Elko, Nevada. And one of the things they were doing was trading women between that compound and Red Wind. In order to live there it was part of the culture."

When I asked if the men made the rules he replied, "I suspect Semu and Rolling Thunder made the rules, although I don't know for sure. But when I showed up there it was already in effect."

George said that after Semu fled the compound, a man named Ernie Peters, also known as Chief Longwalker, had taken over to "clean the place up." The men wanted Semu back because he "made things happen," like concerts to raise money and other activities. "Semu was like a rock star," he said.

After several days, George left with a feeling of shock. He said it seemed like it was just a hippie encampment with a mutiny taking place.

The Red Wind commune was founded by Semu to revive Native American traditionalism, based on a blending of multiple tribal traditions he'd picked up along his journey of transformation from Paul Olivas from Pomona to Grandfather Semu, the Chumash medicine man. What began as a beautiful dream for Native American cultural resurgence, however ill-conceived, turned into a scandalous hippie commune run by men with unchecked power and marginal if not outright fake Native identities. It was an experiment gone horribly, tragically wrong. There are people alive today who lived through it and are still too traumatized to tell their stories publicly, and others, no doubt, who have their own reasons not to speak of it.[39]

Semu was believable because, like Sacheen Littlefeather, Buffy Sainte-Marie, Cher, Iron Eyes Cody, and many others in early Hollywood, he knew how to play to certain audiences. He proved resourceful at crafting an aesthetic that could easily be taken for an authentic, traditional Indian by those who didn't know better, just as Sacheeen's aesthetic at the 1973 Academy Awards sent a very specific message to an unknowledgeable audience. The same can be said for Mati Waiya's appearance.[40] It is evident, however, that Semu was not raised with any Chumash traditions or identity and that he spent time in a variety of other tribal contexts so he would have picked up enough elements from different tribal cultures to be convincing.[41] Meanwhile, the evangelizing of the Hopis and other tribal traditionalists about prophecies and the ways they were being framed for non-Native people, and Native American spirituality more broadly, spread like wildfire through the counterculture, reflected in many popularly circulating texts of the times. These include Frank Waters's *Book of the Hopi* (1963), John G. Neihardt's *Black Elk Speaks* (1932), Hyemeyohsts Storm's *Seven Arrows* (1972), Richard Erdoes's *Lame Deer: Seeker of Visions* (1972),

Robert Boissiere's *The Return of Pahana: A Hopi Myth* (1990), Peter Matthiessen's *Indian Country* (first published in 1979) and *In the Spirit of Crazy Horse* (1983), the wildly popular but fraudulent series by Carlos Castaneda about the sorcerer Don Juan Matus, and many other New Age books by neo-Indians and non-Indian cultural appropriators in the 1980s and '90s. It was part of the larger back-to-the-land hippie movement that drew heavily on romanticized ideas about Native American "old ways" beginning with the Hopi traditionalists and their New Age allies who intentionally targeted the counterculturalists.[42]

The irony of the traditionalist movement as it took shape at Red Wind and other communes,[43] and in other pan-Indian spaces like LONAI is that those who adopted traditionalist identities who were not raised in tribal communities or were not verifiably Native, inevitably portrayed themselves as more Indian than those who actually had legitimate ties to tribal communities. They produced "medicine people" and "cultural experts" who continue to pass down their dubious teachings to the spiritually hungry and culturally disconnected with self-appointed authority. In Santa Barbara and other California communities, they populate cultural monitoring firms competing for lucrative contracts, often in competition with companies tied to federally recognized tribes. This observation prompted Haley, Wilcoxon, and others to write about it, including in a *Los Angeles Times* article in 1987 highlighting the lack of genealogical accountability in some of the Chumash cultural monitoring firms and the conflict it generated with the federally recognized Santa Ynez Chumash.[44]

The discussion about Red Wind and traditionalism brings us back to the story of Mati Waiya, the executive director of the Wishtoyo Chumash Foundation, whose self-proclaimed Chumash roots proved nonexistent. As the example of Red Wind shows, stories about countercultural neo-Indians and neo-Chumash can be hard to trace due to lack of documentation. Communes like Red Wind and Meta Tantay came and went well before the internet and social media, and were over before the end of the 1980s. Those communities could be secretive, but their impact lingers. Mati Waiya/Frank Rocha descended from a cultural lineage that connects him with Rolling Thunder and Semu, through one of the original neo-Chumash, Kote Lotah. Kote Lotah, sometimes referred to as Dr. Kote Lotah though he appears not to have a medical or doctorate degree, was mentored by Semu, who gave him the name Kote Lotah (his birth name is George Barbin).[45] Lotah was closely associated with Rolling Thunder and Meta Tantay.[46] Waiya, who was mentored by Kote Lotah, may have spent time at Red Wind as a young man, considering his relationship with him.[47] The 1987 *Los Angeles Times* article about undocumented Chumash cultural monitors named Lotah as a founding member of the United Chumash Council. John Johnson in that story recounted that the founding members of the Council requested his help finding their Chumash heritage. When his research turned up proof of no Chumash ancestry, predictably the research was angrily rejected.[48] United Chumash Council is known today as the Coastal Band of the Chumash Nation.

The story of the Hopi traditionalists shows us that Indians played a role, perhaps inadvertently, in the rise of neo-Indianism in the 1960s as they worked for their own intratribal agendas. Other traditionalists arrived in the following decades, driven by their own motivations but still contributing to non-Native peoples' fantasies about Indians. Yet the neo-Indian phenomenon was much bigger and far more complicated than a few Indians taking advantage of disaffected white and other racialized youth.[49] California's unique social landscape created an opportunity for the convergence of specific circumstances at a particular moment in time. Census-based race-shifting and urban pan-Indianism rose in tandem with Southern California's brand of bohemianism and a romanticized reimagining of tribal traditionalism. The anti-war movement fueled anti-American sentiments as well, giving people even more reason to distance themselves from white colonial Americanism. It was also a time when Hollywood was shifting its approach in the way Indians were being represented in film and television, with the release of sympathetic treatments such as *A Man Called Horse* (1970), *Billy Jack* (1971), *Little Big Man* (1970), and the Iron Eyes Cody "Crying Indian" commercial (1971). Never mind that the lead characters were typically played by non-Native actors; that, too, was a reflection of the times.

While Southern California was a magnet for neo-Indianism, the San Francisco Bay Area mirrored what was happening four hundred miles south, especially considering the flashpoint that was the Alcatraz Island occupation from 1969 to 1971. California in the 1960s and '70s created a cultural vacuum into which anyone could step and re-imagine themselves in new ways. It wouldn't be surprising, then, that a young mentally unstable, ambitious Mexican American woman from Salinas with a malleable appearance and a desire for fame would reinvent herself as an Apache Indian named Sacheen Littlefeather. Or that others, such as Paul Olivas, John Pope, or Craig Carpenter, would seize the opportunity to elevate themselves in ways that garnered attention and adoration from people who wouldn't question their identities. But their lingering influence, seen in examples like the proliferating neo-Chumash communities and phony Cherokee tribes, raises a great many questions about the nature of American Indian identity, race, culture, sovereignty, and legitimacy—and how we talk about it all.

FIGURE 4–1: *New Age and Pretendianism Genealogy*

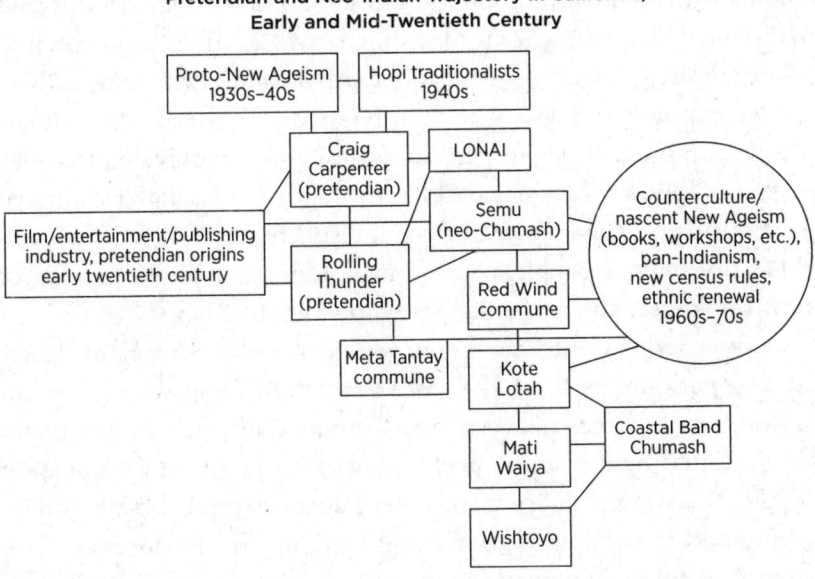

This figure illustrates the genealogy of contemporary pretendianism as it developed in Southern California. We see its merging with the 1960s and '70s counterculture and nascent New Age era, linkages with pan-Indianism, the ethnic renewal movement, and the neo-Chumash.

CURRENT NEO-CHUMASH ISSUES

It's clear that the confusion surrounding Native identity today stems from centuries of colonial domination and the desperate need to survive genocidal violence, especially in California. The result is a muddy mix of narratives that blend truth and fiction in assertions of neo-Native identity. Stories about survival tactics in California closely resemble those told in other places. Families who could pass as white—or in California's case, Mexican—did. In fringe Cherokee groups, a common story is that their ancestors escaped the Trail of Tears or hid in the hills for generations. Similar stories about hiding circulate in California to explain a lack of cultural continuity beyond family rumors of Indian ancestors; other stories doubt the accuracy of recordkeeping of Indian ancestry in the Spanish, Mexican, and early American periods. California Indian persistence was unforeseen, so when social values changed in the twentieth century, leading to land claims to right some of the historical wrongs, it opened the door to both justice and opportunism. Not all tribal identities were abandoned or lost to history, though, and many tribes and individuals never lost contact with their cultural roots and communities. Tribal identities are maintained through sustained kinship networks, always anchored to ancestral places. Those with unbroken tribal connections, especially in small communities, know who their relatives are, so when unfamiliar people pop up claiming to be Chumash without family connections, suspicion follows. Tensions build in the face of unverifiable claims to places, the performance of inauthentic spiritual practices, questionable stories about people, places, and traditions, and the rallying of anthropologists and archeologists who validate them.[50]

Exacerbating California Indian problems today is a lack of clearly defined parameters from the state for determining who is Indian in non-federally recognized tribes. Certain California Indian issues are mediated by the state's Native American Heritage Commission (NAHC) "as the primary government agency responsible for identifying and cataloging Native American cultural resources . . . to prevent irreparable damage to designated sacred sites, as well as to prevent interference with the expression of Native American religion in California . . . [and] provide protection to Native American human

burials and skeletal remains from vandalism and inadvertent destruction."[51] To accomplish these specific goals, NAHC maintains a list of
Most Likely Descendants (MLDs), consulted when human remains
are uncovered in development projects (places other than dedicated
cemeteries). The MLD list is not a system of state tribal recognition
as in other states. Determining MLDs is a complex bureaucratic process with criteria based on "geography, kinship, biology, archeology,
anthropology, linguistics, folklore, oral tradition, historical evidence,
or other information or expert opinion that reasonably lead to such
a conclusion . . . genealogies, ethnographic studies, anthropological
or historical studies or other credible evidence tracing a California
Native American tribe's genealogical lineage to the Indigenous ancestors who occupied the traditional tribal territory, known tribal reservation or tribal rancheria or traditional tribal village site where the
remains were discovered."[52] These criteria pertain to who qualifies
as MLDs for the purpose of reinterring Indigenous human remains
but say nothing about what defines California Indian tribes and individuals for other purposes. Thus, there is nothing to stop any group
from claiming to be an Indian tribe or any individual from claiming
to be a member of a self-proclaimed tribe.

The freedom from rules restricting claims to being a tribe means
that groups can organize land or environmental projects under the
guise of a tribe without an actual political relationship to the US or
an individual state. It also means they can raise money based on overt
or covert claims to being a tribe, similar to what Mati Waiya's Wishtoyo Chumash Foundation in Malibu does. With a powerful board
of directors, skillful fundraising, and local influence, Wishtoyo has
developed a vibrant outdoor cultural education center on four acres
with a stunning ocean view, on a documented ancient village site, in
partnership with Los Angeles County Department of Beaches and
Harbors. On the reconstructed village site, classes are held in the
Chumash language, basketmaking (taught by Kote Lotah's daughter,
Tima), and *tomol* boatbuilding, as well as multiple K–12 educational
programs in partnership with local schools. The site is not open to
the public except by appointment. The organization also serves as a
hub for regional environmental protection initiatives including stream

restoration, endangered species projects, and marine protected area (MPA) advocacy.[53] On Wishtoyo's website is something of a disclaimer about the contested nature of Chumash identity claims: "Since the Chumash had no written language (until recent years), the birth records identifying Chumash people is complex and incomplete, and as a result, some longtime residents with Latino, French, English and other foreign surnames in Santa Barbara, Ventura, Los Angeles and San Luis Obispo Counties today, can track their lineage of Chumash descent *through oral rather than written history* [my emphasis]."[54]

Wishtoyo's work is impressive by any measure; it's not hard to see why it garners so much local support. Their environmental work benefits everyone who cares about protecting sensitive ecosystems in the face of the relentless development that characterizes Southern California, and they appeal to white fantasies about traditional, primitivist Indians. Wishtoyo is not the only Chumash-identifying group in the area engaged in coastal conservation. Just a short distance up the coast, a group calling itself the Northern Chumash Tribal Council launched a campaign to establish a federal MPA under the name Chumash Heritage National Marine Sanctuary. The brainchild of self-proclaimed Northern Chumash Fred Collins begun in 2013, the proposed marine sanctuary spans 140 miles of coastline from Point Conception in the south to Cambria in the north, extending to the Santa Lucia Bank along the Santa Lucia Escarpment in some of the most pristine stretch of ocean on the 1,100-mile California coastline.[55] On land it will protect many Chumash sacred sites within the Western Gate/Point Conception area. Collins's nomination, accepted by the National Oceanic and Atmospheric Administration (NOAA), is lauded as the first "tribally" nominated marine sanctuary in the US. The project has gained support from a wide array of entities and officials at the highest levels of federal, state, and local governments, including former vice president Kamala Harris and Laguna Pueblo tribal member and former secretary of the interior Deb Haaland, to some of the most influential Big Green groups, such as the Sierra Club, Surfrider Foundation, and Greenpeace. Over thirty thousand people had sent public comments in support by February 2017.[56]

Not everyone, however, was enthusiastic about the proposed sanctuary. Some feared the restrictions would impact local businesses, represented by local fishers, ranchers, farmers, and chambers of commerce; the San Luis Obispo County Board of Supervisors voted against it in 2017.[57] Other opposition came from the Santa Ynez Band of Chumash Indians and the Salinan Tribe of Monterey and San Luis Obispo Counties. In November 2021, Santa Ynez reversed their opposition through a resolution formally supporting the sanctuary.[58] The issues for Salinan were more complex. The boundaries of the proposed sanctuary overlap with the traditional territory of the Salinan and encompass the Salinan sacred site Morro Rock, already the subject of a long-standing dispute with Collins. The conflict escalated when Collins's Chumash identity claims were challenged by the Salinan. They hired a genealogist, who found "collateral" Chumash family members in Collins's lineage but no direct California Indian lineage, Chumash or otherwise.[59] The Salinan communicated the report to the Sierra Club, local political representatives, the Native American Heritage Commission, and a local newspaper, which Collins responded to with an anti-SLAPP (Strategic Lawsuit Against Public Participation) suit attempting to silence the Salinan's findings, claiming defamation. The court decided in favor of the defendants "because issues regarding the proposed marine sanctuary, access to Morro Rock, and Collins's status as a Chumash advocate and spokesman were of public interest."[60] Collins, therefore, lost the case; not only he did he never prove he was of Chumash descent, but it was proven that he was not of Chumash descent.

Fred Collins passed away in 2021. The proposed sanctuary remains in the final stages of approval. Collins's daughter, Violet Sage Walker, whose supposed Chumash ancestry she inherits from Collins, took the reins from her father. She has been successful in raising money for the project, something of a media darling, and was rumored to have been invited to the White House. In the summer of 2022, the Northern Chumash Tribal Council, which according to its website exists exclusively to comply with state laws to support the family cultural monitoring business,[61] posted a job announcement for an environmental campaign manager specifically for the sanctuary designation.[62] They have been actively fundraising for the marine sanctuary project for years and boast a long list of high-powered partners.[63]

The examples of Wishtoyo and the Northern Chumash Tribal Council illustrate how precarious the situation is when it comes to advancing work that is otherwise righteous but carried out under the guise of questionable if not outright fraudulent claims to tribal identity in California. First, when Indigenous ecological knowledge has increasingly been seen as critical to environmental protection and in recent years has been funded at unprecedented levels through state and federal legislation and philanthropy, claims to Indian heritage come not just with cultural clout but economic incentive. Second, it shows that the general public wants to believe claims to indigeneity but struggle to discern truth from fiction, easily duped into supporting people, projects, and institutions built on foundations of lies, half-truths, and a shortage of integrity. Third, these examples drive home the deep and ongoing influence of Paul Olivas/Semu Huaute as the originator of neo-Chumash traditionalism and identity, and the central role he plays in California as one point of origin of contemporary pretendianism. Here is where we return to the questions these issues and histories raise.

Neo-Chumash identity, like that of the fringe Cherokee groups and urban pan-Indian reclaimers, hinges on claims of having Chumash "blood" in an equation where blood determines identity. It's a conception that reinforces Indian identity as racially determined. But what does it mean to claim Chumash, or Indian, blood when there is no actual evidence of ancestry or connection to an Indian community inherited in a family? What do claims of being a "traditional" Indian mean when there is no evidence of tribal ancestry? What does "traditional" mean, especially in the absence of connection to a tribal community through kinship? Furthermore, what are the implications for claims to sovereignty made by groups and individuals with no political relationship to the US state, and little to no evidence of ancestral ties to a tribal community, as is allegedly the case with most of the individuals in the Coastal Band of Chumash?[64] When groups raise money for public projects under the banner of a nonexistent or illegitimate "tribe," does this defraud the public? Even if cultural sovereignty is what's asserted (the right to cultural self-determination), what is cultural self-determination without verifiable ancestry in the culture? If claims to Chumash or other Indian identity are based on the racialized notion of blood, even fictitiously, how does this compromise the sovereignty of federally recognized tribes, especially now when sovereignty is under direct attack?

\\\\\\\\\\\\\\\\\\\\\\\\

In 1984, Vine Deloria Jr. and Clifford M. Lytle, in writing about the nature of tribal sovereignty and nations, observed:

> A parade of white imposters pretending to be Indians has become a common phenomenon in many tribes. Articulation of tribal traditions can be the province of almost anyone willing to put himself forward as an expert on these matters. Consequently, the younger generation is never certain what is acceptable tribal behavior and what is not. The majority of adult Indians feel that they have no right to ask questions of people posing as Indians or call obvious fakes to account. Hence the tradition of many tribes has become what the most aggressive people say it is . . . Traditional Indians have tended to prostitute their own knowledge by making it available to the wandering scholar, the excited groupie, and the curious filmmaker and writer. The cultural landscape is now so littered with erroneous information that it is extremely difficult for the serious Indian youngster to learn the truth about his past.[65]

Deloria's voice is all over this passage. By the early 1980s he could see the writing on the wall; he was signaling a warning about the fallout from the previous decade and a half of urban Indian activism with the troubling merging of traditionalism and fakery. But it took time even for Deloria to see it. In his first book *Custer Died for Your Sins*, written in 1969, he extolled the virtues of LONAI, whose demise was only a year or so away. Even he seemed unable to recognize that by that point the organization had been infiltrated by imposters, including Paul Olivas/Semu Huaute, John Pope/Rolling Thunder, Craig Carpenter, and many others.[66]

The Red Power movement had ignited a long smoldering fire in Indian country and it was the youth who burned the hottest with their direct-action campaigns like Alcatraz, the Trail of Broken Treaties, Wounded Knee, and many others. Some were from reservation communities, many had been relocated, and all were the products of the US' abysmal assimilation policies. During those years, I was too young to have attended protests, but I was old enough to notice Indian activism and the refrains of Indian pride playing out on the evening news while being told by my parents to be proud of being Indian. And I was proud to be Indian, ever since I could remember. I had a general sense of what being Indian was, having grown up with my mother's stories about life on the reservation, so far away in Washington. I knew the stories of the injustices and discrimination our family had experienced and how the United States stole our land and tried to make us out to be ignorant savages. When we went to the Colville reservation to visit relatives, it was life-altering for my twelve-year-old self; I felt my connection to the land and my ancestors in the core of my being, even at such a young age. But what I didn't know was what it meant to be Colville in Los Angeles. We had lost our language, we had no spiritual traditions, there were no beautiful cultural heirlooms passed down in our family. All we had was our stories, alcoholism in every one of our family members, and our reservation family connections, and even those were fading with the passing of time. As a Native American person, I was lost.

As a young adult in the 1980s, I began asking the deeper questions about my identity, especially about my Native heritage. I got myself registered as a tribal descendent because my mother hadn't done it for us as kids. I needed to know how being an adult child of an alcoholic had affected my life, which meant digging deeper into our family heritage. That led me back to the rez, where I reestablished neglected family ties. But I was living in California, still not really knowing what it meant to be Colville outside of the reservation. By then I had moved to Sonoma County, the northern part of the San Francisco

Bay Area, a stronghold of the counterculture in wine country. I'm a baby boomer, so the counterculture was part of my generation; I had grown up amidst its emergence in California and it shaped a lot of who I was. There was also a vibrant Native community there in the heart of Pomo, Wappo, and Coast Miwok territory. There were hubs of Native gathering places including Sonoma County Indian Health, Santa Rosa Junior College's Jesse Peter Museum, and the campus Native American Club and annual powwow, and Ya Ka Ama out in Forestville, a magical 125 acres of redwood forest and open land on the banks of the Russian River, surrounded by vineyards. There were lots of cultural events and activities held there, and I volunteered and participated for many years. Local reservation communities also had their own doings that were often open to the public.

Sonoma County's hippie counterculture was giving birth to the New Age movement, and there was a terrain of intersection between New Age and pan-Indian cultures. Sweat lodges, Native American Church peyote meetings, traveling medicine men conducting ceremonies (almost always Lakota), and other pan-Indian activities attracted a variety of Native and non-Native people, making it easy for non-Natives to play and become Indian. Non-Indians with vague claims to Indian heritage were ubiquitous, and rarely questioned. I had friends who many today would call cultural appropriators or pretendians, but at the time, I didn't have an awareness of cultural appropriation. I don't think the phrase had even been coined yet, or if it had, I hadn't heard it. I participated in all of it, for years. I went to Lakota-style sweat lodges, pipe ceremonies, and peyote ceremonies with rez Indians, mixed-blood city Indians like me, neo-Indians, and white hippies.[67] I fell into many of the traps, not always clear on what or who to believe. I was bamboozled by frauds peddling their versions of shamanism, or fanciful family stories about Indian ancestry. It didn't occur to me that people would lie or stretch the truth about being Indian, nor did it seem the least bit strange for non-Lakotas and non-Natives to be practicing Lakota spirituality. Lakota spirituality seemed like universal Indian culture that was available to anyone, as George described the scene that surrounded Red Wind. In my extensive road-tripping in the 1990s, I saw it happening all over California, the Pacific Northwest, the Southwest, Hawaii. I know there were a lot of other places where pan-Indian traditionalism was playing out, including Europe. The strange irony was that for young, displaced Natives like me urban pan-Indian culture was a doorway into their own Indianness. For me, it was a stepping stone to a deeper understanding of myself as an Okanogan/Sinixt Colville, a journey fraught with painful and embarrassing lessons.

I was exactly the "serious Indian youngster" Vine Deloria described, who would have an extremely difficult time finding their way through the littered cultural landscape to learn the truth about her own past.

Clarity came as I learned more of my own Colville history, connected with family, and became a moderately successful beadwork artist in the small but significant world of Indian art. In time I got involved in Native and environmental activism in Sonoma County and began writing about those issues as a citizen/grassroots journalist. That meant learning about tribal sovereignty and federal Indian law. It was this process of education that taught me why Indian identity is a matter of sovereignty and nationhood, not self-identification. That lead me back to college and a couple of degrees in American Indian and American studies. It was all part of my journey to understand who I was as a nontribally enrolled American Indian person, officially classified as a tribal descendant in a federally recognized tribe, neither fully Indian or non-Indian in a legal sense, born and raised in the vast post-relocation urban Native diaspora. I was immersed in, and a product of, the immensely confusing social landscape of California at the time of the emergence of contemporary neo-Indianism and pretendianism, and it's only now, in hindsight, the significance of that historical moment is legible to me in such terms.

CHAPTER FIVE

KILL THE INDIAN
TO SAVE THE PER CAP

*Settler Capitalism and Tribal
Belonging and Unbelonging
Through Disenrollment*

I N DISCUSSIONS ABOUT what constitutes Native identity, there is a
saying in Indian country: it's not about what you claim, it's about
who claims you. That is, through recognition by a legitimate tribal
government, which presumes a fair governing process, one can be
said to be authentically Native. Anyone can claim anything, but without a family and tribal community to verify that you are who you
say you are, it's meaningless. As this book maintains, the premise
for legitimate claims to being American Indian must be mediated by
a legitimate tribal government as a matter of sovereignty or other
formal recognition by the US. This constitutes the realpolitik of the
government-to-government relationship within the context of the US
settler-state system. As I also show, a core component of colonialism
was the forcible conscription of Native people into the American capitalist economy, leading to the commodification of Indianness, which
is the first step in a process that grows throughout the twentieth century for Native American ethnic fraud to take hold. In addition to
giving birth to contemporary pretendianism, the twin processes of colonialism and capitalism are responsible for other detrimental impacts
on Indian country, namely the surge of tribal disenrollments in the
past three to four decades. Disenrollment is the act of being formally
evicted from a tribal roll—the stripping of tribal citizenship—which
often leads to a cascade of deleterious material and psychological

effects for those who have been disenrolled. It is seen by many as a violation of the civil and/or human rights of tribal members.

What's insidious about disenrollment, however, is that while it is more in the domain of tribal, not the federal, government, it is directly linked with capitalism in how it reproduces the kind of abuse and trauma inflicted on tribal communities by the US settler state. Settler capitalism denotes the specificity of capitalism's relationship to colonialism in a tribal context. As tribes have adapted to their colonial realities and learned to play by the rules of settler colonialism in late-stage capitalism, the phenomenal success some have achieved by excelling at so-called casino-capitalism has come with devastating consequences to thousands of Native people who have been jettisoned from their tribes and families, or "dismembered."[1] So, while it may have been true in the past that being Native is about who claims you, in a world where tribal members can be unclaimed through the whims of despotic tribal politicians and undemocratic tribal policies and practices, we cannot assume that tribal governments are always fair and objective arbiters of Indianness and belonging. In this chapter, I argue that for Native Americans there are two uniquely, equally damaging sides to the metaphorical coin of settler capitalism that impact identity: the commodification of Indianness combined with the rise of Native ethnic fraud and the robbing of tribal belonging to maximize profits for those who remain. The net result is the weaponization of identity for the sake of maximized profit sharing among as few people as possible, and California once again stands out as the epicenter of both processes.

THE SCOURGE OF TRIBAL DISENROLLMENT

In July 2023, a news story about Indigenous land reacquisition in the affluent area of Marin County in Northern California quietly broke, reported on by a handful of local sources. The Coast Miwok Tribal Council of Marin had purchased a twenty-six-acre parcel in the semirural town of Nicasio, halfway between Highway 101 and the Point Reyes National Seashore—a relative stone's throw from George Lucas's Skywalker Ranch. It is some of the most valuable real estate in the world today. The story caught my eye because Marin is not far from my old stomping grounds in Sonoma County, and Marin, and Sonoma more broadly, are the ancestral lands of the Coast Miwok and Pomo people. The tribes are closely related through historical and contemporary kinship ties, but there are no federally recognized tribes in Marin. I had never heard of this group. The closest tribes are the Federated Indians of the Graton Rancheria in Rohnert Park, who are predominantly Coast Miwok, and several Pomo bands, including the nearby Dry Creek and more distant Lytton, Cloverdale, Hopland, and Kashia, among others farther north. My first take was that it was just one more in a long succession of groups in California in recent years claiming to be original tribes, like the Northern Chumash Tribal Council and numerous others in Southern California. Many of these groups have compelling stories of indigeneity that appear legitimate until one digs deeper to learn about the people involved and their true ancestry. Like other groups within and beyond California that claim to be tribes, the Coast Miwok Tribal Council of Marin are organized as a nonprofit entity. This one, called Huukuiko, Inc., raised the $1.3 million to purchase the parcel located close to one of the original Coast Miwok villages. The plan is to use the land for growing traditional foods and other plants, ceremony, and other cultural practices.[2] Without federal tribal recognition, the group could never develop a casino.

Upon closer inspection of the Coast Miwok Tribal Council, I noticed that one of the leaders was an old friend whom I had lost contact with many years before. I knew him to be legitimately of Pomo and Coast Miwok ancestry, with family who are respected members of the Sonoma County Native community.[3] I didn't know until I spoke with him about the land purchase, however, that he had been disenrolled from Dry Creek. And even with documented connections to Graton Rancheria, he was ineligible for enrollment there due to tight enrollment rules and a de facto enrollment moratorium. Dry Creek and Graton have successful gaming operations, and my friend had effectively been rendered tribeless by both. I came to realize that the formation of the Coast Miwok Tribal Council was directly attributable to disenrollment and enrollment moratoriums.

To my knowledge, it is the first instance of a group forming a tribe under such conditions.

Dry Creek has experienced numerous waves of disenrollment since at least 2004. That's when a tribal member challenged the tribe's leadership, running against the incumbent for tribal chair after a decision was made to cut seventy-three adults and seventy children from the 565-member roll, a full 25 percent of the membership. At stake was a monthly per capita payment of approximately $650 and other benefits such as medical coverage and housing.[4] This is often the focus of media stories about disenrollment. Beyond the material aspects of disenrollment, though, is the psychological harm of being ejected from a tribal community. The Dry Creek story is a typical example of how disenrollment battles unfold in gaming tribes; while it may seem to be about money, which is problematic enough, disenrollment carries far greater emotional costs, affecting a person or a family's sense of identity and belonging in a community they have always been part of.

THE GOLD STANDARD: PER CAPITA

To understand the inner workings of disenrollment, we need to follow the money in tribal communities. Per capita payments are central to this discussion. Per capita, or per cap, payments are distributed on an annual, semiannual, quarterly, or monthly basis to enrolled members of federally recognized tribes. It is not welfare money handed down from the federal government for distribution to tribal members just because they are Indians. They are generally derived from revenue generated by tribal businesses and other activities that could include land claims settlements or government management of tribal trust lands or other resources; the amounts are evenly distributed among tribal members/citizens. The larger the membership, the smaller the per caps, and vice versa. In tribes with gaming operations, the Indian Gaming Regulatory Act (IGRA) governs how tribes can spend their profits through revenue sharing in the following ways: (1) funding tribal government services; (2) providing for the tribe's general welfare; (3) promoting economic and community development; (4) donating to charitable organizations; and (5) aiding local governments.

Tribes can distribute profits as per capita only after the approval of the secretary of the interior[5] through Tribal Revenue Allocation Plans (RAP).[6] Wilkins and Wilkins report that since 1993, 130 tribal governments have received federal approval to distribute gaming revenue in per capita payments—78 percent of tribes with gaming operations.[7] Indian gaming continues to grow, having weathered the Great Recession of 2007 and the COVID-19 pandemic. In 2022, the Indian gaming industry recorded an astonishing $43 billion in revenue, generated from 504 casinos run by 246 tribes.[8] Of Class III gaming operations (casinos with slot machines, table games, and other high-stakes gambling), sixty-six are in California,[9] and the American Gaming Association reported, as of 2016, California accounted for $8.6 billion in gross gaming revenue.[10] In other words, California, home to 13 percent of the country's Indian casinos, generates approximately one-quarter of Indian gaming revenue nationwide.

Not all tribes issue per capita checks, but by far the biggest per caps come from tribes with successful casinos. Research shows that per capita payments have both positive and negative effects for tribal members.[11] On the positive side is the reduction in poverty, especially on reservations where unemployment levels are typically the highest nationwide. Reduced poverty means greater access to credit, greater tribal civic engagement, and better psychological and educational outcomes for children. Negative impacts include a "culture of dependency" and reduced incentive to work or engage in other productive activities. Higher per caps are also linked to increased high school dropout and substance abuse rates. In the Seminole Tribe of Florida, as per capitas increased, life expectancy dropped.[12] Per capita payments are tied to political power for tribal politicians; increasing per caps is commensurate with tribal politicians staying in power while conversely, lowering per capita payments is equated with political suicide.[13] Tribal leaders have even borrowed money to keep the per caps flowing.[14] The Ninth Circuit Court of Appeals found that per capitas in gaming tribes are linked to disenrollment. However, Adam Crepelle notes that disenrollment is not always linked to gaming or even money: "[d]isenrollment usually occurs when those in power believe it is in their best interest to do so."[15] Disenrollment is ultimately a matter of power and is tied to money, since money is also a lever of power. But some data also suggests that other factors play a role in whether a tribe disenrolls, especially in California.

DISENROLLMENT AND ITS CAUSES

As this book attempts to show, California has been a site where the complexities of Native identity have converged with settler capitalism and resulted in systemic Native ethnic fraud, or pretendianism. The state also displays a unique role in the phenomenon of tribal disenrollment. As gaming revenue has increased, so has tribal disenrollment, and scholars have struggled to understand the connection. The task is further complicated by the lack of transparency and tribal governmental data, as tribes are not legally required to publicly disclose financial information. It's easy to attribute disenrollment to tribal politicians' desire to maximize per capitas, which helps maintain their power, and there is no doubt that per capitas play a significant role in tribal disenrollment. There are certainly examples of tribal politicians who have remained in power for decades and also lead tribes that have disenrolled members or enacted enrollment moratoriums, all of which contribute to the maximization of per capitas. According to the 2017 study from David Wilkins and Shelly Hulse Wilkins, seventy-nine tribes have either disenrolled or banished tribal members, thirty of which—38 percent—are in California.[16] Of those, at least twenty distribute per capita,[17] ranging from a few hundred dollars to $20,000 per month or more.[18] Other research complicates the per capita explanation to some extent. One study, for example, found a correlation between California gaming tribes that have disenrolled and were also terminated and later reinstated, and those that have IRA constitutions and tribal court systems. The research revealed that of the subset of gaming tribes that had been terminated, 59 percent of them had disenrolled; all but two of the disenrolling California tribes did not have IRA constitutions, and only 17 percent of the disenrolling tribes have viable tribal court systems. The research suggests a "nexus between gaming and termination as twin causes of disenrollment," and that IRA constitutions and viable court systems seem to act as deterrents to the civil rights abuses of disenrollment.[19]

Still, there does seem to be a preponderance of evidence suggesting that disenrollment is most closely associated with the distribution of per capitas. David Wilkins points out in another source the roles of political power and personal vendettas, as alleged in the Dry Creek case.[20] Between five thousand and ten thousand tribal members have been disenrolled since the entry of tribal gaming[21] "without any concern for human rights, Tribal traditions, or due process, arbitrarily and capriciously . . . as a means to solidify their own economic and political bases and to winnow out opposition families who may be disapproving of the direction the nation's leadership is taking the community,"[22] Wilkins contends. Whatever the decision is based on, disenrollment is always done in the name of tribal sovereignty and self-determination. Reasons can stem from family feuds that become blood quantum issues, ostensibly from an error in previous recordkeeping. Such "errors" can go back generations, resulting in the ghoulish expulsion of people long dead. Well-established facts and previously relied upon documentation are often discarded, and truth loses all meaning. If one ancestor is classified as having insufficient blood quantum, declared adopted, said not to have lived on the reservation when it was established, or denied their tribal heritage altogether, their descendants will be kicked off the rolls as well. Other reasons have been treason (which could be as simple as challenging tribal leadership), criminal activity, or inexplicable denial of membership. Adding further injury, there is virtually no due process or means of recourse to contest such decisions, particularly when a tribe has no court.

The Picayune Rancheria of Chukchansi Indians in California's Central Valley has disenrolled more members—more than a thousand—than any other US tribe in several waves of disenrollment since at least 2003. One Chukchansi disenrollee said the tribe started disenrolling before it began distributing per caps. Leadership ousted one-third of its membership before it submitted an RAP to the Bureau of Indian Affairs to begin issuing per capitas. After six hundred people had been cut from the rolls, per caps began in late 2007. Per caps increased with the next wave of expulsions in 2010 and 2012.[23]

A CASE STUDY IN DISENROLLMENT: PECHANGA

Of the dozens of tribes that have disenrolled, few stand out more than Pechanga Band of Luiseño Indians in the Temecula Valley in Riverside County in Southern California. As with all disenrollment cases, the issue is so divisive that both sides—tribes and disenrollees—are hopelessly polarized. Disenrollees with no legal recourse are understandably aggrieved, whereas tribes rest on self-righteous arguments about the sanctity of tribal sovereignty and shroud themselves in sanctimonious rhetoric that these are internal matters. But Pechanga's story has, like other disenrollment cases, been covered extensively in television news segments, articles, and academic studies. I draw on many of these sources, including a personal account from an outspoken Pechanga disenrollee, John Gomez, to sketch a broad outline of Pechanga's disenrollment history. As disenrollment cases go, as disturbing as Pechanga is, it's fairly typical. But there is one aspect that deserves attention for the critical questions and larger implications it raises: the role of the tribe's long-standing chairman, Mark Macarro. The questions involve larger issues of power, representation, and influence, as well as who gets to control narratives and at whose expense.

The Pechanga band is one of the wealthiest and most powerful tribes in the US, and by some accounts, it eclipses all gaming tribes in California. But like all California tribes, Pechanga is preceded by a history of surviving against overwhelming odds in the face of a state policy of extermination, aided and abetted by the federal government.[24] For the purpose of this discussion, Pechanga's history begins in the American period with the Treaty of Temecula, one of eighteen unratified California Indian treaties, one of only two in Southern California. Collectively, the treaties would have set aside around seven million acres for reservations, but because the treaties were never ratified by the US Senate, land was taken anyway, with very little reserved for the tribes. The Treaty of Temecula, or Treaty K, was signed in 1852 by representatives of tribes known today as Agua Caliente Band of Cahuilla Indians, Pechanga Band of Luiseño Indians, San Manuel Band of Missions Indians, and Ramona Band of Cahuilla in the village of Temécku in the Temecula Valley, the location of today's Pechanga reservation.[25] The treaty negotiations and signing were held at the adobe home of Pablo Apis (pronounced "Apish"), a tribal leader of the Temecula Luiseño, also known as Payómkowichum. Although Apis was not a signatory to the treaty, one member of the Apis family was—Pablino "Coo-hac-ish"—Pablo Apis's stepson from Pala.[26] Pablo Apis was born at the village of Gaujome where Mission San Luis Rey was located, about twenty-five miles west of the Temecula Valley, and was raised in the mission. He was officially an alcalde and *capitán* because of his relationship to the Spanish at the mission; he also became known as a chief and headman of the Luiseño. Researcher Sean Milanovich notes that although Apis was not a traditional tribal headman, or *nta* (a term John Gomez attributes to the Kumeyaay, not Luiseño), he became known as a leader among the Luiseños because he advocated for the return of Indian lands during the period of Mexican secularization. He was jailed briefly for leading a revolt against the mission. In 1843, Apis was granted 2,333 acres under Governor Pio Pico for his services as alcalde;[27] today's Pechanga casino now sits on a portion of that land.[28] Apis passed away in 1853 or 1854 at about the age of sixty-one.[29] His rancho lands were gradually sold off in parcels, and the Temecula Indians were evicted in 1875.[30] The Pechanga reservation was established by executive order of President Chester A. Arthur in 1882.

Pechanga's tribal government was not formally organized until 1979. Few people lived on the rural, economically depressed and underdeveloped reservation. A total of 456 people were registered in the original enrollment book under the tribe's constitution over a sixteen-month period.[31] In 1989, six Apis descendants were disenrolled for being adopted, in contradiction of Article II of the constitution, which allowed the enrollment of people accepted in the "Indian way" prior to 1928. The tribe began its gaming operation in 1995, leading to an influx of new enrollment applications. The following year, a moratorium was placed on all new adult and child enrollments; it was intended to be temporary, but the moratorium was never lifted after repeated approval by the general membership.[32] In 2002, a review of the Enrollment Committee's work found unprocessed applications from prior to the moratorium in violation of the tribe's constitution and by-laws, leading to a request for an internal audit. Outside legal counsel was obtained, then promptly replaced by the tribe's internal legal counsel, John Macarro, brother of tribal chairman Mark Macarro. The audit may never have been conducted. Eight members of the eleven-member Enrollment Committee, including John Gomez, were ousted, and some, like Gomez, later disenrolled, leaving only three members. Within a few months, the whittled-down committee, overseen by the tribal council and Chairman Macarro, who Gomez alleges ran the council, instigated a new round of disenrollments, supported by a group calling itself the Concerned Pechanga People.[33]

This second wave of disenrollments allegedly targeted over two hundred descendants of Manuela Miranda, a granddaughter of Pablo Apis.[34] The committee questioned Miranda's tribal affiliation and her status as one-half Pechanga.[35] Subsequent news coverage showed Mark Macarro beginning to reject Pablo Apis as Pechanga; he may have been from another band of Luiseño but "just not Pechanga."[36] Without a fair and independent court, tribally based legal remedies were unavailable to the disenrolled, and outside legal action proved fruitless; state and federal courts deferred tribal enrollment matters to tribes. A petition circulated by a Miranda/Apis descendant requesting an end to the disenrollments in 2005 was passed overwhelmingly by the general membership. "Under the provision of the Band's Constitution and By-Laws," Barker writes, this process and vote had the force of making it tribal law.[37] However, it appears to have been ignored by the band's elected officials, given the lack of evidence that the disenrollments were overturned.

Meanwhile, the tribe had hired John Johnson—the same John Johnson Coastal Band Chumash members, including Wishtoyo's Mati Waiya, had consulted—to conduct a genealogical investigation of Paulina Hunter. Johnson found, first with 90 percent and later 100 percent confidence, that Hunter, a survivor of the 1846 Temecula massacre who received a land grant of twenty acres from President McKinley (and has a street named for her on the reservation), was a legitimate Pechanga ancestor from whom many Pechanga members traced their descent. But based on Johnson's initial comment about 90 percent certainty, a third wave of disenrollments followed after Paulina Hunter was posthumously removed as a Pechanga ancestor in 2006. Ninety of her descendants were disenrolled. At least three hundred people have been disenrolled from Pechanga since 1989, and according to one claim, another four hundred are prevented from membership due to a moratorium.[38] In 2004, just prior to his disenrollment, Gomez said per capitas were around $14,000 a month. After the disenrollment of the Paulina Hunter line, per caps had gone up to $32,000 per month. In 2008, per caps were reported to be $40,000.[39]

IMPLICATIONS OF CALIFORNIA TRIBAL GAMING AND QUESTIONS OF POWER

Mark Macarro has been the chairman of Pechanga since 1992, stewarding the tribe's journey from rags to riches in a Cinderella story most tribes and corporations would find enviable. The effectiveness of his leadership in California Indian gaming is unquestionable. He became the face of Indian gaming in California when tribes were fighting to protect their rights to Class III gaming under the federal Indian Gaming Regulatory Act, which faced opposition from a number of sectors bankrolled almost entirely by Nevada gaming interests. In 1998, 107 tribes backed an initiative called Proposition 5 to push the state into negotiating compacts that allow Class III Las Vegas–style gambling. They had spent a total of $69 million[40] on a marketing campaign featuring Mark Macarro. He recorded so many commercials pushing the proposition, the Los Angeles Times called him "Prop. 5's pitchman" with a "starring role."[41] Even though Prop 5 was passed by voters in a landslide, opponents immediately mounted two separate lawsuits. Labor unions contended that the initiative didn't adequately address the labor rights of tribal employees, while business interests claimed racial discrimination because tribes received special rights as a racial group,[42] a similar argument would be levied against the Indian Child Welfare Act years later. The California Supreme Court overturned the legislation.

Anticipating the court's decision, tribes mobilized again, this time behind Prop 1A, dubbed the Indian Self-Reliance Amendment. Macarro reprised his role selling the virtues of Indian gaming to a public simultaneously enthusiastic, ambivalent, and hostile toward Indians with casinos. He was videogenic, appearing affable, trustworthy, articulate, and unintimidating. Another resounding success, Prop 1A amended California's constitution to permanently authorize Class III gaming in tribal casinos in 2000; it also gave the state authority to strictly regulate it through the oversight of the state gambling commission.[43] Indian country's newfound wealth and political power was threatening to the Las Vegas gaming establishment, which despised Indians infringing on their turf. While both Prop 5 and Prop 1A seriously compromised tribal sovereignty by giving the state so much authority over tribal matters, it was deemed a risk worth taking because no one wanted to return to the poverty of California Indian life before gaming. Framing the issue as self-reliance was a brilliant strategic move that resonated with American bootstrap ideology, making Indians more relatable to the wider public. It also cemented Macarro's reputation as an effective tribal leader throughout Indian country.

Less than two years after the passage of Prop 1A, Pechanga's political leadership was shoring up its disenrollment efforts, beginning with the firing of the Enrollment Committee members. Coincidence? John Gomez thinks not. But whether Pechanga's disenrollment campaign was related to amending the California constitution, Macarro was suddenly on the defensive in news reports that cast a sympathetic light on disenrollees' stories. He continued reiterating his dubious claim that Pablo Apis, Manuela Miranda, and Paulina Hunter were not Pechanga Indians to justify the cruelty of the dismemberments he oversaw. Gomez told me that the tribe's enrollment records are stored in a bank vault, subject to strict secrecy; one member of the Enrollment Committee was even fired for violating the secrecy regulations. With this level of opacity, lineages, even Mark Macarro's, are shielded from scrutiny. But Gomez and others have pointed out that the Macarro lineage, also known as Macarria, is not even listed on the original enrollment, whereas Apis and Hunters "are all over the place."

John Gomez was once a political representative and lobbyist for Pechanga, playing a key role in helping to establish today's Pechanga's gaming enterprise. Disenrolled members lost per capitas, cars, homes, health benefits, and education subsidies. Some, like Gomez, lost jobs, and some went into bankruptcy.[44] As painful as the loss of material things can be, by far the toughest impacts disenrollees report is being robbed of their standing as tribal members, as citizens of their tribal nations. Being cast out from a community and the ripple effects it has on family relations and sense of identity causes the most injury. To be rendered tribeless is the most culturally traumatic event that can happen to an Indigenous person. There is a paucity of research on disenrollment; the research that does exist tends to highlight case studies of different tribal examples, focusing on the legal aspects and potential solutions. Less research is dedicated to understanding the psychological ramifications of being dismembered from a tribe, although media documentation typically shares these personal stories of anguish and grief. The Association of American Indian Physicians, however, passed a resolution effectively condemning disenrollment and urging tribes that have disenrolled to reenroll. The resolution was backed by three briefs citing "critical issues concerning tribal disenrollment [such as] the psychiatric implications and other medical issues that affect the morbidity and mortality of all members. It is important to note that not just current families are affected but families of future generations as well." The statements highlighted how disenrollment exacerbates high rates of mental health and social problems stemming from trauma caused by cultural loss, including depression, PTSD, substance abuse, suicide, homicide, domestic violence, child abuse, and accidental death.[45]

One study addresses disenrollment specifically in California.[46] The study involved in-depth interviews of seven individuals—two from the Pala Band of Mission Indians (a band of Luiseño not far from Pechanga), four from Pechanga, and one from Pinoleville (Pomo) in Northern California. Unsurprisingly, common themes and patterns emerged from the testimonies. Some of the most poignant themes include the belief that their disenrollments were driven by the greed of tribal councils; that these disenrollments occurred after they questioned how tribal funds were being managed by councils and administrators; and that all were accused of failing to prove tribal affiliation, even with indisputable evidence. Proof was simply disregarded. This last point leads the researcher Dayna Barrios to conclude that the underlying reason for disenrollment is the maintenance of power. As we observed earlier, tribal politicians who can assure lucrative per capitas are guaranteed to retain their positions. Disenrollment was especially hard on elderly members, and although the act of disenrollment cannot strip people of their inherent Indianness, concern for children growing up without access to their cultures is acute. Depression and stress—from being exiled and from being thrust into poverty, exacerbating already existing conditions of intergenerational trauma that Native people live with daily as survivors of genocide—were common. Barrios argues that hegemony, capitalism, and inequality are all interrelated components of disenrollment in what she terms "casino-capitalism,"[47] and contends that "tribal elite dominate modes of representation of their people, which in turn supports the existing power relations with claims to legitimate heritage and traditional social relations."[48]

Prior to gaming, Indians had little to no political power in the US. Since gaming, as research clearly shows, tribes have achieved unprecedented levels of power and influence, especially at the state level, as this is what money buys in politics.[49] Nowhere has this proved truer than in California. The concentration of power by some tribal politicians needs to be addressed, however, and Mark Macarro is the best example. Since his election to the position of tribal chairman in 1992, Macarro has been appointed or elected to numerous bodies, including the Riverside County Historical Commission; the California Workforce Investment Board; the Democratic Party Platform Committee; the Democratic National Convention; the Electoral College (Voting Member), California, US Presidential Election; the Harvard Project on American Indian Economic Development; the Native American Rights Fund board; the Indian Gaming Association; the American Gaming Association; the University of California President's NAGPRA (Native American Graves Protection and Repatriation Act) Native American Advisory Council; and the California Truth and Healing Council. In October 2023, Macarro was elected president of the National Congress of American Indians (NCAI), the oldest and most powerful Native American rights policy and advocacy group in the US. His presidency was preceded by his two-year tenure as vice president of the organization.[50]

As critics relentlessly point out, disenrollment is not traditional and does not reflect the values of inclusiveness and generosity that shaped precolonial tribal societies. Historical processes that forced tribal communities into the settler capitalist state have resulted in Faustian bargains eroding otherwise predominantly egalitarian Indigenous value systems. The settler capitalist state rewards greed at the expense of human well-being, and disenrollment is a perfect reflection of that. More recently, we see troubling interlinkages between Pechanga, trends in the nonprofit and philanthropy sectors, and Native Hollywood's infrastructure. This new generation of wealth has spurred an insidious jockeying for power and access based on the kind of toxic competition, exclusion, and nepotism that capitalism inherently engenders. The access that wealth buys means those with the money have power to exert influence in high places; in this case, influence in Hollywood drives what kinds of film and television shows are produced, and who gets to make them. In the philanthropy world, grantmaking opens doors of opportunity that have the power to define social priorities and shape narratives.

As president of NCAI, Macarro has an influence that reaches all the way to the White House, in addition to other political spheres of influence, including the California governor's office. Macarro doesn't work alone; besides the tribal council that supports him decade after decade, his wife, Holly Cook Macarro, is also every bit as ambitious as her husband. Enrolled at Red Lake Nation, Cook Macarro has worked as a political lobbyist for two decades (unsurprisingly, Pechanga is one of her clients), and she serves on the advisory boards, boards of directors, or in other affiliated roles in many leading Indian country organizations, including Native Forward Scholars Fund (formerly American Indian Graduate Center), Advance Native Political Leadership, ICT (Indian Country Today), National Native American Hall of Fame, NDN Collective, Decolonizing Wealth, and IllumiNative. The latter three organizations are part of a recent trend in philanthropy that has seen record-breaking amounts of money funneled into Native and BIPOC (Black, Indigenous, and People of Color) nonprofits.[51] In 2021, NDN Collective received an astounding $50 million from the Bush Foundation for a range of BIPOC community projects, including their #landback initiative. Cook Macarro is also NDN Collective's official lobbyist. Native Forward, which grants college scholarships to Native students, received $20 million from MacKenzie Scott, former wife of Jeff Bezos.[52] It was part of a give-away of $1.7 billion to 116 organizations addressing racial equity, climate change, public health, and other social concerns begun during the pandemic in 2020.[53]

The Decolonizing Wealth Project, founded in 2018 by Edgar Villanueva, who identifies as Black and Indigenous and who wrote a popular but problematic book of the same name,[54] announced a commitment of $20 million over five years to Black reparations projects in 2023. Villanueva, a member of the controversial Lumbee tribe of North Carolina (which has only a partial form of federal recognition), grew up in the Deep South. In 2019, Villanueva launched Liberated Capital, a "fund of Decolonizing Wealth" as a passthrough organization that distributes grants to California Indian entities from the state of California's Indian Truth and Healing Council funds. Decolonizing Wealth's board of advisors includes Chrissy Castro, a member of the board of directors for Advance Native Political Leadership as well as the California Native Vote Project. Also on Decolonizing Wealth's Philanthropic Advisory Group is Nick Tilsen, president and CEO of NDN Collective.

The connections between these organizations and individuals reveals the reach of the Macarros' influence and their enmeshment in centers of power and financial resources (see figure 5.1 for a visual representation of these relationships).

These new cash infusions into Native (and Black) organizations have enabled much-needed community development and social justice initiatives. What is troubling, however, are the linkages between some of the players and the outsized influence they possess in steering wealth and directing social narratives. IllumiNative is especially instructive here. IllumiNative is a Native nonprofit, founded in 2018, to combat negative stereotypes with its Reclaiming Native Truth project, touted as "the largest public opinion research and strategy-setting project ever conducted by, for, and about Native peoples,"[55] with $3.3 million in

FIGURE 5–1: *Power Map*

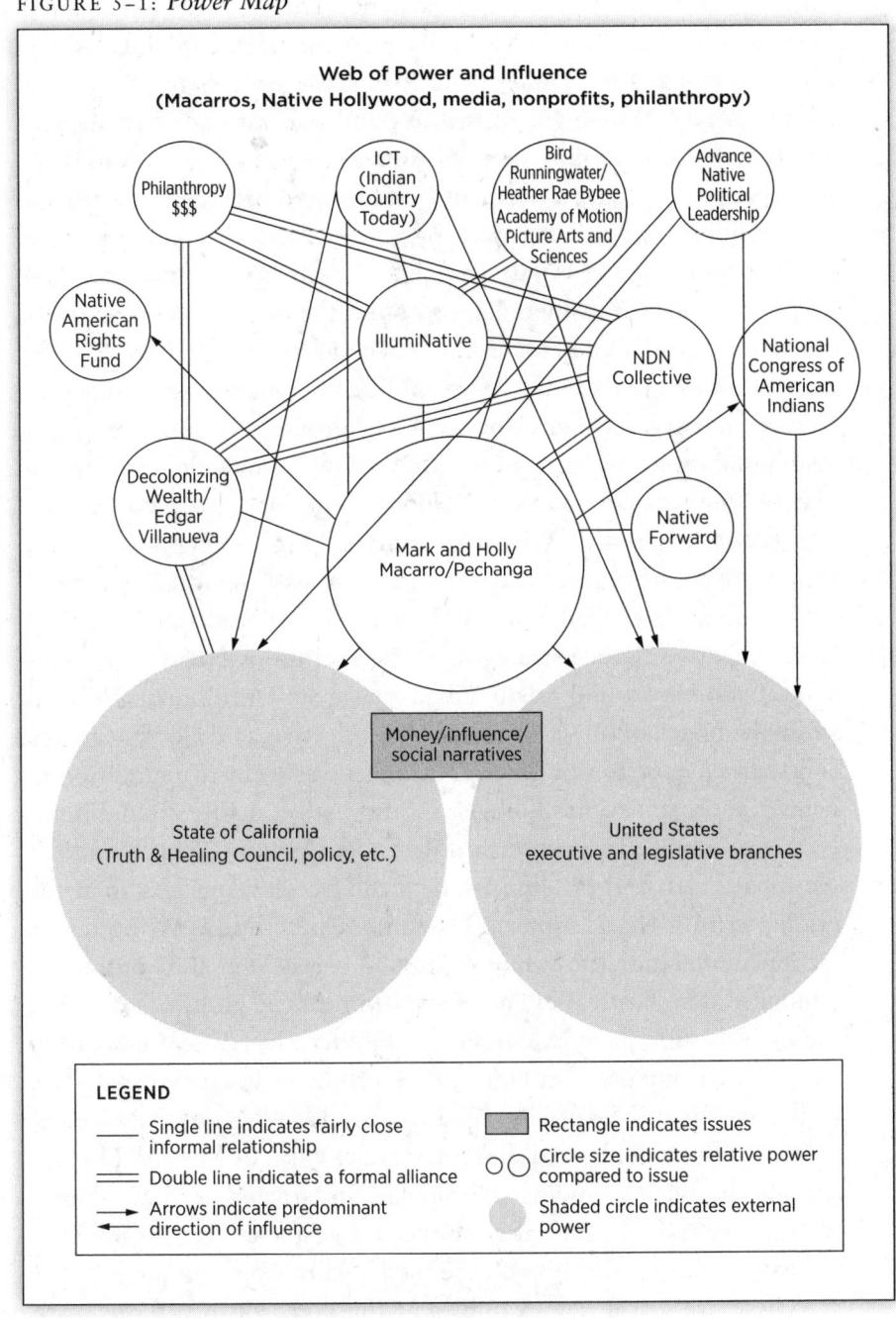

Web of Power and Influence
(Macarros, Native Hollywood, media, nonprofits, philanthropy)

Philanthropy $$$

ICT (Indian Country Today)

Bird Runningwater/ Heather Rae Bybee Academy of Motion Picture Arts and Sciences

Advance Native Political Leadership

Native American Rights Fund

IllumiNative

NDN Collective

National Congress of American Indians

Decolonizing Wealth/ Edgar Villanueva

Mark and Holly Macarro/Pechanga

Native Forward

Money/influence/ social narratives

State of California (Truth & Healing Council, policy, etc.)

United States executive and legislative branches

LEGEND

_____ Single line indicates fairly close informal relationship

===== Double line indicates a formal alliance

→ Arrows indicate predominant
← direction of influence

▬ Rectangle indicates issues

◯◯ Circle size indicates relative power compared to issue

⬤ Shaded circle indicates external power

funding.[56] Over its few years of existence, we can see mission creep into other realms of influence with a growing interest in film and media. Its mission is to "build power for Native peoples by amplifying contemporary Native voices, stories, and issues to advance justice, equity, and self-determination. We utilize research, narrative and culture change strategies, movement-building, and organizing to disrupt the invisibility of Native peoples, re-educate Americans, and mobilize public support for key Native issues." IllumiNative has since raised millions of philanthropy dollars to build the organization, which is expanding into TV and film production and financing with the launching of IllumiNative Media.[57] Crystal Echo Hawk, the organization's founder and executive director, has a background as a consultant "advising philanthropic institutions about how to make investments in Native American communities."[58] Holly Cook Macarro, Echo Hawk's best friend, chairs the board of directors.[59] Bird Runningwater and Heather Rae, from the Academy's Indigenous Alliance, are integral to IllumiNative as well, with Bird on the board and Rae IllumiNative's narrative change strategist, a title that followed her from Amazon. Echo Hawk and Edgar Villanueva from Decolonizing Wealth sit on the board of directors for NDN Collective, and Cook Macarro is listed as a contributor on NDN Collective's website in addition to being the organization's lobbyist. Additionally, in July 2023, IllumiNative announced a partnership with Decolonizing Wealth and the National Truth and Healing Fund, with Decolonizing Wealth as the grant program's fiscal sponsor. The same year, IllumiNative hosted its second annual Indigenous House, the first was held in 2022 during the Sundance Film Festival in Park City, Utah. At the Hollywood soiree, the organization gave Native Power Builder awards to *Reservation Dogs* showrunner Sterlin Harjo, *Prey* producer Jhane Myers, NDN Collective director of policy and advocacy Jade Begay, US Representative Sharice Davids, and the San Manuel Band of Mission Indians. Among the event's funders is Pechanga. In November 2023, IllumiNative and NBC Universal announced a new partnership aimed at increasing Native visibility on the media giant's platforms.

These are just a few examples of the kinds of incestuous institutional relationships enabled by the combination of philanthropy wealth and tribal gaming wealth. The ubiquity of the Macarros should be deeply concerning to anyone who cares about the civil and human rights of disenrollees. With Mark and Holly Macarro wielding so much influence in Indian country grant funding programs, film, television, and news media, the crisis of disenrollment will never get its deserved attention—as long as they are gatekeeping the resources that can make a difference. We might wonder if Maccaro's role in NCAI's leadership has a chilling effect on the organization's approach to disenrollment. In 2020, for instance, before Macarro became vice president, NCAI had passed Resolution #PDX-20–001, the Tribal Citizenship Policy and Protection Task Force. It was the first time in NCAI's seventy-six-year history that the organization had ever moved to protect the rights of tribal citizens, affirmed with references to the United Nations Declaration on the Rights of Indigenous Peoples and "a growing body of Indigenous scholarship warn[ing] that arbitrary and incongruent governing authority and definitions of tribal citizenship threaten the future of Indigenous citizenries and nations."[60] This was arguably a direct reference to disenrollment. However, after Macarro became vice president, the task force was "all but dead" by October 2022, as attorney Gabe Galanda wrote.[61] We need to ask the serious but obvious questions: What are all the impacts of the Macarros' influence, not just in NCAI, but in the philanthropy world and other Native leadership organizations? How does their influence affect what and who gets funded for community development projects and so many other efforts to safeguard Native interests? How does their sphere of influence shape Native media representation and social narratives about Indian country? And how do we make sense of their alliance with Heather Rae and her dubious Native claims on the one hand, and Mark Macarro's role in Pechanga's cruel disenrollments on the other? Mark Macarro will not be Pechanga's chairman forever, and in time, the tribe's council may change their enrollment policies. But with one hundred tribes now practicing disenrollment—17 percent of all federally recognized tribes—the dynamic of power concentration and unchecked structural alliances that ignore the injustices inflicted upon the disenrolled still exists. Only the names will change.

Power on its own is not necessarily the problem, but how power is wielded and where it is concentrated is a problem, especially in a state like California, which is the fifth-largest economy in the world. Pechanga has been wildly successful in achieving wealth and political influence in the state, leading the charge for changing the literal fortunes of people who have been most victimized by California's dark history of violent domination. It has extended its influence into the spaces of narrative representation and entertainment. For most of the past thirty years, Mark Macarro has been at the helm of this transformation, but as this research shows, Pechanga's road to success is littered with casualties. Hundreds of Pechanga lives alone have been harmed as a result of Macarro and the tribe's concentration of power, all in the name of tribal sovereignty. Macarro's website biography extols his "service to Indian country." But as we ask of any non-Native politician: What is the difference between public service and leadership on one hand and greed and the quest for power on the other? The same question can be applied to any tribal chair or council person responsible for disenrollments in their tribes. How is the web of power and influence here any different than the way power and influence has been concentrated in the hands of a few media and business conglomerates in the past few decades, or more recently, in the executive branch of government during Trump's second presidential term? What are the implications for Indian country in the long run, even after the Macarros? And most importantly, what is the way forward in a settler capitalist infrastructure that we have collectively been dragged into without our consent?

SETTLER CAPITALISM: NATION BUILDING OR SOMETHING ELSE?

Exposing disenrollment as fallout from casino-capitalism leads us again to a broader interrogation of the settler state's impact on American Indian identity through assimilation to settler capitalism. If we understand the US's nineteenth-century Indian policy to forcibly assimilate Native Americans as not just cultural but economic, it casts a different light on the policy decisions that followed in the first decades of the twentieth. It also alters how we might view today's tribal governments and the choices made available to them that shape their own policies of inclusion and exclusion. Tracing the emergence of Native American ethnic fraud to the commodification of Indianness, as we have seen, opens the door to understanding how capitalism leads to misconceptions of what constitutes Native American identity. In the same way, examining the origins of the modern Indian tribe reveals the ways capitalism shapes ideas of tribal membership, citizenship, belonging, and unbelonging. It then exposes how traditional values rooted in kinship, inclusiveness, and generosity have been dislodged by capitalist logics rooted in exclusion, scarcity, and greed.

The irrefutable goal of the federal policy of assimilation, or as historian Tom Holm worded it, the "vanishing policy," was disappearance.[62] Individualizing Indians and extinguishing the tribal bond through Americanization in boarding schools and land allotment was expected to take just a generation or two. But, as Holm wrote, "instead of becoming everyday white Americans, many Native Americans essentially became American *Indians* [emphasis in the original] who, despite their clothing, speech, and religion, continued to orient themselves toward Native American communities."[63] In some ways, the boarding schools backfired, failing to achieve the intended outcome. Indian students had a tendency to band together, reinforcing their cultural identities. With a new appreciation for education, many went on to college and began using the skills they had learned to push back against the federal abuses of allotment, the Religious Crimes Code, and other offenses they'd endured. As the progressive movement built through the first decades of the twentieth century, there was also a burgeoning of reform-minded organizations and initiatives to address Indian issues, including the Society of American Indians (SAI), established in 1911. It was the first society exclusively formed and run by Indians themselves. SAI reflected a new pan-Indian organizational sensibility, dedicated to uniting Indians from all over the country, some of them employees of the Indian Bureau (an older term for the BIA) working for reform from the inside. These were Indians still connected to their reservation communities, who believed in "racial pride and uplift" while also recognizing the need to adapt to their changing world, which Thomas Maroukis argues in his book *We Are*

Not a Vanishing People was not about assimilation as some have con-tended.[64] Progress in this new era of Indian activism was instead di-rected away from federal guardianship and toward self-determination, precisely what assimilation robbed tribal communities and individ-uals of, even though the language of self-determination was not yet fully articulated.

As Indian policy reform developed, it increasingly became framed in economic terms, and as the evidence about the boarding schools in chapter 3 shows, Indian integration into the American economic system, not just acculturation, had always been the goal of assimi-lation. The Dawes Act was designed, after all, to move tribes into a European-style farming lifeway, which required individually owned private land, ostensibly the purpose of allotment. Success was deter-mined by a number of measures and can be observed in the historiog-raphy of the early reservation days. For instance, one part of the job of the Indian agent was to oversee the allotment process; documentation from the early years of the Colville reservation provides an example of how the Indian agent assessed his duty. A journal kept by Major Richard Gwydir, one of the first Indian agents in the Upper Colum-bia Plateau, includes his recording of traditional stories, observations of community social life, and reports for the commissioner of Indian Affairs. Gwydir, a former Confederate soldier from Kentucky, arrived in Spokane in 1886 in Washington Territory, charged with overseeing the tribes of the Colville, Spokane, and Coeur d'Alene reservations. The tribes were still governing themselves based on the traditional leadership of chiefs, albeit under the changed conditions of imposed reservation boundaries, which had a destabilizing effect. Gwydir's reports to the commissioner document the general condition of the tribes—which he described one year as "miserable"—assessing the work of the Jesuit missionaries, the condition of the agency buildings, stock laws, education, alcohol use, and health. The central concern of the reports was how well the Indians were adapting to the farm-ing and ranching economy. Some were more successful than others, depending on how much whiskey was consumed and gambling was done, how many children were being sent to school, and how ara-ble the allotments were (many were of poor quality for farming or ranching).[65] Other publications from this era and region also documented how productive Indian farming and ranching activities were.[66]

In the 1920s and early 1930s, a slew of reports, studies, and legislative hearings assessing conditions on the reservations and the work of the bureau pointed to the need for substantial change. A plethora of problems were identified: health conditions were abysmal, poverty and land loss were rampant, tribal land leases under BIA management were yielding poor returns, and tribes lacked formal governing councils that the federal government could officially interact with,[67] to name just a few. The Meriam Report of 1928, the best known of the studies, was clear that allotment had been an abject failure.[68] Tracing the trajectory of federal action, the reform movement in this era emphasized loosening the restrictions on Indian social life through the valuing instead of denigration of culture, and encouraging tribal community and individual economic self-sufficiency. The imposition of the settler capitalist system on Indian life in the nineteenth century meant that reform would naturally be conceived of within that framework in the twentieth. Capitalism became inescapable; now American Indian success (or failure) would be defined implicitly or explicitly in colonially based economic terms. Thus, when the Indian Reorganization Act, also known as the Wheeler-Howard Act and the Indian New Deal, was passed in 1934, it was designed to facilitate economic development through limited tribal self-governing power by organizing tribes as a type of federal chartered corporation that they could choose to accept or decline.

In their detailed account of the process of the passage of the IRA, Deloria and Lytle show how dramatically the final bill had changed compared to the original concept as imagined by its architect, John Collier. As initially drafted, the bill imagined far broader tribal powers and far less BIA oversight than was finally achieved. Collier was a visionary who understood the value of restoring traditional tribal life and that's what he was striving for. But Deloria and Lytle point out this New Deal era brought a new generation of Indians, who had adapted to their changing world. While they wanted to preserve their old customs, they were also ready to experiment with new ways of doing things. These were also the Depression years of great hardship, demanding the kind of innovative approaches the Roosevelt administration was known for. "Hence," Deloria and Lytle wrote, "the revolution that Collier had wrought, when it reached the reservations, manifested itself in new economic activities, not political sophistication."[69]

NATION BUILDING AT WHAT COST?

Greater political sophistication indeed came in the mid- to late-twentieth century, but often not in ways that have been nurtured by the intrinsic values that can be found in precapitalist, precolonial tribal societies. There were traces of it in the Red Power movement, with calls for the revitalization of tribal traditionalism, but in the context of urban pan-Indianism, movement rhetoric and tactics sometimes went astray, as we saw with activists' misguided attempt to reclaim Alcatraz Island under the Fort Laramie Treaty of 1868. We also saw how Native American traditionalism in that era was widely co-opted and led to pretendianism as we know it today. By the mid-twentieth century, the newly corporatized tribes were concerned not only with surviving the onslaught of termination, but ongoing land incursions by exploitative mining interests and other polluting industries, infrastructure projects (dams and pipelines), protecting treaty rights to hunting and fishing, and land claims settlements. With the shift in federal Indian policy after the passage of the Indian Self-Determination and Education Assistance Act in 1975, or P.L. 93–638, tribes were newly empowered. P.L. 638 created greater tribal autonomy largely through the direct management of government contracts for services and programs, which was enhanced with the passage of the Tribal Self-Governance Act of 1994. This act made permanent the self-governance demonstration project and established the Office of Self Governance (OSG) in the BIA through an amendment to P.L. 638 as Title IV. The OSG "is responsible for implementation of the Tribal Self Governance Act of 1994, as amended. The OSG operates as a one-stop-shop that provides financial management, budgeting, accounting and contracting services for self-governance tribes and assists with the development and implementation of regulations, policies, and guidance in support of self-governance initiatives."[70] By the end of the century, tribal sovereignty and nation building was the name of the game. In this new era, it was all part of what it meant to run a tribe as a business.

Within this federal framework of tribal sovereignty as self-governance, tribes increasingly became the equivalent of administrative wings of the BIA. They gained greater control of economic resources and decision-making, and were able to provide much needed jobs in poor rural reservation communities. At the same time, they also became capitalists, and with gaming wealth, they became capitalists of the highest order, as in the example of Pechanga. After being sucked into the vortex of settler capitalism, one of the biggest challenges tribes faced was how to stabilize their economies, as Deloria and Lytle put it,[71] and simultaneously maintain their cultural values without succumbing to capitalism's worst and darkest impulses. A significant strand of Indigenous and non-Indigenous scholarship today focuses on self-determination as nation building, which is equated with economic development. This is best exemplified by the Harvard Project on Indigenous Governance and Development at the Harvard Kennedy School, formerly known as the Harvard Project on American Indian Economic Development. Its presence at Harvard University conveys a sense about the prioritization economic development research gets in university funding. Founded in 1986 by economist Joe Kalt, sociologist Steve Cornell, and later joined by Manley Begay (Navajo), the Harvard Project is a well-funded institute that generates research and policy briefs across a range of topics, including federal policy, social issues in tribal communities, Native American education and healthcare, cultural revitalization, environment and energy, and of course, economic policy. Without a doubt, these are all important aspects of rebuilding tribal nations, yet there is a conspicuous absence of more critically grounded scholarship. What is hard to find is research that questions the broader systems of power within which tribal nations exist, which have led to the kinds of problems tribes now must address, or investigations into the ways these systems contribute to the excesses and abuses within tribes themselves, such as disenrollment. Capitalism remains the default structure influencing research on tribal economic development.

CASINO CAPITALISM AND THE ABROGATION OF ORIGINAL INSTRUCTIONS

Native and non-Native scholars and intellectuals writing from critical perspectives have highlighted the many ways settler capitalism adversely affects tribal communities. One of the most obvious impacts is seen in how tribes have been drawn into industrial development, often because of the valuable natural resources on their reservations. In his book *The Invasion of Indian Country in the Twentieth Century: American Capitalism and Tribal Natural Resources*, Donald Fixico gave numerous examples of how "American capitalism, deriving from a tradition of Eurocentrism, has continued through the twentieth century to exploit tribal nations for their natural resources, thus forcing Indian leadership to adopt modern, corporate strategies to ensure the survival of their nations and people."[72] These strategies are constitutive of the Faustian bargains in which tribes are pushed into choices about fossil fuel development, for example, based on circumstances not of their own making but originating from desperate poverty.[73] Poverty was the direct result of land dispossession, coupled with the destruction of traditional lifeways during the allotment years.

In another lucid critique of capitalism's impact on Indigenous people, Leanne Betasamosake Simpson writes about how capitalism is a foreign concept in the Nishnaabeg nation, an assessment that would apply to virtually all Indigenous cultures. This knowledge is contained in tribal creation stories, known more succinctly as a culture's Original Instructions.[74] For the Nishnaabeg, traditional stories center Nanabush, a trickster-like character, in warnings of the disasters that result from the accumulation of excess, driven by greed and selfishness. Indigenous people in Canada, Simpson comments, "too often start from the place that global capitalism is permanent and our survival depends on our ability to work within it . . . placing Indigenous people in a never-ending cycle of victimhood and Canadians in a never-ending cycle of self-congratulatory saviorhood, while we both reinforce the structure of settler colonialism that set the terms for exploitation in the first place."[75]

One of the most insidious aspects of capitalism is its intransigence, or as Eric Cheyfitz puts it, "the limits of capitalism's imagination."

Cheyfitz shows how elite neoliberal world leaders believe that capitalism can be made more inclusive, moral, or conscious to curtail the ravages of growing wealth inequality by restoring waning global faith and trust in the system, thus protecting the status quo. This belief ignores certain contradictions, that as a structure capitalism requires the kind of exploitation of humans and the natural world that results in the economic hierarchies at the root of so much human misery and now climate change. Cheyfitz concludes with the argument that so many are increasingly reaching: capitalism is antithetical to all human and nonhuman life, and that Indigenous cultures contain keys to imagining a way of living on the planet outside capitalism's destructive tendencies.[76]

Mohawk professor Taiaiake Alfred minces no words when he writes, "In recent years, one of the motivating forces behind Native politics has been the belief that increasing material wealth of Native people will solve all the problems of colonization . . . [b]ut development is not a panacea. In fact, without a sound traditional basis, it becomes a real danger." He goes on:

> Unfortunately, many Native politicians share a political vision that mirrors the worst tendencies of mainstream society. In a capitalist economy, financial resources are obviously a precondition for community autonomy. But it is one thing to see money as a competitive lever and a measure of collective strength; it is quite another to see self-government as an exercise in accessing financial resources, or the accumulation of wealth as an end in itself. An ideology of accumulation, even if it's collective rather than individual, plays right into the consumptive commercial mentality shaped by the state corporatism that has so damaged both the earth and human relationships around the globe. From an indigenous perspective, appropriate economic development entails taking advantage of opportunities to build self-sufficiency in order to preserve the essence of indigenous cultures and accomplish the goals that emerge from that culture. That is quite different from tying a community to an exploitative economy promoting objectives that contravene traditional values.[77]

Without saying it explicitly, Alfred describes precisely the way capitalism has been operationalized by tribal governments, resulting in the epidemic levels of disenrollment we see today. Disenrollment has emerged as a crisis not only attributable to extreme forms of capitalist-driven nation building, but to the abrogation of Indigenous values rooted in kinship, generosity, fairness, respect, reciprocity, and responsibility. What the Original Instructions of virtually all tribal cultures share are these and other attributes that ensured community continuity and stability and thus their sustainability. Settler capitalism and the quest for revenue and profit has become so normalized as a result of US intrusion into tribal life, it's altered the way Native people interact with the natural world. In addition to the Faustian bargains some tribes have made relative to fossil fuel–based economic development, their land management practices have come to reflect more the bureaucratic imperative of the BIA than a culturally based kinship orientation. Clint Carroll illustrates this in his study on Cherokee medicinal plant protection. Carroll finds that within Cherokee Nation, as is true with most tribal communities, there is a dichotomy between community approaches to the natural world and that of the tribal government. Stemming from paternalistic federal oversight, in its environmental governance the Cherokee Nation eschewed a historical kin-based view of land and nature and adopted instead a management perspective that viewed the environment as a resource. Because the bureaucratic approach of "natural resource management is the process of allocating and administering the resources themselves to achieve mostly economic goals," the ability to protect medicinal plants was compromised to the detriment of the community's needs.[78] This is just one example of how traditional tribal values have been usurped by the settler capitalist state.

Perhaps the most devastating impact of settler capitalism on Native communities is the disruption of Indigenous kinship systems. By privatizing land, allotment eroded how Indians related to it and the natural world, enabling their severance from it through no choice of their own. Assigning monetary value to what can be extracted from the land alters the choices tribes make about how they interact with the land and nonhuman relatives. Land went from being kin to being a commodity. Disenrollment, moratoriums, and blood quantum policies disrupt human kin relationships through the centering of foreign value systems. In a world where survival depends on respecting the limits nature imposes, not a desire to conquer, a worldview centering the ethics of kinship is the result. Kinship assured the ability of tribal communities to thrive in even the harshest of environments; kinship is the essence of sustainability. The lack of respect for kinship is the path of destruction, against a tribal community's original instructions. Like the commodification of land, disenrollment, enrollment moratoriums, and blood quantum are all a choice for death, not life.

CHAPTER SIX

SLIPPERY POLITICS

Why Claims to Indianness
Are So Common

CONVERSATIONS ABOUT Native American identity exist within a broad sociocultural context rooted in American citizenship. The "hyphenated American" is always American by default and the hyphen emphasizes race and/or ethnicity. Race, though socially constructed, is naturalized as a given state of being with European whiteness presumed as the standard against which all "others" are understood. However, American Indians are the only "ethnic group" with a political association to the US as a legal category. This political association is rooted, as already noted, in the nation-to-nation relationship that was established from the earliest days of contact between Europeans and Indigenous populations. Over time, American Indians became racialized while the US sought Native elimination and the commonsense understanding about what constitutes Native American identity became defined by the concept of Indian blood, measured in diminishing fractions. For tribal communities, Indian identity, inseparable from kinship, eventually became conflated with colonial notions of blood. As "American Indian" became normalized as race in popular thought and unmoored from tribal belonging, Indian identity became a matter of personal claims with varying degrees of legitimacy; Indian self-identification invokes Indianness through the "right" to claim, and is always imbricated with power relations as political processes. In this chapter, I examine these dynamics of personal Native-claiming to dissect motivations, uncover what's at stake, and maintain that while the desire for material gain is a major factor, it's not always the raison d'être that can explain the prevalence of Native-claiming.

THE TRIBAL FOUNDATION OF NATIVE IDENTITY

When I was growing up, it was common for people to talk about their national heritage. It seemed uniquely American to discuss where ancestors came from, especially when they were from Europe, even if people didn't know much beyond their grandparents' countries of origin, and to query others unselfconsciously about their ethnic origins. It was natural for me to say that I was Italian (or Sicilian) on my father's side and Indian (later, Native American) on my mother's side. This almost inevitably met with the question: "How much Indian blood do you have?" I noticed that people didn't ask me how much Italian blood I have. It was usually followed with a comment about my looks: some saw my Indianness while others didn't, but either way, they seemed entitled to reflect how they saw me. It always felt intrusive and vaguely insulting, but I never felt comfortable saying so. What business is it of anybody to demand that information? To me, it was like asking someone how much they weigh or how much money they have; it's just not polite and it's no one's business. When I was around other Native people, that question was almost never asked. Instead, they asked: "What tribe are you?" Depending on social context, that conversation usually leads to questions about who your family is, the connections you might have to each other, and how you might be related. It's just how Native people talk.

Nowadays, with the growing diversity of the US population, asking about someone's ethnic heritage does not seem as socially acceptable as it used to be. Native American heritage queries are especially fraught, given the pervasiveness of pretendianism. Conversations about ethnic heritage are conversations about identity, and identity is typically assumed to be a matter of how one perceives oneself. Theories about identity can be found in many fields of study including philosophy, sociology, psychology, ethnic studies, religion, even political science ("identity politics"). It's generally recognized that identity exists on multiple levels that intersect the personal and social realms. There is no one theory or cohesive definition of what exactly identity is or how it is determined.

Questions about American Indian identity involve questions about self-perception, the perception of others, and the rules that govern the recognition of people as American Indian in tribal communities and at the level of the federal government. Tribal criteria vary dramatically from tribe to tribe, and can vary from federal definitions. Within the federal schema, Eva Marie Garroutte found that in 1978 there were at least thirty-three different definitions of *Indian* in federal legislation.[1] Federally, one can qualify as Native American for some things, but not for others. One might be seen by others as Native, but not enjoy recognition by a tribal community or the federal government. Conversely, an individual may qualify for recognition by a tribal or federal government, but reject any sense of Native identity for themselves. Native identity, however defined, though, is not synonymous with tribal belonging, and as we've seen, not all "tribes" are legitimate. And we've also seen how tribes possess unchecked authority to disenfranchise their members.

Federal law has long affirmed that federally recognized tribal governments have the authority to determine who their members are, based on whatever criteria they deem appropriate.[2] As we've seen, the United States introduced the concept of blood quantum during an era when tribal elimination via assimilation was its primary Indian policy goal. As the research of Desi Rodriguez-Lonebear demonstrates, tribal enrollment criteria hinge on base rolls created by the federal government in this time period. It's important to remember that, by and large, those base rolls were created at the behest of the federal government largely for the purpose of issuing land allotments. While Rodriguez-Lonebear's study found a current trend of tribes slowly abandoning blood quantum, 59 percent still use it in some form.[3] Her point is that while tribes may freely choose to use blood quantum, "the federal government cannot easily disentangle itself from [it]." Besides blood quantum, the research found that the most common enrollment criteria are based on lineal descent and/or residency in the tribal community. Lineal descent presumes direct descent from an ancestor on an original base roll, regardless of blood quantum.

Tribal enrollment is formal acceptance into a tribal community. It is a marker of belonging and identity. In many though not all tribes, membership is being reconceived as citizenship, emphasizing that tribes are nations, not private clubs. As nations, the ability to confer membership or citizenship is a function of tribal sovereignty. Together, American citizenship and tribal citizenship constitute a form of dual citizenship.[4]

FEDERAL ACKNOWLEDGMENT

Federal recognition is a framework whereby the United States acknowledges its legal relationship with a tribal entity, and thus its trust responsibility to them. For many tribes, the relationship is based on treaties that created reservations through land cession agreements (albeit agreements made under duress), but for others, the relationship descends from the executive branch when reservations were set aside by presidential order. Such was the case with the Colville reservation, established by executive order in 1872. A few tribes that were small, isolated, or otherwise not a threat to white settlement continued existing from the historical period into contemporary times and were simply ignored by the government.[5] Over one hundred tribes were stripped of their federal recognition during the termination era, some of which have since been restored, though many still have not been, particularly in California. In 1978, the Bureau of Indian Affairs created a process for establishing that "an Indian group exists as an Indian tribe,"[6] administered through the Office of Federal Acknowledgment (OFA). OFA oversees one of three possible paths toward federal recognition, in addition to a congressional act or order by a US court.[7] Any group applying for federal recognition through OFA must meet all of seven criteria that substantiates the continued existence of a tribe as a distinct community that has exercised political influence over its members since 1900.[8] The criteria is strenuous, the process takes many years, often decades, is extremely expensive, and in the end, most groups fail to meet the criteria. Since OFA's inception, thirty-four groups that went through the federal acknowledgment process (FAP) were denied acknowledgment while eighteen were granted.[9] In 2012, the General Accounting Office (GAO) found approximately four hundred groups that identified as tribes in a study on non-federally recognized tribes that received federal funding, revealing the pervasiveness of groups with claims to indigeneity.[10] Federal recognition entitles tribes to a government-to-government relationship with the United States and resources set aside for tribal governments, as well as the right to gaming as economic development under the Indian Gaming Regulatory Act.

Some states have a formal process for recognizing tribes within their borders, and there are a few state-based reservations. In 2016, the National Conference of State Legislatures (NCSL) reported that eleven states recognize sixty-three tribes, mostly under the authorization of state legislatures.[11] Occasionally, state recognized tribes achieve federal recognition, as was the case in 2015 when the state-recognized Pamunkey Tribe in Virginia was granted federal recognition, and in 2019, with Little Shell Tribe of Chippewa Indians in Montana. Six state recognized tribes in Virginia were granted federal recognition via legislation in 2018. It seems to be more a rule than an exception that state-recognized groups are denied federal recognition.[12] The procedures for state recognition are not consistent across states, and tend to be significantly less arduous than the federal process.[13] This is exemplified in a 2023 study of four state-recognized Abenaki "tribes" in Vermont, which highlights that a key problem with the state's recognition is a lack of genealogical substantiation.[14] State recognition is also controversial among some federally recognized tribes. The Narragansett Indian Tribe, the only federally recognized tribe in Rhode Island, for instance, opposed bills that would create a state recognition process, claiming that the legislation lacked the kind of anthropological and genealogical rigor that should be applied in such a process.[15] In 2019, the chairman of the Eastern Band of Cherokee Indians, Richard Sneed, delivered testimony before Congress opposing the federal recognition of the state recognized North Carolina Lumbee tribe, which Sneed said have wrongly claimed to be Cherokee and "many other tribes."[16] The Cherokee Nation (Oklahoma), whose research in 2007 found over two hundred "bogus Cherokee tribes,"[17] has long opposed state recognition. In 2023, Cherokee Nation principal chief Chuck Hoskin publicly opposed the Indian Arts and Crafts Act's clause that authorizes people from state recognized tribes to sell their work as "Indians," encouraging support for a change in the law.[18] In another 2023 news story, Ben Barnes, chief of the federally recognized Oklahoma-based Shawnee Tribe, said that the proliferation of fake tribes is far more extensive and problematic than the GAO report outlines. In addition to the hundreds of faux Cherokee tribes, Barnes notes over eighty fake Shawnee tribes, numerous illegitimate Delaware (Lenape) tribes, and even a Lakota tribe of West Virginia (the actual Lakota tribal groups are based in the Great Plains). Barnes pushed back on state recognition, pointing out that "legislatures are ill-equipped and ill-educated to make these decisions—at least at a state level—on who is and who is not an Indian," and emphasized that tribes themselves are much better equipped to make such decisions.[19]

THE "BENEFITS" OF NATIVE CLAIMING

There is no denying that the processes of colonization have severely disrupted American Indian life. Forced removal, assimilation through Christianization and education, the intentional breakup of Indian families and communities, the banning and criminalization of Native religions, termination, racialization, discrimination, blood quantum, disenrollment, enrollment moratoriums—all of it over four centuries is the historical context for the chaos we see today when it comes to understanding and legally defining what is an Indian tribe and who is an Indian. There are many ways people who legitimately descend from tribal families can lose their connections to tribal communities or their ability to prove kinship to those communities. At the same time, there is an also argument to be made that American Indians have been exhaustively documented since the arrival of foreigners. Mission and church records, Spanish presidio records, Spanish, Mexican, and American census records, other federal and state documents, tribal base rolls, and genealogical records are established methods of enumerating Native individuals. Given how much Indians have been documented, we might question the reliability of narratives that attempt to explain why ancestors were never enumerated as Indians, and who doesn't appear in Indian genealogical searches. To what extent is state tribal recognition legitimate, and what are we to make of state criteria that recognize tribes without the kind of rigor the federal government employs? Do we understand federal recognition of Native people as merely an act of colonial domination, as some who don't have it contend, or as a function of the modern Westphalian US state that, while deeply flawed, still nonetheless preserves tribal nationhood as the basis for the government-to-government relationship? At the individual level, how do we understand Sacheen Littlefeather's claim to being White Mountain Apache and Yaqui when the evidence clearly shows she had no awareness of White Mountain Apache or Yaqui people in her family? What do we make of the fabricated claims of Paul Olivas, also known as Semu Huaute, to being the last full-blood Chumash when his last full-blood Chumash ancestor was five generations in the past? What about the unsubstantiated claims of John Pope, also known as Rolling Thunder, to Cherokee heritage that so many people accepted without scrutiny? Self-identification is not enough when it comes to the federal acknowledgment process nor, for the most part as the GAO study found, for receiving program benefits earmarked for American Indians. Are there times when self-identification should be an acceptable basis for a person's claims to indigeneity, and if so, under what conditions? How well, we might ask, has that worked in Native Hollywood? We already know the answer to that question.

IN IT FOR THE MONEY

All these questions and more invite an examination on how we might analyze the growing phenomenon of American Indian identity claiming, especially in the absence of documentation of American Indian heritage. We are tempted to reach for easy explanations, and chief among them is that people claim Native heritage for material gain. There is, after all, abundant evidence supporting such a conclusion. Recall the *Los Angeles Times* exposé on the hundreds of millions of dollars in government contracts intended for Native American–owned businesses that went to people with unsubstantiated Native American claims. There is also evidence that when the US opened up claims processes to account for unjustly taken land, notably in California in 1928, a substantial number of individuals submitted applications asserting claims to California Indian heritage, often successfully, with thin or no evidence that could be found in pre-American era mission records.[20] There are ways in which people are creatively deceptive too. In one particularly bizarre 2016 story, a man was sentenced to three years in prison for selling memberships in a fake Yamasee tribe to 144 undocumented immigrants who were trying to avoid deportation.[21] This wasn't even the first time such a scam occurred. In 2008, Malcolm Webber was sentenced to five years in prison for selling memberships in the fake Kaweah Tribe to undocumented immigrants, promising a path to US citizenship.[22] Webber's group had applied for and was denied federal recognition in 1985.

A common misconception among those seeking to trace their American Indian heritage is the belief that Indians receive free government money solely for being Indian, or that they can get a free college education because they're Indian. There is no such thing as free money just for being Indian; while Native people do have the possibility of attending one of thirty-two tribal college or universities (TCUs), mostly located on or near reservations, scholarships for Indians are not so abundant. There is access, however, to jobs in academia as colleges and universities seek to diversify their academic offerings and staff and faculty lines. In the United States, proof of ancestry is not required from applicants who claim minority status. Applicants for ethnic studies and American Indian studies need only a convincing claim for tenure and non-tenure track teaching jobs as a Native American diversity hire. Once hired, they can perform Indianness in their teaching and research without accountability, to the detriment of colleagues and students who trust them not only to present accurate knowledge but to be honest about who they are.

There are many examples of professors who have built entire careers on misrepresenting themselves as Native Americans due to the lack of accountability.[23] One high profile case came to light in 2022, coincidentally two days after the death of Sacheen Littlefeather. A statement was posted online by Elizabeth Hoover, a professor at University of California, Berkeley, known for her scholarship in Native American environmental justice and food sovereignty.[24] Hoover long claimed Mohawk, and to a lesser extent Mi'kmaq, but could never identify linkages to a documented Mohawk person, family, or community of origin; many in American Indian studies had doubted her claims for years. Titled "Letter of Apology and Accountability," Hoover wrote, "I am a white person who has incorrectly identified as Native my whole life, based on incomplete information."[25] The statement was a rare and stunning admission after more than a decade in the field. She disclosed that after studying her genealogy she could not trace descendancy from any Mohawk family, despite being told her whole life the family was Mohawk. The statement was met with sharp criticism, though, because instead of apologizing and withdrawing her claims, she seemed to double down on them, justifying why she had done it.

The Hoover case dredged up long-standing resentments about the problem of Native American ethnic fraud in the academic world. Pressure had been mounting for years with the discrediting of once respected academics Andrea Smith and Ward Churchill. Smith's fall from grace was a direct result of her persistent Cherokee claims. Churchill, a prolific writer on Native American issues with a bombastic personality, was fired from a tenured professorship at the University of Colorado, Boulder, in 2007 for research misconduct that included allegations of plagiarism, falsification, and misrepresentation.[26] Ethnic fraud was not a factor in the sacking, but his questionable claims to Cherokee heritage contributed to his lack of credibility. Over the years Churchill had made numerous conflicting statements about his supposed Cherokee heritage that were not validated by any Cherokee tribe and refuted by at least one. As the Churchill conflict was intensifying, Smith was a rising star in American Indian and ethnic studies for her incisive Indigenous feminist political analysis and scholarship. As with Hoover, for Smith, there were doubts within the American Indian studies community about the veracity of her claims that had become full-blown accusations of fraud by 2008 with the publishing of an article by the renown late Cherokee legal scholar Steve Russell. Russell and subsequently numerous others exposed the fact that Smith had sought out Cherokee genealogists, who had told her definitively that she was not Cherokee. After being denied tenure at University of Michigan, she landed a position at University of California, Riverside. Meanwhile, media scrutiny of her unrelenting Cherokee claims continued, culminating in a *New York Times Magazine* article in 2021.

In 2023, after a group of thirteen UC Riverside faculty members filed a complaint about Smith's ongoing Cherokee claims violating the university's Faculty Code of Conduct, it was announced that Smith would resign with emerita status as of August 2024. It was not, to the dissatisfaction of many, an admission of wrongdoing. The approach was effectively only a workaround for a problem with no structural or legal solutions. The Smith case illustrates how academia enables Native American ethnic fraud.[27]

California, renowned for its prestigious public universities, is regrettably fertile ground for pretendianism. In this state, its frequency is deeply entrenched; some individuals occupy academic positions for multiple decades under questionable or outright false American Indian identities. The term *Indigenous* is often used indiscriminately by individuals who not only secure tenure and authority through deception but have also hindered genuine Native American academics from progressing. The masquerade often involves participating in cultural events and conveniently shifting tribal affiliations to evade scrutiny. A comprehensive examination across California's vast higher education system, which includes 116 community colleges, 10 University of California campuses, and 23 California State universities, would likely reveal a significant number of cases. The ubiquity of this phenomenon underscores the urgent need for rigorous verification processes to protect the integrity of Indigenous representation and scholarship.

Academic pretendianism is particularly harmful because it undermines the integrity and representation of genuine Indigenous voices within academic circles. Individuals who falsely claim Indigenous identity personally and financially benefit from positions, scholarships, and endowed chairs meant for authentic Indigenous scholars and also serve as gatekeepers and experts. This fraudulent behavior robs real Indigenous academics, including those who may be white or Black passing, of opportunities and also imposes additional trauma. They sometimes threaten litigation or overshadow the voices of actual tribal communities, creating an environment where the true and diverse experiences of American Indian people are obscured or ignored. This hampers the progress and understanding of Indigenous scholarship and disrespects the very communities they falsely claim to represent, perpetuating cycles of harm and misrepresentation. They provide the worst examples possible to students charged to their care.

The phenomenon of academic ethnic fraud in higher education is a serious issue that goes beyond personal gain. Such individuals insist on inclusion in diversity committees and other bodies critical in shaping the future of American Indian studies and related curricula. By demanding a voice under false pretenses, imposters misrepresent minority voices and exert undue influence over decisions and discourse, guiding them toward their own skewed visions. This behavior misappropriates opportunities meant for actual Indigenous scholars and distorts the representation and understanding of Indigenous cultures and experiences in the academic sphere. They create an environment of good Indians versus bad Indians, for example, as they move easily among white people, with administration, and tend not to challenge colonial structures, leaving authentic Indians to be criticized when they stand up against academic colonialism. Their presence and influence can lead to the promotion of inaccurate or harmful narratives, which directly affects the authenticity and efficacy of educational programs designed to advance true diversity and inclusion. Finally, academic frauds make it more difficult for California Indians to secure tenure track positions in California institutions, partly because of the pretendendians holding space but also for their fear of scrutiny when an Indian person from the local tribal community is hired.

NOT IN IT FOR THE MONEY

Critics have been increasingly outspoken about the problem of ethnic fraud in academia, pointing out that when people are hired for prestigious academic jobs, which can lead to lucrative publishing deals, research grants, or consulting positions based on unverifiable or false Native American identity claims, it siphons resources away from actual American Indian people.[28] It's a serious problem that needs to be addressed. But while much of the prevalence of Native American identity claiming can be attributed to the desire for material gain, that's not always the case. We need a way to understand the persistence of Indian claims as they appear, for example, in family lore, and in census box-checking. As I've suggested in previous chapters, there are other intangible, affective, psychological benefits people get from their Native claims. As we have observed, a trajectory links cultural appropriation in the form of playing Indian to the impulse to become Indian at particular historical moments. As Philip Deloria noted, Americans have been playing Indian as early as the Boston Tea Party, and, similarly, Shari Huhndorf found that Americans' ongoing compulsion to "go native" has always been a way to evade association with the violence that characterizes the origin of the US.[29] "Throughout the twentieth century," she writes, "going native has served as an essential means of defining and regenerating racial whiteness and a racially inflected vision of Americanness . . . reaffirm[ing] white domination by making some (usually distorted) vision of Native life subservient to the needs of the colonizing culture."

Playing Indian and going native go to the next level of *becoming* Indian when (usually racially white) people narrate or re-narrate their family histories. These histories often include a long-lost Indian ancestor and use that as a basis for claims to *being* Indian typically without, sometimes with, evidence, however thin. And arguably, as the example of Sacheen Littlefeather shows, race-shifting moves into indigeneity or Indigenous hybridity are not always moves away from whiteness. The transition into indigeneity can be seen as the reinforcement of the *logics* undergirding and animating colonizing culture, in Huhndorf's terms. If we understand colonizing culture as a United States shaped by racial whiteness, other dynamics become visible that can help explain the strange phenomenon of Indian-becoming and why it is not always about what one can materially gain but is nonetheless tied to capitalist logics. The clues are in how the desire for whiteness itself shape-shifts, and how it is simultaneously useful and discardable, depending on historical context and the social mood of the country.

Older studies on the resurgence of Indian identity that link the resurgence with the protest movements of the Red Power era, such as Joane Nagel's well-known 1996 sociological study, didn't anticipate the extent to which the post-1960s wave of Native-claiming would evolve into today's phenomenon of rampant pretendianism.[30] A decade later, Kathleen Fitzgerald's 2007 research among reclaimers—those who racially present as white and recently discovered Native heritage in their families, or recently began identifying as Native—found that "as culturally diverse as Native Americans are, there is now a self-conscious Indian identity, as distinct from tribal identity."[31] She sees reclaiming as a move away from whiteness, and wonders if "reclaimers view this search for a heritage in political terms, or cultural terms, or as an individual identity issue?"[32]

The question about Nativeness as an individual identity[33] detached from tribe, clan, family, and place is gaining salience among scholars who study Native identity. What some call reclaiming, others call race-shifting, or self-indigenizing. We've already observed Sturm's framing of race-shifting in the context of Cherokee identity. Self-indigenizing is another way of characterizing groups and individuals who make identity transitions toward indigeneity. In his 2019 study *Distorted Descent: White Claims to Indigenous Identity*, Darryl Leroux sees the growing phenomenon of white French Canadians' reclaiming of a long-lost Indigenous ancestor hundreds of years in the past as a clear example of race-shifting, and in this case, for quite nefarious purposes. His research shows that using genealogy French Canadians reject not just white identities but settler identities, legitimizing their ability to speak for all Indigenous people. Cloaked in the language of decolonization they form themselves into Métis, Abenaki, or other "tribes" and then challenge the legal rights of actual tribes to gain access to territory and resources. "At the centre of these efforts to redefine indigeneity is the practice of self-identification, which sociologist Eva Marie Garroutte has critiqued for its emphasis on an individualism that undermines Indigenous sovereignty and self-determination," Leroux writes.[34] He argues that genealogy as a "blood logic" does not stand in for community belonging and kinship as a determinant of indigeneity.[35] Similarly, Canadian legal theorist Pamela Palmater contends that on its own blood is an inadequate concept for determining Indigenous identity, and that it must be balanced with kinship and familial connections to a home community.[36]

Here again we see the vexed deployment of blood as that which conveys identity. The physical substance that flows through human veins is understood as having almost magical power to impart both culture and identity. Blood in this sense is typically used metaphor-ically to describe how we understand ourselves through biological inheritance, even things like individual behavior or belief systems, out-side social processes. Genealogy can operate in the same way, where blood or biological material is seen as the linkage between us and our ancestors and the vehicle that delivers identity in a physiologically deterministic way.[37] In today's world of consumer DNA ancestry test-ing, for example, conversations about ancestry, genealogy, and blood are never far from discussions about personal identity. Studies show that people get DNA tests to understand themselves medically and to better understand their identities. One longitudinal study published in 2021 found that among 322 people who responded to a survey about ancestry test results (most of whom self-reported as racially white and mostly college educated), 40 percent indicated changes in perception about their cultural roots, and 21 percent indicated changes that re-shaped their personal identity.[38] Additionally, according to another market demand–based study of over one hundred thousand people, those least likely to express interest in genetic ancestry testing were those within one or two generations of immigration in a receiving country, and Asian populations. In other words, unsurprisingly, it is those with less ancestral certainty who are more likely to seek genetic ancestry testing.[39] Direct-to-consumer genetic testing companies cap-italize on that uncertainty, dangling the carrot of Native American heritage in their marketing schemes to attract customers as TallBear's work on Native American genetic testing showed.

For Leroux, Palmater, Sturm, and others, the "logic" of blood is not enough to understand how indigeneity is a function not only of genealogical inheritance, but also, and more importantly, as the main-tenance of kinship and family within a community of people who have maintained their relationship to ancestral places over periods of time that span thousands of years. So, what then can explain how and why reclaimers, generic Indians, race-shifters, neo-Indians, and self-indigenizers—whatever we want to call them—ignore the rela-tional and place-based aspects that are the very definition of indige-neity? One explanation hinges on the idea of identity as a personal possession, an idea several prominent theorists have advanced.

IDENTITY AS CAPITALIST POSSESSION

Property rights are indisputably one cornerstone of the capitalist, racial, settler state. In 1993, legal scholar Cheryl Harris, one of the early voices of critical race theory, provocatively proposed that over time whiteness became a form of property protected in the law. The origin of property rights, Harris argued, are rooted in racial domination of Blacks and Native Americans through slavery and conquest. The right to own slaves and to expropriate Native American land, both constructed as property for which rights are required, was always reserved for white people. Property, Harris argued, is understood legally not so much as a thing but as a right.[40] As Blacks and Native Americans could be justifiably owned and conquered through the sanction of law, whiteness and white identity became defined and protected by law. Harris wrote, "Whiteness defined the legal status of a person as slave or free. White identity conferred tangible and economically valuable benefits and was jealously guarded as a valuable possession allowed only to those who met a strict standard of proof. Whiteness—the right to white identity as embraced by the law—is property if by property one means all of a person's legal rights."[41] Whiteness thus evolved to be inseparable from property as a right one owns, protected by law.

Similarly, Indigenous Australian scholar Aileen Moreton-Robinson elaborated that from an Indigenous lens, whiteness is not confined just to the realm of individual identity but constitutes the character of the nation-state itself through the logics of (patriarchal colonial) dispossession, domination, and sovereignty. She argues, "Australian national identity is built on the disavowal of Indigenous sovereignty because the nation is socially and culturally constructed as a white possession."[42] It is an argument that can easily be applied to the US context not just because both are settler states with similar histories, but because Indigenous sovereignty, or "quasi-sovereignty," in the US is incomplete; constrained by domestic American law, it is not equivalent to Westphalian state sovereignty. Through racialized domination of American Indians, the logics of the (white) settler capitalist state simultaneously disavows indigeneity and colonization as the very foundation of the state as it seeks to make both invisible to legitimize its existence.[43]

Whiteness as a possession also explains a phenomenon called reverse passing. The idea of passing is an adaptive strategy used historically by people from racially mixed backgrounds who could pass as white to hide their racial otherness. Reverse passing, on the other hand, as the term implies, describes ways people who are otherwise racially white pass themselves off as nonwhite. Rachel Dolezal is a notorious example that authors Khaled Beydoun and Erika Wilson give: as a white woman, Dolezal insisted she was Black and took a leadership role in the Spokane chapter of the National Association for the Advancement of Colored People (NAACP), graduated from Howard University (a historically Black university), and obtained a teaching position in Africana studies at Eastern Washington University. Dolezal, who performed blackness by tanning and adopting Black hairstyles, was exposed by her white parents and others in 2015, when they publicly contradicted her claims that her father was African American. The first to name and analyze reverse passing, Beydoun and Wilson argue that reverse passing was enabled initially by post-civil rights affirmative action policies. Top-down racial assignment via census and other legal mechanisms that ended in the 1950s led to today's diversity doctrine, replacing remedial affirmative action programs, where racial and ethnic diversity is now the gold standard of public and private institutions concerned with social equity. Diversity, determined by and achieved through self-identification, has unintended consequences because it incentivizes identity fraud as individuals seek benefits like college admissions and employment. Reverse passing depends on how well white people can perform racial otherness, absent the lived experience of oppression, and can easily be articulated "by simply checking a box."[44]

Reverse passing can describe the false adoption of any race, but given what we know about the explosion of the Native American population based on census numbers, it's fair to say that reverse passing is far more common when it comes to passing from white to Native American than to any other race or ethnicity. It offers a reliable explanation for passing from whiteness to Indianness for material gain. Yet it can't fully account for the millions of people who have claimed Native American heritage since 1960, most of whom are likely not claiming it just for filling out college, job, or grant applications. We are left with the need for a broader explanation for why people lay claims to Indianness. Whiteness as a rights-protected possession provides a clue for how we might understand the phenomenon, because if whiteness as race is property, as Harris and others have shown, then by extension, identity itself is also property in a conceptual sense, if not a legal sense. And if identity is understood as property, that which one owns, it stands to reason it would be defended as something unassailable, not subject to the scrutiny of others. It is free to do with what one wants, protected by free speech principles, regardless of the norms and definitions of what it means to be connected to a particular community, in this case, a tribal community.

In her sociological study of New Age practitioners who appropriated Native American culture, Lisa Aldred found that consumerism was the mechanism for people seeking Native American spirituality; non-Native people she interviewed shared feelings of spiritual emptiness and longing through purchasing Native American products and "experiences." She noted that when confronted with Native American objections to misappropriation, interview subjects justified their actions by couching them in First Amendment terms. "New Agers consistently argued that their right to religious freedom gave them the 'right' to Native American religion," Aldred writes. Arguments justifying cultural appropriation as a First Amendment freedom of religion is just a step away from claims to Native American identity as a freedom of speech issue. The close relationship between capitalism—commodified cultural appropriation—and American democratic principles framed as legally protected individual rights (the right to culturally appropriate) conditions consumerist values that mediate the way people see and present themselves to the world. The nexus of capitalism/property/rights is thus inextricably linked to American expressions of self-perception and identity in ways that seem perfectly natural, if not predetermined.[45]

Kim TallBear, a Sisseton-Wahpeton Dakota citizen, in the evolution of her work on genetic testing and Native American DNA has come to deconstruct popular narratives about "identity" showing how they cloud the meaning of indigeneity. She points out that identity as it is commonly deployed exists in the context of settler society, shaped by laws and ideas grounded in individuality and rights, juxtaposed to the rights and responsibilities of tribes as collectives. This colonial framework destabilizes how we think of identity as emerging from kinship and community, as she elucidates here:

> I want to offer a word of caution about the term "identity," and ask us to think very carefully before we pull it off of our word shelf. Is it the best term for what we are trying to say? It is usually an individualistic word that pertains to our individual bodies and things we consider our bodies' property: "*My* ancestors, *my* genealogy, *my* ancestry, who *I* am, *my* rights." Can we instead use more collective terms that get at what is at stake for Native nations or Peoples in combatting this problem? Relatives, relations, citizenship, kinship, and who we are or become together as collectives? I listen closely when we Native people use the identity word; I understand, we are operating in English and it is a much-loved word in this language. But in almost every instance when I hear us use "identity," we could instead use another term that more closely reflects what we really mean. We do not want to reinforce the individualism that roots often false claims and help further erase the fact that we are making collective claims and asserting collectively-forged ideas and cultural and political authorities.[46]

TallBear understands non-Native obsession with Indian identity as the "final Indian bounty," where Indianness itself is the only thing left for settlers to extract from Native communities after the theft of lands, resources, children, and governance systems.

For those who claim to be Native without the kind of accountability fostered by connection to place, kinship, and community, the individualistic "right" to self-identity is all there is, with no real social barriers to prevent it. Without any built-in social penalties to discourage it, claiming to be Indian with little or no evidence is socially acceptable, whether for material gain or not.

In a social system where the freedom to claim an Indian identity outside the authority of a legitimate tribal entity is not viewed as theft but as an individual right, these claims serve another function in the settler state. In the widely cited essay "Decolonization Is Not a Metaphor," Eve Tuck and K. Wayne Yang make the case that well-intended advocates of decolonial discourse often reduce the meaning of decolonization, which must center Indigenous lands and futures, to something less than the actual dismantlement of colonial structures. The tendency to conflate decolonization with other forms of social justice equivocates all forms of oppression in a society that disavows its always already colonial nature, even for immigrants and people of color. The result is a desire to disassociate with settler social structures, which takes several forms of what they call "settler moves to innocence."[47] "Settler moves to innocence are those positionings and strategies that attempt to relieve . . . feelings of guilt or responsibility without giving up land or power or privilege, without having to change much at all,"[48] they write. Settler nativism describes the individual impulse to become Indian as a "common move to innocence because it is an attempt to deflect a settler identity while continuing to enjoy settler privilege and occupying stolen land."[49] Race-shifting, neo-Indianism, reclaiming, and self-indigenizing are other terms for Tuck and Yang's settler nativism. Framed as a settler move to innocence, Native-claiming outside tribal structures of belonging is operationalized by the normalization of the idea of identity as a personal possession—an inherent entitlement to claim—versus a community conferred recognition and mode of belonging. As a process shaped by US subjectivity, it reinforces state domination over American Indians because it rejects the collectivist paradigm affirmed by tribal communities. That is, when non-Native people assert Native identity as a right, they ironically are at odds with the values and worldviews of the very people they embrace and claim to be part of.

LEGITIMACY AND THE NATIVE AMERICAN IDENTITY SPECTRUM

Words have power and how people describe themselves matters. It matters to the communities being claimed. It matters to university faculty and staff search committees. It matters in corporate and nonprofit diversity hiring and granting initiatives. It matters to Indian preference hiring in federal agencies, and to the Office of Federal Acknowledgment. It matters to publishers, who trust that authors are honestly representing themselves. It matters to Indian art show juries, and it should matter in casting and audition rooms. It matters to generations of audiences who take for granted a high-profile person's claims—like Sacheen Littlefeather or Buffy Sainte-Marie. When a person indicates they *are* Native American without having to produce any kind of evidence or explanation, the lack of accountability may all too easily lead to ethnic fraud. There is a difference between claiming to be Native American and expressing a belief that there might be Native American heritage in the family tree. One suggests a kinship-based relationship to a legitimate tribal community, while the other stops short of asserting community belonging. The rise of urban pan-Indianism during the Red Power era ripened the conditions for promiscuous claiming of Native American identity because there was little to no expectation for individual accountability to those claims. In urban Native communities where Native people come from tribes all over the country, there are no built-in institutional or community-based methods to check people's claims like there are in tribal communities where there is long-standing knowledge of each other through family and clan relationships. The emergence of generic Indian or Native American identity separated from tribal-specific identity, as Vine Deloria Jr., Kathleen Fitzgerald, and others observed, was possible because there are no accountability mechanisms.

On a spectrum of Native identity—Native American, American Indian, Alaska Native—I suggest measuring the legitimacy of claims on a scale that ranges from legitimate at one end, to illegitimate on the other, with a large area of ambiguity in between. Legitimacy in this sense derives from tribal sovereignty, understood as originating from the political relationship between tribal nations and the United States. Legitimate claims are characterized by enrollment in a federally recognized tribe while illegitimate claims constitute blatant ethnic fraud. The ambiguous claims can be quite subjective, while on the extreme ends of the continuum, legitimacy and illegitimacy are more objective. With the exception of those who have been disenrolled or subject to enrollment moratoriums, tribal enrollment and citizenship are objectively legitimate because through sovereignty they exist within the domain of political relationship to the state, whereas illegitimate claims are often intentionally deceptive and evade sovereignty. For those with enrollment in a federally recognized tribe, the assertion of indigeneity (or even Indigenous "identity") is uncontestable.[50] The claim to "being Indian" or being "[fill in tribe]" is verifiable and legitimate. And there are many ways one can "be Indian" without enrollment or citizenship in a federally recognized tribe, existing in a large grey area on the spectrum.

AMBIGUITY

Ambiguity is a zone of contingency, exposing the ways colonialism destabilizes tribal existence and reshapes terrains of Native life in a range of complicated ways. It tends to be messy, typically defying easy definitions for what it means to be American Indian based on a relationship to a tribe and the US state. Individuals can be authentically Native but be disenfranchised for many reasons. We can identify categories where common experiences of marginalization worked to diminish or erase a person or family's connection to their heritage. A perfect example is in cases of adoption, as in my family, where children were taken without consent or relinquished willingly and grew up not knowing they come from a Native family or knowing they were Native but lacking the information to reconnect to the tribal community. Another experience of ambiguity revolves around descendancy. While it's true that the term is often disingenuously used by people with no verifiable tribal heritage, one can be a tribal descendant as an official tribal designation and form of recognition, as is the case with me, since as a matter of policy, the Colville Confederated Tribes recognizes descendants three generations from an enrolled member through the issuing of descendant letters. A person can be the child or grandchild of an enrolled tribal member and not have a descendant designation because the tribe does not extend such a policy; many don't. There are people who can document descendancy from a historic tribe that has never had recognition or who have relations in a tribe from which they have been disenrolled or has imposed an enrollment moratorium that prevents membership even if they meet the criteria, as is the case in some California tribes. As is often the case in California, people can possess a federally issued CDIB (Certificate of the Degree of Indian Blood) without any formal tribal affiliation.

The term *Indigenous* should be mentioned here as well because it can be exceedingly murky and misleading. As discussed in chapter 2, *Indigenous* is a term we see particularly in the international arena for the ways it makes distinctions between colonizers and the colonized in the modern state system; it has become a descriptor for American Indians in recent decades. *Indigenous* appropriately describes people with legitimate American Indian heritage and/or federally recognized tribes, but when used for individuals or groups said to be Indigenous on a broader scale, it can incorrectly conflate all Indigenous people in ways that misrepresent Indians in US-based tribes. This is especially true when the term *American Indian* is applied to Indigenous people from Latin America. Los Angeles has the largest and most diverse "Indigenous" population of any US city. The 2020 census counted 156,646 people either fully or partly American Indian or Alaska Native based on racial self-identification in LA County. Under the category of American Indian, the largest "tribal affiliation" listed was "Mexican American Indian" at 19,911. The *Los Angeles Almanac* explained:

> In recent census counts, more Hispanic or Latino persons elected to identify their race as fully or partly American Indian. Recognizing this trend, the U.S. Census Bureau, in 2015, added "Mexican American Indian," "South American Indian" and "Spanish American Indian" to the list of tribal affiliations, under the American Indian racial category. This has resulted in Mexican American Indians now identified as the sixth largest American Indian tribal population in the United States (and largest in Los Angeles County).[51]

Other research suggests the total of Latin American Indigenous people in LA is likely much higher; one estimate of the Zapotec population alone exceeds 200,000. Researchers note that these populations are difficult to count because many still speak only their Indigenous languages. They also may be reluctant to identify themselves out of fear of discrimination.[52] Census numbers gathered this way reinforce the problematic racializing of Native Americans of the US. The categorizing of self-identified Latin American Indigenous people as "American Indians" confers the misnomer of "tribal affiliation" to describe what are in fact immigrant populations, if we understand indigeneity as being defined by Indigenous populations' relationship to states. While Indigenous people globally and in the US tend to make common cause with each other and recognize each other relationally—and recognize state borders as colonial constructions—conflating immigrant Indigenous populations with Native American populations contributes to the invisibility of the original people of the United States. It raises questions about how this kind of data may be used to allocate resources that are, or should be, meant for American Indians—people original to the Unites States. Just as census self-identification did beginning in 1960, it falsely inflates the number of American Indians with a political relationship to the US and contributes to the general confusion of what indigeneity means.

In addressing terms of ambiguity that can muddle American Indian identifiability on a proposed spectrum of Native identity, I will tackle the more common ways this grey area of Native identity claiming shows up in legitimate and illegitimate ways.

DESCENDANCY

The term *descendant* rests on a very slippery slope depending on how it's used. Critics of pretendianism coined the term *descendian* as a pejorative of those who misuse the term, though it's not always clear who they are referring to. "Descendant" as a claim verges on illicit when it is used to manufacture a Native identity based on descent from several generations in the past without connection to a tribal family or community. Other common terms are *Native American heritage* or *ancestry*. Claims to Native American heritage or ancestry may be authentic when there are verifiable familial ties to a tribal community, but without kinship ties, they veer into inauthenticity. Claiming descendancy, ancestry, or heritage is especially egregious when leveraged for financial or professional gain. A distant ancestor may even have been verifiably Indian but, through generations of intermarriage and abandonment of tribal cultures and communities to assimilate to dominant, usually white society, lose the lived experience that comes with *being* American Indian or Indigenous. They may be the reclaimers Kathleen Fitzgerald and Michelle Jacobs studied, as well as some of the white French Canadian self-indigenizers in Darryl Leroux's research or the neo-Chumash and other neo-Indians in the work of Brian Haley and Circe Sturm. They often rely heavily on genealogy to produce long-lost ancestors who serve as the foundation of their claims to indigeneity, whether or not the records are reliable.

The term *descendancy* can describe a wide swath of those who have legitimate tribal ties without enrollment. They can be people with documented Native heritage outside tribal structures as well, such as disenrollees or people with government-issued CDIB cards naming federally or non-federally recognized tribes. For tribes that recognize descendancy status, documentation of descendancy entitles one to some federal services like Indian Health Service and potentially tribal benefits too. This can be seen as evidence of some level of political relationship to a tribe and/or the federal government on an individual basis, since services are provided under the legal principle of the trust doctrine. This relationship can exist even in cases where there may not be tribal descendancy status. An example is holders of fractionated allotment interests and Individual Indian Money (IIM) accounts. These people inherit interests in their ancestors' allotments that the federal government manages as the trustee; no law requires inheritors to be enrolled tribal members, but they are subject to the government's paternalistic federal Indian land policies.[53] Where a person verifiably descends from a tribal family and community, even though there may not be a formal relationship with a tribe, they cannot accurately be called non-Indian.

Legitimate descendancy outside tribal enrollment is not merely a label; it's a testament to enduring lineages from formidable forebears. Descendants are the living legacy of the ancestors' strength and resilience. The word embodies kinship, genealogical continuity, and a cultural through line from the past to the present. Disparaging or misusing the term disrespects ancestors and diminishes the rich tribal heritage of those who rightfully inherit it. *Descendant* should not be a term of shame or minimalization; it should be embraced with pride, representing our collective journey and the unbreakable bond we share with those who came before us.

DNA TESTING

Claims to Native American identity are on the inauthentic end of the spectrum when consumer DNA tests are the sole basis for claims. We saw this situation play out in Elizabeth Warren's DNA debacle in her feud with President Donald Trump in 2018, during the lead-up to her 2020 presidential bid. For years, the Democratic senator from Massachusetts had variously claimed Cherokee and Delaware, based on family stories, and there was speculation that she had used it to gain an advantage in her law career. It was never proven that she benefited from her claims of being a racial minority. But her ongoing claims evoked criticism in Indian country at least as early as 2012 and became political fodder for Trump, who had taken to calling her Pocahontas in his characteristically caustic and offensive manner. Trump challenged Warren to take a DNA test to "prove" her Native American heritage, offering to donate $1 million to charity if she could show she was "an Indian." Warren's DNA test, meant to prove Trump wrong, spectacularly backfired, unleashing a torrent of controversy that put her in even deeper hot water with Indian country. The test revealed "strong evidence" of an Indian in the family tree "six to ten generations ago," which Trump predictably misconstrued, saying she had "far less [Indian blood] than the average American"—a patently absurd statement—and accused her of scamming and lying.[54] Meanwhile, Native critics went on the defensive, furious that Warren had doubled down on her claims to Indianness, confusing the public even more by perpetuating the myth that DNA tests can determine Native identity. Warren spent months on the campaign trail apologizing profusely for the misstep, but the damage had already been done, both to Indian country and to her campaign, and in the end, it's doubtful that she ever (re)gained Indian country's trust and support.[55]

Elizabeth Warren's DNA fiasco sparked intense public debates on social media, with many people supporting her against Donald Trump's attacks; after all, there was the genetic evidence to back up her family's claims to indigeneity. But American Indian commentators were adamant that DNA tests that showed evidence of Native American biological material was not enough to justify claims to being Indian without tribal recognition, and that Indianness is a matter of tribal sovereignty, not personal claims. It was especially true in Warren's case as Cherokee genealogists had declared in 2012 that she had absolutely no connection to the Cherokee Nation and asked her to stop claiming it. It was a useful if painful lesson for the public at large, illuminating the common misconception of the infallibility of direct-to-consumer (DTC) DNA tests and that genes alone can confer identity.

We turn again to Kim TallBear, known for her penetrating analysis of genetic science and DTC testing. In her book *Native American DNA*, TallBear interrogates, among other things, the foundational assumptions of the DTC industry. Based on her research into several DTC companies, TallBear finds overall the genetic testing industry reinforces the concept of race as biologically deterministic and predicated on the idea of racial purity. TallBear sees "gene talk" as a new form of "blood talk," where the quantifying of Native American genes is deployed metaphorically in the same way blood quantum represents a measure of culture and identity. She writes that the insight she gained clarified for her that outside the context of tribal life, "dominant cultural understandings of kinship and race, more than tribal understandings, give concepts of genetic ancestry their power and salience in our national culture."[56] Genetic research can and does undermine tribal governmental authority over numerous domains of influence, including how genetic samples are used and how indigeneity is conceived and marketed to the public. One of the most important points about DTC tests is that even when they show markers of indigeneity, they cannot pinpoint a tribe or community. In other words, when it comes to determining Native American identity, DNA ancestry testing has only exacerbated the public's already confused comprehension about what it means to *be* American Indian.

ILLEGITIMACY

Outside the realm of ambiguity on the extreme end of the Native identity spectrum are various types of illegitimate claims. They can overlap with narratives about descendancy, heritage, or ancestry (conceived in terms of genetics), but claims lack believability when there is no evidence or tribal community affiliation. The most recognizable among them are family lore, playing Indian, and outright lies about tribal heritage. Family stories are perhaps the most common. These are the tales passed down for generations about a long-lost Indian in the family, usually a great-grandmother, often though not always Cherokee. These stories of the Indian ancestor explain why someone has a darker complexion, why they tan so well in the summer, or has black or straight hair, or high cheekbones. It can even explain why someone was skilled at hunting or handicrafts or was prone to alcoholism. It can be Grandpa's deathbed confession about Indian heritage that the family was too ashamed to talk about. I have heard these and countless other stories in my life, and I have had many conversations with Native friends who have too. People adhere to their stories with stubborn conviction, despite all evidence to the contrary. I once was in a conversation with a woman who recounted a family story of Cherokee ancestry to me in front of her daughter, my friend and university colleague. Embarrassed by her mother's claim, my friend immediately jumped in to debunk the story, reminding her mother that the DNA test she took showed no Native American genes whatsoever.

Family lore often leads to playing or becoming Indian. As Michelle Jacobs found in her study on reclaimer communities in Ohio and Kathleen Fitzgerald found in her work before that, when white-passing people truly believe they are Indian, they are prone to performing Indianness. It becomes a role they play, and in the absence of actual American Indian heritage, their believability is dependent upon how "authentic" they can appear, how well they can talk the talk, and who they associate with. Indian players gather at urban powwows, Indian centers, backyard sweat lodges, ayahuasca ceremonies, Native American retreats, Sun Dances, and Native American Church meetings. They populate boardrooms; university faculty lines and department chairs; research institutions; film industry writing rooms, director's chairs, and producer roles. Groups of Indian players become "tribes." They might coalesce around a charismatic leader like Semu, Rolling Thunder, or Sun Bear aka Vincent LaDuke, the New Age guru who founded the Bear Tribe in the early 1970s. More commonly they become what are in effect hobby clubs, formed as nonprofits where they sell "tribal membership" cards. Sometimes they insert themselves into local civic roles and politics, and as we've seen, if they are convincing, they can achieve state recognition and vie for the holy grail of federal recognition.

At the extreme end of the Native American identity spectrum are the outright frauds, who adopt an American Indian persona knowing full well they come from no American Indian family lineages. They can be non-Native people who ingratiate themselves to Native people who then "adopt" them, which gives them a story to help pass themselves off as Indigenous. These claims are characterized by deliberate deceit, which requires a well-constructed tale designed to enhance believability. The most obvious examples of this category are Sacheen Littlefeather, Iron Eyes Cody, Archie Grey Owl, Chief Buffalo Child Long Lance, Rolling Thunder, Craig Carpenter, Harley Swift Deer Reagan, and Hyemeyohsts Storm.[57] Others have claims to indigeneity that may be more opaque or implied but have built public reputations based on their proximity to real or fictional Indigenous people. Author Carlos Castaneda, for example, didn't become famous for claiming to be Indian but for his stories about the alleged Yaqui "sorcerer" don Juan Matus, who supposedly mentored him. Castaneda's book series was debunked long ago as a work of fiction rather than a serious anthropological study that earned him a doctorate at the University of California, Los Angeles, but it remains widely read and likely believed.[58]

Why people invent false Native identities, a question I and so many others have asked, has no easy answer, even in the cases of previously mentioned high-profile frauds. In cases where high-paying jobs in academia, entertainment, publishing, or government contracting are at stake, we might attribute false claims to economic opportunism. For "plastic shamans" like Semu, Rolling Thunder, Harley Swift Deer Reagan, and Hyemeyohsts Storm, there were brands, reputations, and positions of power to maintain. Yet it does not fully explain why Sacheen Littlefeather stuck to her many lies for nearly half a century; based on what I saw, she was not living a lavish life of economic privilege. She did not appear to benefit financially in any substantial way from her make-believe life. In the case of Iron Eyes Cody—who made a living in a time when authenticity was not a prerequisite for playing Indian in the film industry—of what benefit was it to him to dress in buckskin, moccasins, and a braided wig when he wasn't on a film set? He maintained an elaborate hoax even when his career didn't depend on it; can we attribute it to a psychological benefit he received, or was it that once the lie is told it must be maintained?

The United States is a country of profound contradictions and more than a few fictions. Narratives of liberty and justice for all don't square with histories of slavery, genocide, and land theft. As much as Americans want to believe the fairy tale of a land where everyone is equal, but manifest destiny was the ideological mechanism that justified the violent extirpation of entire cultures to make room for their existence, there will be confusion about their roles and that of their ancestors, and what side of history that puts them on. Cognitive dissonance is the result of a reality that doesn't match the stated ideals that Americans are conditioned to believe their country rests on. Within the ruptures of those interstitial spaces of the psyche, individually and collectively, are the conditions for denial of all shades to bloom.

THE LESSONS OF TRICKSTERS

What Coyote Teaches Us

A S THIS STUDY HAS SHOWN, of the many questions posed, some have easier answers than others, and some may be unanswerable. The twin process of colonialism and capitalism have resulted in what my Passamaquoddy friend, Roger Paul, calls "twistory." Roger, a gifted linguist, is a rare example of someone born in the United States whose first language was an Indigenous language. Twistory is a word he heard from his elders, a combination of the words *twisted* and *history*. Twistory can be used in all kinds of ways, but in essence, refers to the whitewashed and sanitized historiography that shapes our collective realities with all their attendant fictions and distortions. How American Indians are viewed by outsiders and how they view themselves today is inescapably altered as a result of the twistory, brought on by the intertwined historical processes of colonialism and capitalism. These social structures, foreign to this continent until only five centuries ago, now influence our understandings of identity and belonging, both tribal and nontribal. On one hand is the propensity of Americans to reimagine themselves as American Indians and on the other is, paradoxically, how American Indians have learned to exclude and deny each other's heritage as American Indians. Undoing the twistory is the work before us now, part of which is determining to what degree that is even possible. I'd like to conclude this study by offering ways we might think through the twistory. One is a social process we have limited power to control but has material consequences to American Indian people. I suggest a culturally based way to understand pretendianism, followed by a brief general discussion leaning into approaches to dealing with it. The other is a problem caused by American Indian people, which tribes themselves can solve with enough political will. I review suggestions made by others about what can be done to address the human and civil rights violations of disenrollment when tribes lack the political will.

PRETENDIANISM AND COYOTE THE TRICKSTER

On the Upper Columbia Plateau, the Original Instructions of the Interior Salish and Sahaptin peoples of the Colville tribes are contained within Coyote stories, known in the *nsəlxcín'* language as *c̓aptik̓ʷɬ*. Called trickster tales, Coyote stories are a story motif that imparts lessons about how to live life by describing relationships between humans and the natural world, with Coyote as the central character. As Jay Miller in 1990 succinctly put it: "Coyote is a complex figure often baffling to a white audience. He is more anti-hero than hero, more buffoon than champion. He is for native people the ultimate negative example . . . His greatest flaw is pride and self-importance."[1]

Many *c̓aptik̓ʷɬ* stories were recorded by Okanogan and Colville (*sx̌ʷyʔɬpx*) tribal member and author Christine Quintasket, also known as Mourning Dove. Quintasket's 1933 collection, simply titled *Coyote Stories,* offers some of the most common stories. The book begins with the tale about how all the animals got their names, clearly establishing the importance of Coyote's role in Salishan culture. In the story, Spirit Chief announces that a new kind of people is coming to live on Earth and that the Animal People all need new names to be given out the next morning at sunrise. The Animal People would be free to choose their own names in the order in which they arrive. Coyote does not like his name, *Sin-ka-lip (snk̓lip)*, Imitator, in English and is not respected because he is arrogant and thinks and acts like he knows everything. Known for playing rude tricks on people and being boastful, he wants a more regal name like Grizzly Bear, Eagle, or Salmon. Fox, the brother of *Sin-ka-lip'*, laughs and says he might have to keep his name because no one else wants it. Coyote is determined to stay awake the whole night to be the first person at Spirit Chief's lodge the next morning. But he becomes sleepy, his eyes grow heavy, so he props them open with two little sticks. He falls asleep anyway, with his eyes wide open.

When he arrives the next morning at the lodge of Spirit Chief with the sun high in the sky because he overslept, *Sin-ka-lip'* requests the names of Grizzly Bear, Eagle, and Salmon, only to be told that the names have already been taken. Spirit Chief explains to *Sin-ka-lip'* that he is meant to keep his name, for he has important work to do. *Sin-ka-lip'* is to be chief of all the tribes and defeat all the People-devouring monsters that keep killing the people and preventing their numbers from increasing. "For doing that, for all the good things you do, you will be honored and praised by the people that are here now and that come afterward. But, for the foolish and mean things you do, you will be laughed at and despised. That you cannot help. It is your way," Spirit Chief says.[2]

In another story about Coyote's habit of imitating others, Chickadee can take his eyeballs out, juggle them, and land them back in their sockets. Insisting that it is he who has this power, Coyote copies Chickadee's trick, juggling his eyes, which get stolen by a pair of ravens, leading to a series of events that ends with him killing Pheasant in order to get his eyes back. Typically, Coyote's behavior is self-serving, rising out of the conceit of his massive ego, and seeking an attribute that was not meant for him. The lessons Coyote teaches Salishan people are, among other things, about the consequences of selfishness and trying to be something you're not. The two are connected. In today's terms, we might see these lessons as warnings about the dangers of inauthenticity and fakery, and the harms hubris and egotism can cause.

The tale of Sacheen Littlefeather is a modern-day Coyote story. For nearly fifty years Littlefeather told a tale about herself based on the need to be perceived as important, to be seen as something she wasn't, peppered with truth and lies large and small, making it nearly impossible for people to tell the truths from the fictions. The Sacheen Littlefeather that appeared on the Oscars stage on March 27, 1973, was a character in costume, an actor performing a role that would last almost half a century. It was the pretense of an American Indian

person whom she had no right to impersonate. She was Coyote trying to convince Spirit Chief to allow him to be Grizzly Bear, Eagle,
or Salmon. She was Coyote trying to appropriate Chickadee's gift for
juggling his eyes. And just as Coyote's antics are manipulative and intended to deceive, so her performance will live on in infamy as little
more than a self-serving publicity stunt, an act divorced from reality.
In a world where identity is a personal possession, entitlement and
hubris follows. This is Coyote's world, and Coyote's game.

We might see all pretendians, Indian-players, race-shifters, self-
indigenizers, and even neo-Indians as a manifestation of Coyote, but
while seeing them through this lens might help us come to terms with
the phenomenon in a cultural way, creating coherent and actionable
strategies to dissuade the wrongful claiming of Native identity, especially when financial resources are at stake, is much more challenging.
What that looks like in the US would depend on context, considering anti-discrimination laws in employment practices, for example.
Because discrimination based on race, ethnicity, sex, disability, age,
or religion is illegal, employers avoid asking personal questions that
could be construed as discriminatory. This obstructs the ability to
assess job applicants' Native claims in places where it would be considered illegal to ask for proof of tribal status, like colleges and universities, or even to pose probing questions about tribal community
belonging. The problem stems directly from the racializing of American Indian people at the expense of tribal sovereignty. One potential remedy might be the passing of laws and policies that allow for
exceptions for inquiries that clarify the Native American claims of
applicants based on tribal citizenship status, like proof of citizenship or immigration status of immigrants. Such inquiries would also
allow those without tribal citizenship to explain their claims, thus
encouraging accountability to the tribes being claimed. In contracting situations, anti-discrimination laws don't apply in the same way,
but as we've seen, the lack of rigor in determining the tribal status
in minority contracting results in the bilking of millions of dollars
in government funding based on false Native American claims. Preventing opportunism in government contracting would involve better

training for decision-makers and perhaps more accurate processes to vet Native American claims.[3] The same applies to private foundation funding intended for American Indians, though the circumstances between tribal entities and individuals may differ.[4] In the film and publishing industries, tribal documentation could be requested as a show of good faith. Or instead of asking for proof of tribal status, better vetting could be accomplished through strategic lines of inquiry that assess an individual's relationship to a tribal community and what it means to be American Indian.

APPROACHES TO DISENROLLMENT

The Coyote metaphor can easily be extended to understand disenrollment; one of the things Coyote is most famous for is his greediness. In this way tribal governments and politicians themselves embody the worst of Coyote's traits, much like Anishinaabeg renderings of Nanabush and other trickster characters in tribal creation stories. The profit motive inherent in casino capitalism conditions the egregious exclusionary tactics of tribal disenrollment. There is little incentive to end or ban disenrollment or to reenroll, although there are examples of both in recent years. The Enterprise Rancheria, Robinson Rancheria, the Modoc Tribe of Oklahoma, and Laytonville Rancheria have all reenrolled members since 2016.[5] Among the few who have ended or banned disenrollment and/or banishment are the Confederated Tribes of the Grande Ronde Reservation (they both ended and banned disenrollment), Pleasant Point Reservation (Passamaquoddy), the Spokane Tribe of Indians, and the Federated Indians of the Graton Rancheria.[6] Most of these tribes have drawn from the wisdom of their cultures to resist the basest instincts of settler capitalism that reject kinship, demonstrating that they are quite capable of handling these issues internally.[7] Enacting values rooted in kinship relative to enrollment issues, as Gabe Galanda suggests, should include abolishing blood quantum, banning disenrollment, lifting enrollment moratoriums and welcoming lost generations, renewing kinship terminology, and ceasing per capita payments.[8]

In a perfect world, tribes would reverse course on disenrollment at their own behest, but because that doesn't appear likely for so many, other suggestions have been advanced. David Wilkins proposes:

- developing an independent, intertribal appellate body that would review enrollment decisions in a fair and impartial way;
- a system of dual tribal courts, as John Collier called for in his initial framing of the Indian Reorganization Act;
- an intertribal treaty to handle human rights violations;
- amending the Indian Civil Rights Act, allowing disenrollees to sue offending tribes in federal court;
- invoking the IRA-era Oklahoma Indian Welfare Act allowing ten or more Indians to organize under an Interior Department cooperative charter for receiving services such as credit administration, production, marketing, consumers' protection, or land management;
- invoking the plenary power of Congress and the Secretary of the Interior to protect the right of enrollment as a property right as part of the government's trust responsibility.[9]

The wisdom of Salish Coyote stories, as in all tribal cultures, lies in the power of metaphor to teach. Metaphors transcend time and reflect aspects of humanity that are universal. Not all cultures are centered around the same kinds of values, but all human cultures warn their young about the dangers of selfishness, greed, lying, and inauthenticity. One of the brilliant and timeless qualities of Salish Coyote stories is their rootedness in change. Coyote is, in a sense, an emissary of change, sent to usher in a new era of new people that demands new ways of thinking and being. Change is full of landmines; it's always dangerous, and we are challenged to maintain our humanity as we adapt to new circumstances. Not all change is good; a crucial part of our learning is discerning what to keep of the old and what to discard of the new. Coyote stories as Salish peoples' Original Instructions are every bit as applicable today as they were five hundred, or a thousand, or five thousand years ago. Only the circumstances have changed. Coyote is a reminder to us all of how we adapt to our colonial conditions, of what we choose to keep and what we leave behind. Our cultures are our medicine, and more than anything, it is the values of kinship and generosity handed down from countless generations of ancestors that define us. If we lose sight of that, we lose who we are. And we must remember that it is always a choice.

FINAL THOUGHTS

I have tried to craft an analysis that can serve as a foundation for coherently addressing how the twinned processes of settler colonialism and capitalism have resulted in the contorted ways Native American identity is viewed today. As is so often the case with research, this study may have raised more questions than it answered. There undoubtedly will be opposition to my primary contention that race must be decentered in favor of the political relationship of tribes to the state, especially since it refuses unqualified self-identification as a legitimate basis for Native American identity. It rejects the American phenomenon of long cherished but often unprovable stories about Native American heritage and challenges core assumptions about identity rooted in free speech and individual rights. At the same time, centering tribal political status is inescapably intertwined with the influence of colonial domination over tribal communities. What we call tribal sovereignty today is shaped by colonial processes, and even terms like *sovereignty* and *decolonization* are often misunderstood, co-opted, and misused. There is no more perfect example than the crisis of disenrollment. Because of colonial influence, tribes have been pressured into accepting definitions of tribal belonging too often based not in cultural values of kinship and generosity but in scarcity driven racial logics, which is what blood quantum is. These contradictions, among others, prompt us to consider issues for further research as we think through what constitutes tribal belonging and Native identity and, simultaneously, the solutions we propose to curtail fraudulent Native claiming. Topics and research questions might include:

Tribal sovereignty: In what ways is sovereignty, as it is often framed today, conditioned by pressure to conform to Euro-American norms? Is it truly tribal sovereignty when rules for belonging are based on nontribal values? How can tribes shape sovereignty in more culturally grounded ways? Is *sovereignty* the right term for understanding tribal agency and authority, and if not, are there better terms?

Indigenization, decolonization, and accountability: In tribal communities, when introducing oneself at formal gatherings it is common to cite family lineage—to establish who one is related to—as a show of respect and accountability to the community. How might a protocol like this be implemented in nontribal settings as a way to indigenize institutional processes in the interest of accountability to the tribe(s) being claimed? Can the voluntary offering of such information be normalized and avoid violating discrimination laws? How can tribal and nontribal institutions decolonize their enrollment, hiring, granting, and contracting practices to be as inclusive as possible, but also ensure individual integrity and accountability? What does decolonization mean in this context?

Research and genealogy: Who is qualified to perform tribal genealogy searches? Are public ancestry database searches sufficient sources to determine the tribal heritage of others, and what are the ethical considerations of conducting genealogical research on others without their consent? Is genealogical certification enough to qualify someone as an expert in tribal genealogy, or should genealogists who do tribal genealogies be required to have more specialized education?

Other considerations: What are other gaps in the research on Native American identity and belonging? What have the preceding questions not covered?

There will undoubtedly be many different approaches to how these questions are answered, and many other questions yet to be posed. I know there will be negative reactions to some of the claims this book has made, while for others there will be a sense of relief that difficult topics often avoided are being raised. As Native people, we must be honest about the impact colonization has had on our precontact tribal ways of living, our relationships to the land, and to each other. As we rightly assert our self-determination and work to heal the traumas that have been inflicted upon us, we must also decolonize our ideas about what tribal belonging is, who our relatives are, and what the future will be like for our descendants. We also cannot lose sight that tribal self-determination as a political project is constrained within legal and economic structures not of our own making. The work is simultaneously about controlling our own narratives—especially about what defines us—and the struggle to transcend our colonial restraints. The challenge is to be clear about the former as we strive for the latter.

ACKNOWLEDGMENTS

THROUGHOUT THE WRITING OF THIS BOOK, I was fortunate to have had the support of key people whose voices in one way or another are echoed in the text. I could not have written this book without them. First, I thank the sisters of Sacheen Littlefeather, Trudy Orlandi and Rozalind Cruz, who gave generously of their time in our many conversations, emails, and texts. It was the Cruz family who has suffered most from Sacheen's lifelong lies. Thanks also to Helen Hagan, who was also harmed by Sacheen Littlefeather. Her contribution was critical to setting the record straight.

Several people kindly read drafts or gave valuable insight through interviews and conversations or in other ways. For their time, energy, and expertise, I thank Eric Reed, Liza Black, Gabe Galanda, Eric Tippeconnic (thanks also for the amazing art that graces the cover of this book), Stan Rodriguez, Bryan Pollard, Darryl Leroux, Kim TallBear, Nicole Myers-Lim, Kevin McKiernan, Dayna Barrios, Julie Tumamait-Stenslie, KC Rodriguez, Brian Haley, John Johnson, and John Gomez. John, I am so sorry for all your family and other Pechanga disenrollees who have suffered as a result of reckless policies and practices. Thank you to Ryan Flynn for his courage in exposing the darkness of disenrollment in the film *You're No Indian*.

A special thank you to Kouslaa Kessler-Mata, Leah Mata-Fragua, Wendy Lucas, Scott Lathrop, chairwoman Mona Tucker, and the tribal council and board of directors of the Yak Tit'u Tit'u Yak Tiłhini Northern Chumash Tribe, who have been so helpful in shedding light on Chumash issues and combating Native American ethnic fraud.

Many of the topics I've tackled in this book are so controversial that few people confront them openly, especially in Native media, academia, and other relevant Native forums. Many fear bullying, retribution, or otherwise turn away because they benefit from their association with people in high places. My stance on Sacheen Little-feather resulted in consequences professionally not long after I began the writing of this book. I couldn't have gotten through this project without the much-needed moral support during the many moments of doubt and angst: Mishy Lesser, Liz Cera, Geri De Stefano-Webre, Nick Reo, Fredi Avalos, Rebecca Robles, and my sister, Sissy, who is always there for me. Thanks to my beloved son, Devyn, for making my life easier by making wise choices and to my husband, Tom, for your steadfastness.

I am grateful to my newfound sisters and brother, who help complete the story of my life; Robert, Sandy Lolos Lee, Anne Allison, and their children, my nieces and nephews. Welcome home to all of you. Thank you, Amy, for being the emissary that brought us all together. You left us too soon.

For their inspiration and leadership, a special thank you to Chris Eyre and Tantoo Cardinal. Shelly Boyd and Rick Desautel, much gratitude and admiration for all you do for Colville and Sinixt people. *Limlmtx* to my *snəqsilxʷ* at the Inchelium Language House for being on this *nsəlxcin'* language journey with me. You enrich my life more than you know.

I extend a deep and heartfelt thanks to the dedication and loyalty of my editors at Beacon Press, especially Joanna Green and Gayatri Patnaik, for believing in this project. Your vision and commitment make Beacon Press the shining example of integrity in the publishing world.

I close with a final difficult conversation. As this manuscript was being copyedited a story broke about Circe Sturm, whose scholarship is cited throughout the text. During her three-decade-long career Sturm has claimed Mississippi Choctaw and distant Cherokee descent, which she has dropped in more recent years. The Tribal Alliance Against Frauds (TAAF) released a statement in February 2025 that genealogical research into her family background revealed no Choctaw or Cherokee ancestry. As with so many other previous disclosures of (alleged) fraud of prominent American Indian studies scholars discussed in this book, the news about Sturm rocked the worlds of many in our field who have studied alongside and under her. Sturm released a six-page statement responding to the allegations explaining that her descendancy claims, which are based on family stories of an undocumented full-blood Choctaw ancestor four generations past, have been backed up by a consumer DNA test showing Indian ancestry. Sturm rejected the accusations of fraud on account of her claims to descendancy not tribal citizenship, and writing from the perspective of an anthropologist, not someone speaking from an American Indian perspective. No apology was offered. While the test results undoubtedly provide her a sense of vindication, it seems disingenuous for a scholar of her stature and experience, who clearly understands the issues of self-indigenization and American Indian racialization, to double down on her descendancy claims without a kinship connection to a tribal community.

Sturm's research has been central to all scholars working in American Indian identity studies, many of whom are cited in this book. The revelations are deeply unsettling to our academic community and have eroded the trust of long-standing colleagues and friends. I am not necessarily suggesting that Sturm is a pretendian or that she misrepresented herself. This example is, however, a testament to the need for maximum transparency and precision with words when working in the space of American Indian identity studies with marginal claims to Indianness. Only under these conditions can academic honesty and integrity be maintained.

NOTES

INTRODUCTION

1. Joseph M. Pierce described settler colonial capitalism as having altered Native relationships to land through the "transformation of relatives into things, bodies into labor, and labor into capital," thus emptying the sacred of its cosmic meaning. By extension, I argue that Nativeness and notions of tribal belonging have similarly been transformed due to the imposition of the foreign system of settler capitalism. See Pierce, "Allotment Speculations," in *Allotment Stories: Indigenous Land Relations Under Settler Siege*, ed. Daniel Health Justice and Jeani M. O'Brien (Minneapolis: University of Minnesota Press, 2021), 64.

2. There is evidence that ethnic fraud may have been rampant in Oklahoma when allotments were assigned to Cherokees in the late nineteenth century. This area needs more research for understanding the extent to which feigning Cherokeeness occurred. My contention, however, is that the film industry in California incentivized ethnic fraud through the commodification of Indianness more broadly, making playing Indian profitable and available to anyone who could adequately perform Indianness.

3. Philip Deloria, *Playing Indian* (New Haven, CT: Yale University Press, 1998), 4.

4. Larry W. Burt, "Roots of the Native American Urban Experience: Relocation Policy in the 1950s," *American Indian Quarterly* 10, no. 2 (Spring 1986): 85–99.

5. Damon B. Akins and William J. Bauer Jr., *We Are the Land: A History of Native California* (Oakland: University of California Press, 2022), 265.

6. Joan Albon, "Relocated American Indians in the San Francisco Bay Area: Social Interaction and Indian Identity," *Human Organization* 23, no. 4 (Winter 1964): 296–304.

7. There are different spellings of Okanogan; I defer to the Colville Confederated Tribes spelling, with an "o" in the middle, not an "a."

8. "A Proclamation: Celebrating 125 Years of Survival (1872–1997)," Colville Confederated Tribes, https://www.cct-cbc.com/proclamation, accessed Nov. 29, 2022.

9. Laurie Arnold, *Bartering with the Bones of Their Dead: The Colville Confederated Tribes and Termination* (Seattle: University of Washington Press, 2012), 10.

10. The lawsuit was filed in 1951, utilizing the Indian Claims Commission "fair and honorable dealings" clause to seek justice for the violation of protected land and water rights. With the settlement, tribal members, including my mom, were paid about $6,000 each in 1995. See Holly Sprague, "Unjust Compensation: The Grand Coulee Dam, Indian Claims, and the Colville Nation," unpublished thesis, University of Massachusetts Amherst, Aug. 2011, https://scholarworks.umass.edu/cgi/viewcontent.cgi?article=1022&context =chc_theses, accessed Nov. 29, 2022.

11. Cultural destruction as the intention of the boarding schools has been the conclusion of scholars for decades. In May 2022 the Department of the Interior under the direction of Laguna Pueblo tribal member Deb Haaland released a report documenting the legacy of the schools as part of the Federal Boarding School Initiative, undertaking an investigation into "the loss of human life and lasting consequences of the Federal Indian boarding school system." It confirmed the existence of 408 schools from 1819 to 1969 that the US operated or supported across thirty-seven states including twenty-one schools in Alaska and seven in Hawaii. The report explicitly states that the broader objective of the schools was to "dispossess Indian Tribes, Alaska Native Villages, and the Native Hawaiian Community of their territories to support the expansion of the United States." Further, "The Federal Indian Boarding School Initiative investigation . . . demonstrates that 'children of the first attendees of [Federal Indian] boarding schools went on to attend, as did their grandchildren, and great-grandchildren leading to an intergenerational pattern of cultural and familial disruption' under direct and indirect support by the United States and non-Federal entities" (90).They "deployed militarized and identity-alteration methodologies to assimilate American Indian, Alaska Native, and Native Hawaiian people—primarily children—through education" (92). See *Federal Indian Boarding School Initiative Investigative Report*, Indian Affairs, US Department of the Interior, May 2022, https://www.bia.gov /sites/default/files/dup/inline-files/bsi_investigative_report_may_2022_508.pdf.

12. Robert is a pseudonym I use out of respect for my brother's privacy.

13. This history is well-documented. See especially Margaret Jacobs, *A Generation Removed: The Fostering and Adoption of Indigenous Children in the Postwar World* (Lincoln: University of Nebraska Press, 2014).

14. Jacobs, *A Generation Removed*, 79.

15. Jacobs, *A Generation Removed*, 82.

16. Cassandra Crandell, "Moving Forward from the Scoop Era: Proving Active Efforts Under the Indian Child Welfare Act in Illinois," *Northern Illinois University Law Review* 40, no. 1 (Nov. 2019): 100.

CHAPTER ONE: A PRETENDIAN PRINCESS

1. Lisa Snell, "What Would Sacheen Littlefeather Say?" *Native American Times*, Oct. 26, 2010, https://web.archive.org/web/20211004010356/https:// nativetimes.com/current-news/49-life/people/4479-what-would-sacheen-little feather-say, accessed Jan. 10, 2023.

2. Examples of some of the inconsistencies of the claims of Littlefeather and other people that won't be covered in detail in this chapter include whether she was actually present at the Alcatraz Island occupation, how she actually met Brando, and the story about John Wayne supposedly being held back from attacking her after she left the stage at the Oscars. See the *Los Angeles Times* article addressing research debunking the story in 2022, "Column: Did John Wayne Try to Assault Sacheen Littlefeather at the 1973 Oscars? Debunking a Hollywood Myth."

3. Allan M. Jalon, "How Marlon Brando Became Godfather to the Jews," *Forward*, Sept. 16, 2015, https://forward.com/culture/320671/how-marlon -brando-became-godfather-to-the-jews/, accessed Jan. 1, 2023.

4. Sherry L. Smith, *Hippies, Indians, and the Fight for Red Power* (New York: Oxford University Press, 2012).

5. Littlefeather claimed numerous times she had starred in a few Italian films, though she appeared in only one Italian film, *Il Consigliori*, filmed partly in San Francisco in early 1973, prior to the Academy Awards, released as *Counselor at Crime* in the US. She played the bit part of Maggie, a prostitute.

6. Personal communication with Sacheen Littlefeather, 2016. The details of how Brando first reached out to her as well as the Coppola story have been inconsistent over the years.

7. The National Native American Affirmative Image Committee was a short-lived, perhaps ad hoc organization that never produced anything of significance.

8. At the time of the Academy Awards, members of the American Indian Movement (AIM) were one month into a seventy-one-day armed standoff with the federal government in the tiny village of Wounded Knee, South Dakota, the site of a historic massacre in 1890 on the Pine Ridge Reservation. The action was a response to a failed attempt to impeach Dick Wilson, tribal council president accused of civil rights abuses against tribal members who organized themselves into the Oglala Sioux Civil Rights Organization (OSCRO). Wilson, seen as a puppet of the federal government, tried to expel all AIM members from Pine Ridge, bringing in armed federal marshals to enforce his order. By February 28, 1973, AIM members and Pine Ridge traditionalists had laid siege to the hamlet and the federal government brought in US marshals and FBI agents, heavily armed with .50 caliber machine guns, grenade launchers, and armored personnel carriers, and other equipment.

9. In *Breaking the Silence*, a newspaper clipping appears, referring to Littlefeather as a "Mexican actress dressed as an Indian princess," a claim she denies in the film. Copious evidence, however, would later show that is precisely what she was—a Mexican American playing an Indian.

10. *Counselor at Crime* (1973), The *Laughing Policeman* (1973), *Freebie and the Bean* (1974), *The Trial of Billy Jack* (1974), *Johnny Firecloud* (1975), *Winterhawk* (1975), *Shoot the Sun Down* (1978).

11. *Breaking the Silence* is notable for several other factual errors and omissions. Seven and a half minutes into the film, Littlefeather tells a story about a murder that occurs at Wounded Knee during the occupation. She says, "A Lakota man was murdered by non-Indian young people like they were

killing a deer for sport. They got off with a hand slap by the law." She then claims that the family called on AIM to stand up for the family and says that the FBI tried to silence them and eradicate them from the reservation. There were two Indians killed at Wounded Knee in 1973—Frank Clearwater and Buddy Lamont. Both died during gunfights with the feds. In the vast documentation on the Wounded Knee occupation, no stories match Littlefeather's account. She appears to have conflated the Wounded Knee occupation with the Raymond Yellow Thunder murder in 1972. A major omission in the film is any mention of Littlefeather's mental illness beyond one reference. She talks about being institutionalized for a year after a nervous breakdown and a suicide attempt in college, blaming it on her father, who she says abused her "during that time, psychologically, emotionally, mentally, and physically." Sacheen's father died in 1966, when she was nineteen in college at San Jose State; he had been profoundly sick with cancer for years before he died, in the hospital for much of that time. It would have been extremely unlikely, if not impossible, for her to have been abused by her father in the way she described. The reality of Sacheen's life, which the film makes no mention of, was schizoaffective and bipolar disorder, a severe condition she lived with the rest of her life.

12. In a 1976 interview with Father Miles Riley, founding director of the Archdiocese of San Francisco's Communication Center, on the TV program *I Believe* on KPIX, Littlefeather talks in a nonspecific way about being White Mountain Apache, with no mention of being Yaqui. See https://www.youtube.com/watch?v=zwoYqoGB-6I, accessed Jan. 6, 2023.

13. Charles Thomas Koshiway obituary, Chapman Black, https://www.chapman-black.com/obituaries/Charles-Thomas-Johnston?obId=23201331, accessed Jan. 2, 2023.

14. Littlefeather referred to Charles as Mr. Charles, but never as her husband in my interviews with her; her journal entries don't refer to him as such either. In one 2012 entry, she refers to him as her boyfriend and says they have been together for twenty-two years. There is a discrepancy about when Sacheen and Charles first got together. Sacheen's former friend Helene Hagan has a letter written in April 1991, confiding how lonely and depressed she was. She and Charles were not in a relationship at the time, so this shortens the duration of their relationship by at least a year.

15. Nicolas G. Rosenthal, *Reimagining Indian Country: Native American Migration and Identity in Twentieth Century Los Angeles* (Chapel Hill: University of North Carolina Press, 2012).

16. Rosenthal, *Reimagining Indian Country*, 79.

17. See, for example, Suzanne J. Crawford, *Native American Religious Traditions* (New York: Routledge: 2007); Greg Sarris, "Telling Dreams and Keeping Secrets: The Bole Maru as American Indian Religious Resistance," *American Indian Culture and Research Journal* 16, no. 1 (1992): 71–85; Diveena Marcus, "Indigenous Activism Beyond Borders," *South Atlantic Quarterly* 114, no. 4 (Oct. 2015): 892–906.

18. After Sacheen's death, her sister Rozalind Cruz remarked in public interviews that she tried several times to contact media sources, including Oprah Winfrey in 2007, alerting them to her sister's fraud to no avail. I also wrote to

editors at Indian Country Today to revisit the article I wrote about Sacheen Little-feather in 2012 and fact-check her identity claims, and received no response.

19. The Colville termination conflict is an excellent study for the ways it divided Indian people over traditional and modern values, mixed-blood and full-blood identities, on-reservation and off-reservation perspectives while also reflecting the rapidly changing times. See Laurie Arnold, *Bartering with the Bones of Their Dead: The Colville Confederated Tribes and Termination* (Seattle: University of Washington Press, 2012).

20. There are different versions of the story of Sacheen Littlefeather's name. She attributed the name Sacheen to a Navajo person at Alcatraz (Jac-queline Keeler, "Sacheen Littlefeather Was a Native American Icon. Her Sisters Say She Was an Ethnic Fraud," *San Francisco Chronicle*, Oct. 22, 2022, https://www.sfchronicle.com/opinion/openforum/article/Sacheen-Littlefeather-oscar-Native-pretendian-17520648.php). In an interview with Father Miles Riley, founding director of the Archdiocese of San Francisco's Communication Cen-ter, in 1976 she claims Sacheen was a family nickname (https://www.youtube.com/watch?v=zwoYqoGB-6I). In her most commonly recounted story, her fa-ther gave her the name Littlefeather because she used to dance around with a feather in her hair (Keeler, "Sacheen Littlefeather Was a Native American Icon"). Her website says, "[she] took the name 'Sacheen Littlefeather' after high school to reflect her natural heritage."

21. This is one of Littlefeather's claims I have not been able to verify.

22. In other published interviews, Littlefeather has said she was three years old when she went to live with her grandparents.

23. On June 18, 2022, Sacheen Littlefeather was interviewed by Academy Museum of Motion Pictures director and president Jacqueline Stewart. The three-and-a-half-hour interview, posted on YouTube, contains the disclaimer that as an oral history based on memories, "interviews should not be under-stood as statements of fact," and that it didn't reflect opinions of "Academy Entities." In the interview, Sacheen says that she has never shared her journal with anyone, which is a blatant lie, since she had given me her photocopied journal six years earlier and had also shared bits of the journal with friend He-lene Hagan. Other misinformation in the interview includes the statement that, at the first Thanksgiving, Native people were poisoned and died. There is ab-solutely no historical evidence to support that claim; it's actually the first time I've ever even heard it said. See "Academy Visual History with Sacheen Little-feather," https://www.youtube.com/watch?v=76jP7wZ5MBY, accessed Jan. 8, 2023 (link now defunct).

24. Sacheen's death certificate lists her legal name as Sacheen Littlefeather Rubio.

25. I attempted to contact the doctor that Sacheen named in the journal, a psychiatrist in Marin County; my message went unreturned.

26. In the beginning of the academy museum interview, Sacheen reads from a journal in her hands and directly quotes this passage about her parents being mentally ill.

27. The Apache Sunrise ceremony or dance is a coming-of-age ceremony for young Apache women.

28. In my survey of Sacheen Littlefeather's print and video interviews, she never referred to any specifics about Apache or Yaqui ancestry.

29. The film's narrative about Sacheen's acting career doesn't match the actual timeline. It shows some of her film roles as happening prior to the Oscars but at least one of them—*Freebie and the Bean*—was after. She claims to have starred in a few Italian films, but I was able to confirm only *Il Consigliore*. Another falsehood in the film is a story Sacheen has repeated numerous times: when she was being escorted offstage at the Oscars and John Wayne supposedly had to be held back from attacking her, she claimed people were doing the tomahawk chop—the racist arm gesture baseball and football fans do at Atlanta Braves and Kansas City Chiefs games. However, the tomahawk chop didn't even exist in 1973; according to one source, it first appeared in 1984 at a Florida State University football game. See https://www.baseball-reference.com/bullpen/Tomahawk_Chop.

30. Keeler later published the entire report on her Substack site. See "Hollywood Fantasy: Is Sacheen Littlefeather Apache: Did the Academy Apologize to a Fraud?" Oct. 22, 2022, https://jacquelinekeeler.substack.com/p/hollywood-fantasy-is-sacheen-littlefeather, accessed Jan. 5, 2023.

31. I wrote the article to share my experience with Sacheen, a story I'd been holding on to for years. Supporting Jackie Keeler's work wasn't in my best interest—she had been excoriated over it and had received a great deal of criticism over her *Alleged Pretendians List*—but it was important to support her work because, as I wrote in the article, I believed it was solid research. See Dina Gilio-Whitaker, "Sacheen Littlefeather and Ethnic Fraud—Why the Truth Is Crucial, Even If It Means Losing an American Indian Hero," *The Conversation*, Oct. 28, 2022, https://theconversation.com/sacheen-littlefeather-and-ethnic-fraud-why-the-truth-is-crucial-even-it-it-means-losing-an-american-indian-hero-193263.

32. Rozalind Cruz gave interviews where she reiterated and built on the claims she had made in the *Chronicle* article. Most notable were the *New York Post* (Josh Rhett Miller, "Sacheen Littlefeather 'Lied' About Being Apache to Work in Hollywood: Sister," Oct. 29, 2022) and the YouTube show *Latino Slant* ("Rosalind Cruz, Sister of Sacheen Littlefeather Talks," Dec. 4, 2022).

33. Laura Clark, "How the Sacheen Littlefeather Controversy Exposes the Complexities of Identity and Who Gets to Call Themselves Native (Guest Column)," *Variety*, Oct. 23, 2022, https://variety.com/2022/film/columns/sacheen-littlefeather-who-gets-to-call-themselves-native-1235412067/, accessed Jan. 6, 2023.

34. Daniel Voshart, "The Crashing of Sacheen's Funeral: How Jacqueline Keeler Used an Incomplete Genealogy and String of Media Errors to Smear Sacheen Littlefeather," *Medium*, Dec. 2, 2022. Sisters Rozalind Cruz and Trudy Orlandi confirmed to me it was not true that they believed they were Apache and that Keeler convinced them they weren't. See https://voshart.medium.com/the-crashing-of-sacheens-funeral-a3c3a7bec173, accessed Jan. 6, 2023.

35. See Russell Means with Martin J. Wolf, *Where White Men Fear to Tread: The Autobiography of Russell Means* (New York: Antenna Books, 1995); Dennis Banks with Richard Erdoes, *Ojibwa Warrior: Dennis Banks and the Rise of the American Indian Movement* (Norman: University of Oklahoma Press, 2004).

36. See "The Road to Wounded Knee II: Chronology of Events at Wounded Knee (Part 2 of 5)," American Archive of Public Broadcasting, https://american archive.org/catalog/cpb-aacip_28-hq3rv0db64, accessed Jan. 8, 2023. In the 2019 documentary *From Wounded Knee to Standing Rock: A Reporter's Journey,* Kevin McKiernan, the film's producer, explains being a rookie reporter at Wounded Knee from the beginning on February 27. McKiernan was smuggled into the Indian compound a day or two after March 27 and gathered stories from inside. In the film, there is no mention of the Academy Awards or Sacheen Littlefeather. According to the film, the media blackout didn't even begin until March 26, so there wasn't much of a media blackout to lift on March 27, the day of the Academy Awards. I asked Kevin McKiernan whether the compound had power the night of March 27, whether Means had been in the compound, and whether the Academy Awards was responsible for lifting the media blackout. McKiernan had not been in the compound the night of March 27 but at the Pine Ridge Airport, where there had been US marshals, airport personnel, and reporters, and watched the Academy Awards there. He said the compound's power, which had been on and off, was eventually cut off completely. Because he was not there the night of March 27, he would not have known whether they had power or if Means was there. He did say that, even with power being cut, the occupiers still received regular news reports at meetings in the trading post. In his opinion, it didn't really matter if the occupiers were actually watching it on TV or not because "it was the news of this that had buoyed people." This raises the question: Why would Russell Means have concocted an elaborate story about watching it on TV when he was likely not even there? I also communicated with Willard Carlson, a Yurok tribal member in McKiernan's film and at Wounded Knee. He said he didn't recall a TV. Responding to my question about whether the Academy Awards was responsible for lifting the media blackout, McKiernan said that was not true because the blackout was only a couple of days old and had lasted all the way through April, until May 8 when the surrender took place.

37. An example of how Sacheen promoted herself as a medicine woman can be found for a New Age shamanism conference called the Society of Indigenous and Ancestral Wisdom and Healing, where she trots out the usual claims about being Apache and Yaqui, saying she was born and raised in the Bay Area, not in Salinas. Her web profile states, "I have worked with Native American tribes across the US teaching Traditional Health and Nutrition, and I am founding board member of the S.F. American Indian AIDS Institute in the 1980's. I worked with and was taught by Mother Teresa herself, in her S.F. AIDS Hospice. I am one of the original teachers of the Traditional Indian Medicine Program at St Mary's Hospital in Tucson, AZ." See http://shamanismconference.org/sacheen -littlefeather/, accessed Jan. 8, 2023 (link now defunct).

38. Helene Hagan shared with me in an email the following message, published with permission:

"Unknown to me, Sacheen contacted One Bowl Productions to create a video of her life story, and furnished the producers of that outfit with a copy of the program I had produced in 1999, *The Russell*

Means Show, to which I, Helene Hagan, had and still have all copyrights. Without my knowledge or consent, One Bowl Productions used some of the footage of that program in their twenty-six-minute documentary, *Breaking the Silence*. I only learned about OBP's use of that footage long after the documentary had been completed, sold as a DVD and submitted to six well-known film festivals. Unfortunately, Sacheen never informed me that she had shared my copyrighted program with OBP, or that she had authorized the use of it in the documentary they created. Immediately upon becoming aware of the contents of *Breaking the Silence*, I had my lawyer contact One Bowl Productions with a cease-and-desist letter and a request to discuss the egregious infringement of my intellectual property rights. Going to court for an injunction would have been expensive and entailed a protracted trial, but a court decision might well have cost them up to a quarter million dollars for what they did. They appealed to my sentiments of friendship for Sacheen, and I issued an agreement authorizing them the use of that footage, under duress, on the condition that they make a tax-free donation of $2,400 to the nonprofit 501c3 charitable and educational organization, The Tazzla Institute for Cultural Diversity, Inc. Sacheen and One Bowl Productions got off cheap on that one, and I do regret not having made them face a well-deserved law suit that I would have won. I never intended that any of my television work would become a commercial venture, and I did not want to profit from it. I deplore that my friendship with Sacheen created an awkward situation in which I was never in the position of making a free ethical decision about whether or not the material I had created as a noncommercial work could be used as a commercial moneymaker. Sacheen and One Bowl Productions changed the nature of my work without my consent. In the end, I signed an agreement with that production company, by which I granted them a license to use that footage, but it terminated my thirty year old friendship with Sacheen and left a sentiment of having been betrayed."

Another troubling situation arose after Sacheen's death. Sacheen had befriended a young Suquamish woman named Calina Lawrence whom she'd met in 2018. In the academy interview, Sacheen and Calina talk in detail about their meeting and about Sacheen and Charles adopting Calina in a Native cultural way. Calina calls Sacheen "Aunt Sacheen," and Sacheen refers to her as her niece. When Sacheen died, she had been estranged from her sisters, Roz Cruz and Trudy Orlandi, for many years, but they were still legally Sacheen's next of kin. They learned of Sacheen's passing in the news. Not long afterward, they obtained a copy of her death certificate and noticed five major inaccuracies, in addition to her race as Apache/Yaqui: that her father's birthplace was listed as Arizona, not California; that her level of education was listed as bachelor's degree (she didn't have one); that she had been widowed (she couldn't have been legally widowed because she wasn't legally married); and that Calina Lawrence, the official informant named in the document, was listed as a niece. This is the intentional falsification of a legal document, a misdemeanor offense under California law. It should have been Trudy or Roz with the legal authority to handle Sacheen's affairs, not Calina, who was not legally related to the deceased.

39. There is paradoxically some evidence of undefined but potential Yaqui Indigenous ancestry in Mexico tracing back four generations that shows up in deep online genealogical searches at Ancestry.com, not unexpected given Sacheen's Mexican heritage. This evidence, however, appears in social media posts only after she died, not known to Sacheen's family or to her.

40. In private and public forums, Trudy Orlandi and Roz Cruz speak about growing up with an ill father and Marie's constant need for attention. This was further complicated by her own patterns of continual physical illness, often imagined, and her increasingly violent psychotic behavior as her mental illness worsened, eventually dominating the family dynamics.

41. Christine Domaniecki, who won the New York regional event, ended up with the cameo in the film. See "And the Winner of Miss American Vampire Is . . . ," Collins Sport Historical Society, Sept. 1, 2015, http://www.collinsport historicalsociety.com/2015/09/and-winner-of-miss-american-vampire-is.html, accessed Jan. 10, 2023.

42. A *San Francisco Examiner* article from March 28, 1971, advertising an upcoming American Indian festival at Foothill College, names "Sacheen Littlefeather (White Mountain Apache) and Cherri Nordwall (Chippewa-Shoshone) participating." See www.newspapers.com, https://www.newspapers.com/newspage /460438038/, accessed Jan. 10, 2023.

43. The question loomed whether the Sacheen Littlefeather persona was a symptom of her schizophrenia, connected to the creation of a false memory from the psychodrama experience. However, there was too much evidence that she deliberately misrepresented herself, knowing full well that she was not Native American. Her sisters, Trudy Orlandi and Roz Cruz, contended, for example, that not long after the Oscars incident, Sacheen had all their birth certificates altered—without their knowledge—to change their father's race from Mexican to Indian. In the interview on *Latino Slant* in December 2022, Roz shared they had only recently learned that the birth certificate changes on file in Salinas were filed six months after the Academy Awards, in August 1973. See minute 51 for her recounting of the story, https://www.youtube.com /watch?v=BTsxn0pb43U.

44. Harmeet Kaur, "The Sacheen Littlefeather Controversy Highlights a Debate over What It Means to Be Native American," CNN, Nov. 5, 2022, https://www.cnn.com/2022/11/05/us/sacheen-littlefeather-native-identity-cec /index.html, accessed Jan. 5, 2023.

CHAPTER TWO: INDIGENEITY, NATIONHOOD, RACIALIZATION, AND THE SETTLER STATE

1. Like the term *hunter-gatherers*, the term *nomadic* implies a form of primitivity that ignores the complex use of land and Native people's general respect for bounded space and the territories of others. See Viola Cordova, *How It Is: The Native American Philosophy of V.F. Cordova* (Tucson: University of Arizona Press, 2007).

2. On traditional land management practices, see, for example, Gregory Cajete, *Native Science: Natural Laws of Interdependence* (2000); M. Kat Anderson, *Tending the Wild* (2005); Robin Wall Kimmerer, *Braiding Sweetgrass* (2015); and Melissa K. Nelson and Dan Shilling, *Traditional Ecological Knowledge* (2018).

3. The Okanogan people, for example, work within a system Jeannette Armstrong calls the "four societies process" in which Okanogan decision-making is shaped by consideration for the powerless, including the land itself. In whatever decisions the community must make the land has a speaker whose responsibility is to consider how the land, water, and food sources will be impacted for present and future generations. See Armstrong's Bioneers talk, "Human Relationship as Land Ethic," https://www.youtube.com/watch?v=qw NoX3MNisE. There are many examples of governing processes that Indigenous people have engaged in, but they are processes that Europeans could not recognize as governance.

4. Some of this work includes the so-called influence theory, which postulates that the US Constitution was influenced by the Iroquois, based on the 1991 work by Donald A. Grinde Jr. and Bruce Johansen, *Exemplar of Liberty: Native America and the Evolution of Democracy*. The book makes a strenuous if tenuous case that the Founding Fathers studied the Iroquois Confederacy's political practices and borrowed heavily from them in conceptualizing the Constitution. The book was controversial among numerous scholars throughout the 1990s who believed Grinde and Johansen took too many liberties in their analysis, overstating the Iroquois influence on the founders.

5. Cayuga Nation, https://cayuganation-nsn.gov/index.html. The Great Law of Peace (*Gayanashagowa*), handed down orally since its inception, is visually represented on the historic Hiawatha wampum belt, made from the purple and white beads of quahog and whelk shells, now the design of the Iroquois Confederacy flag.

6. Vine Deloria Jr. and Clifford M. Lytle, *American Indians, American Justice* (Austin: University of Texas Press, 1983).

7. Steve Patton, "The Peace of Westphalia and Its Affects on International Relations, Diplomacy and Foreign Policy," *The Histories* 10, no. 1, art. 5, https://digitalcommons.lasalle.edu/cgi/viewcontent.cgi?article=1146&context =the_histories, accessed Feb. 3, 2023.

8. In the field of international relations, most scholars generally agree that the genesis of the modern state system is the Peace of Westphalia. Mahmood Mamdani, however, argues that it is more accurate to understand the modern state as emerging from European colonialism, beginning in 1492. For more on Mamdani's theory, see *Neither Settler Nor Native: The Making and Unmaking of Permanent Minorities* (Cambridge, MA: Harvard University Press, 2020).

9. Rudolph Rÿser, *Indigenous Nations and Modern States: The Political Emergence of Nations Challenging Modern States* (London: Routledge Press, 2011), 17.

10. Indigenous scholars contest the idea of sovereignty, arguing that it is a colonial, Eurocentric concept. See especially Taiaiake Alfred, *Peace, Power, Righteousness: An Indigenous Manifesto*, 2nd ed. (Oxford: Oxford University

Press, 2009), and Joanne Barker, ed., *Sovereignty Matters: Locations of Contestation and Possibility in Indigenous Struggles for Self-Determination* (Lincoln: University of Nebraska Press, 2005). Legal scholar Gabe Galanda also notes that nationhood, as Europeans understood it, was foreign to Indigenous peoples who were organized by interrelated clans, villages, and bands through kinship relations not centralized institutions. "Nationhood terminology was superimposed upon Indigenous societies by European colonies and the United States in order to justify settler dispossession of Indigenous homelands under international legal process, particularly treatymaking," as Galanda writes (p. 9). See Gabriel Galanda, "In the Spirit of Vine Deloria, Jr.: Indigenous Kinship Renewal and Relational Sovereignty" (Mar. 20, 2023), available at *SSRN*, https://ssrn.com/abstract=4338913 or http://dx.doi.org/10.2139/ssrn.4338913.

11. Rÿser, *Indigenous Nations and Modern States*, 12. The concept of precolonial Indian nationhood is contested by some commentators. Cherokee legal scholar Steve Russell, for example, contends that tribes conceived as nations in federal Indian law (as in the doctrine of domestic dependent nations articulated in *Cherokee Nation v. Georgia*, 1831) was a "magical creation": "It is important we are 'nations' so we cede land in treaties only lightly dipped in the blood of conquest, 'domestic' so that when we disappear our land titles escheat to the United States, and 'dependent' so the United States can choose the time and manner of the disappearance." See Steve Russell, "The Racial Paradox of Tribal Citizenship," *American Studies* 46, nos. 3/4, Indigeneity at the Crossroads of American Studies, *Indigenous Studies Today*, Issue 1 (Fall 2005/Spring 2006): 163–85.

12. Patrick Wolfe, "Settler Colonialism and the Elimination of the Native," *Journal of Genocide Research* 8, no. 4 (2006): 387–409.

13. Deloria and Lytle, *American Indians, American Justice*, 4.

14. Deloria and Lytle, *American Indians, American Justice*, 3.

15. Robert J. Miller, *Native America, Discovered, and Conquered: Thomas Jefferson, Lewis and Clark, and Manifest Destiny* (Lincoln: University of Nebraska Press, 2008), 9.

16. Miller quoting the 1845 editorial by John L. O'Sullivan that gave birth to the slogan "manifest destiny"; Miller, *Native America, Discovered, and Conquered*, 119.

17. Legal historian Greg Ablavsky convincingly argues that the framers designed the Constitution with the intent of coast-to-coast territorial conquest. See especially "The Savage Constitution," *Duke Law Journal* 63 (2014): 999–1089.

18. Not all tribes had treaties, and many were simply pushed off their lands and incorporated into other reservations, or left to scatter. In California, eighteen treaties were made reserving seven million acres of land for tribes. The treaties were unratified, and thus null and void, but most of the land was taken anyway, contributing to a profound state of disarray that still characterizes California Indian life.

19. The Fourth World nations framework emphasizes American Indian peoples as nations with pre-constitutional national existence completely independent of the Westphalian state system, rather than as primitive tribes that were destined to be brought into civilization by the colonizing state,

as conventional histories tend to be written. Rÿser draws the term from Secwépemc leader George Manuel and his 1974 work (cowritten with Michael Posluns) *The Fourth World: An Indian Reality* (Minneapolis: University of Minnesota Press), written during a time of building Indigenous cultural and political resurgence in the US and Canada.

20. For a country that prided itself on its Christian values, the teaching of selfishness is more than a little disingenuous. But instilling selfishness in the Indians was discussed openly among lawmakers, who were well aware of Indian generosity. In most Native cultures, respect in a community derived not from what one accumulated but how much one gave away. The potlatch ceremonies practiced by Northwest tribes is a perfect example of this.

21. Sarah Fling, "The Myth of the Vanishing Indian: Art in the White House Collection," White House Historical Association, https://www.whitehousehistory.org/the-myth-of-the-vanishing-indian, accessed Feb. 9, 2023.

22. Martin Berny," The Hollywood Indian Stereotype: The Cinematic Othering and Assimilation of Native Americans at the Turn of the 20th Century," *Angles* 10 (2020), https://doi.org/10.4000/angles.331, accessed Feb. 9, 2020.

23. When Europeans, especially the English and the Spanish, began washing ashore on Turtle Island in North America, their views toward "Indians" weren't as equals. The difference they perceived was not based predominantly on race; what mattered most was that they were not Christians and their cultures, especially religious practices and use of the land, were dramatically different. As "savages" with societies Europeans did not consider civilized, their very humanity was in question. The concept of race was still emergent in Europe, most fully articulated in Spain, under the control of the Roman Catholic Church. The concept of blood purity took hold in fifteenth-century Spain to expose "secret Jews" who had converted to Christianity. As Maria Elena Martinez writes, the concept of *limpieza de sangre* ("purity of blood") described those of "pure" blood whose ancestors were only Christians. Martinez contends that scholars have not sufficiently addressed the question of how blood purity came to signify race and to become imbricated with class, and became disaggregated from religion in colonial Mexico. Her point can fairly be applied in the US American context as well. But as Doug Kiel pointed out, "[t]he Spanish imported these [genealogical] obsessions to their first settlements in North America, and over the course of two centuries the distinction between Christian and non-Christian blood morphed into ideas of immutable racial difference." See Maria Elena Martinez, *Genealogical Fictions: Limpieza de Sangre, Religion, and Gender in Colonial Mexico* (Stanford, CA: University of Stanford Press, 2008); and Doug Kiel, "Bleeding Out: Histories and Legacies of Indian Blood," in *The Great Vanishing Act: Blood Quantum and the Future of Native Nations*, ed, Kathleen Ratteree and Norbert Hill (Golden, CO: Fulcrum Press, 2017), 83.

24. Paul Spruhan, "A Legal History of Blood Quantum in Federal Indian Law to 1935," *South Dakota Law Review* 51, no. 1 (2006): 5.

25. "Anti-Miscegenation and the Negro Woman," Digital Georgetown, Georgetown University, https://repository.library.georgetown.edu/handle/10822/1051098, accessed Feb. 15, 2023.

26. Spruhan, "A Legal History of Blood Quantum in Federal Indian Law to 1935," 8.

27. A study of the allotment councils on the Colville reservation from 1907 to 1917 is instructive. Author Alexandra Harmon shows how federal agents tried to educate tribal councils on legal concepts to guide the councils' determination for who should be counted as Colville Indians for the creation of a tribal roll. Her research shows councilmembers were not swayed by the agents' efforts to racialize people through blood quantum but determined members through more culturally based, expansive understandings of the concept of "tribal relations." See "Tribal Enrollment Councils: Lessons on Law and Indian Identity," *Western Historical Quarterly* 32, no. 2 (Summer 2001): 175–200.

28. In the 1831 case *Cherokee Nation v. Georgia*, the Supreme Court first articulated the concept of tribes as domestic dependent nations and characterized Indians as "wards of the government." As the US continued to tighten the stranglehold on Native nations throughout the nineteenth century and into the twentieth century, in *Lonewolf v. Hitchcock*, decided in 1903, the Supreme Court confirmed that Congress had "unfettered power as guardians over Indians and their lands" (Spruhan, "A Legal History of Blood Quantum in Federal Indian Law to 1935," 40).

29. See Judith Royster, "The Legacy of Allotment," *Arizona State Law Journal* 27 (1995). Royster reports that between 1917 and 1920, more than 17,000 fee patents were issued, twice as many as were issued in the previous ten years (p. 12).

30. Royster, "The Legacy of Allotment," 12.

31. For example, in 1934, this was explicitly stated by Senator Burton K. Wheeler from Montana, coauthor of the Wheeler-Howard Act, also known as the Indian Reorganization Act, which overturned the Dawes Act and ended assimilation as official federal Indian policy. In debates about how to define "Indian," in response to Commissioner of Indian Affairs John Collier, who thought that it should include all those of Indian descent who were members of recognized tribes, their descendants who lived on reservations, and all others of one-fourth or more Indian blood, the senator balked, saying: "If you pass it to where they are quarter blood Indians you are going to have all kinds of people coming in and claiming they are quarter blood Indians and want to be put on the government rolls, and in my judgement it should not be done. What we are trying to do is get rid of the Indian problem rather than add to it." Quoted in Spruhan, "A Legal History of Blood Quantum in Federal Indian Law to 1935," 46.

32. Kirsty A. Gover, "Genealogy as Continuity: Explaining the Growing Tribal Preference for Descent Rules in Membership Governance in the United States," *American Indian Law Review* 33 (2008): 243–49.

33. David E. Wilkins and Shelly Hulse Wilkins, "Blood Quantum: The Mathematics of Ethnocide," in Ratteree and Hill, *The Great Vanishing Act*, 217.

34. Nicolas G. Rosenthal, *Reimagining Indian Country: Native American Migration and Identity in Twentieth-Century Los Angeles* (Chapel Hill: University of North Carolina Press, 2012), 2.

35. Donald Fixico, *Termination and Relocation: Federal Indian Policy 1945–1960* (Albuquerque: University of New Mexico Press, 1986), 183.

36. "Status and Needs of Unrecognized and Terminated California Indian Tribes," University of California Los Angeles American Indian Studies Center. According to UCLA's document, all but twelve of the terminated tribes have been restored through judicial decisions or settlements. See https://www.aisc.ucla.edu/ca/tribes14.htm, accessed Mar. 4, 2023.

37. An oft-cited statistic from census data says up to 78 percent of American Indian people live in urban areas. However, a 2017 report from First Nations Development Institute claims this number is misleading due to the way "urban" is defined. Their report maintains that 54 percent live in rural and small towns, whereas 30 percent live in suburban and exurban areas and 16 percent live in high-population-density urban areas (p. 4). See Sarah Dewees and Benjamin Marks, "Twice Invisible: Understanding Rural Native America," *Research Note* (Apr. 2017), https://www.usetinc.org/wp-content/uploads/bvenuti/WWS/2017/May%202017/May%208/Twice%20Invisible%20-%20Research%20Note.pdf, accessed Mar. 4, 2023.

38. Elizabeth Prine Pauls, "Tribal Nomenclature: American Indian, Native American, and First Nation," Britannica.com, https://www.britannica.com/topic/Tribal-Nomenclature-American-Indian-Native-American-and-First-Nation-1386025, accessed Mar. 6, 2023.

39. Lola García-Alix, *The Permanent Forum on Indigenous Issues* (Copenhagen: IWGIA, 2003), 19.

40. Rÿser, *Indigenous Nations and Modern States*, 202.

41. "Who Are Indigenous Peoples," *Indigenous Peoples, Indigenous Voices Fact Sheet, United Nations Permanent Forum on Indigenous Issues*, https://www.un.org/esa/socdev/unpfii/documents/5session_factsheet1.pdf, accessed Mar. 6, 2023.

42. Non-federally recognized tribes do not have a political relationship to the US; in some states that have regimes of state recognition, state-recognized tribes have a political relationship to the individual state. Such a relationship, however, is outside the established federal structure.

43. Jonas Bens, *The Indigenous Paradox: Rights, Sovereignty, and Culture in the Americas* (Philadelphia: University of Pennsylvania Press, 2020). Timo Duile notes that Indigenous paradox is not a new concept and relies on a framework of relation and difference. Understanding Indigeneity dialectically, Duile instead emphasizes "that paradoxes of indigeneity are a form of a dialectical process (rather than an issue of relation and difference)" (p. 375). See Timo Duile, "Paradoxes of Indigeneity: Identity, the State, and Economy in Indonesia," *Dialectical Anthropology* 45 (2021): 357–81.

44. Under certain conditions, some Canadian Indians possess privileges to work, study, immigrate, retire, and/or invest within the United States under the Jay Treaty, signed between the US and Great Britain in 1794.

45. Vine Deloria Jr. and Clifford M. Lytle, *The Nations Within: The Past and Future of American Indian Sovereignty* (Austin: University of Texas Press, 1984), 235.

46. See chapter 6 in Deloria, *Playing Indian,* "Counterculture Indians and the New Age," for Deloria's enlightening analysis of this era of Indian cultural appropriation.

47. Circe Sturm most clearly articulated this idea in *Becoming Indian: The Struggle over Cherokee Identity in the Twenty-First Century* (Santa Fe: SAR Press, 2010). Also notable, in the conclusion of *Playing Indian,* Deloria contends that "[Indian play] offered the concrete ground on which identity might be experienced, but it did not call its adherents to change their lives. Only a handful of Indian players ever went native and they tended to do so in the mid to late twentieth century when the borders were blurry enough to slip across with minimal difficulty" (p. 185). Since *Playing Indian* was published in 1999, we can see that pretendianism has exploded as a phenomenon. It is the blurriness of the borders that people slipped across that commentators on Indian ethnic fraud are addressing.

48. Russell Thornton, "Who Counts? Indians and the U.S. Census," in Ratteree and Hill, *The Great Vanishing Act,* 150–51. As Thornton writes, census "self-identification changed everything. Now 'Indian' simply exists in someone's mind." Dwanna McKay reports that of the 5.2 million people who self-identified as American Indian on the 2010 US census, only 1.9 million people were enrolled members of federally recognized tribes, meaning that 67 percent of those who identified as American Indian did so without official tribal membership status. See McKay, "Real Indians: Policing or Protecting Authentic Indigenous Identity?" *Sociology of Race and Ethnicity* 7, no. 1 (2021): 12–25.

49. Thornton, "Who Counts?" 154.

50. Sociologists use the term *ethnic revival* to describe this era of identity shifting in the US. See Kathleen J. Fitzgerald, *Beyond White Ethnicity: Developing a Sociological Understanding of Native American Identity Reclamation* (New York: Lexington Books, 2007).

51. In Circe Sturm's work on Cherokee identity, she uses the term *race-shifting* to explain the phenomenon of white people crossing racial borders, leaving behind whiteness for often imagined and unverifiable Cherokee identities, connecting it to this era of changing census data. In 1980 alone, the census recorded a 251 percent increase in Cherokee claims. In his study on race-shifters in Canada, Darryl Leroux shows how white French Canadians use genealogy to dig up an Indigenous ancestor from hundreds of years ago to legitimize neo-Indigenous identities. See also Leroux, *Distorted Descent: White Claims to Indigenous Identity* (Winnipeg: University of Manitoba Press, 2019); Eva Marie Garroutte, *Real Indians: Identity and the Survival of Native America* (Oakland: University of California Press, 2003); Circe Sturm, *Blood Politics: Race, Culture, and Identity in the Cherokee Nation of Oklahoma* (Berkeley: University of California Press, 2002); Shari Huhndorf, *Going Native: Indians in the American Cultural Imagination* (Ithaca, NY: Cornell University Press, 2001).

52. Sturm, *Blood Politics,* 19.

53. The three federally recognized Cherokee nations have varying enrollment criteria. The United Keetoowah Band of Cherokee Indians requires

one-quarter blood degree, the Eastern Band of Cherokee Indians requires one-sixteenth blood degree, and the Cherokee Nation of Oklahoma requires only documented descent from an ancestor listed on the Dawes Rolls.

54. Thomas Constantine Maroukis, *We Are Not a Vanishing People: The Society of American Indians, 1911–1923* (Tucson: University of Arizona Press, 2021), 14.

55. Deloria and Lytle, *The Nations Within*, 236–37.

56. Renya Ramirez, *Native Hubs: Culture, Community, and Belonging in Silicon Valley and Beyond* (Durham, NC: Duke University Press, 2007).

57. See especially Anita Herle on how pan-Indian powwow culture fosters tribal diffusion and ambiguity: "Dancing Community: Powwow and Pan-Indianism in North America," *Cambridge Anthropology* 17, no. 2 (1994): 57–83.

58. Rose Soza War Soldier, "'To Take Positive and Effective Action': Rupert Costo and the California-based American Indian Historical Society," PhD diss., Nov. 2013, https://keep.lib.asu.edu/items/152393, accessed Mar. 31, 2023.

59. One study found that in the 2000 census, one-third of those who identified as multiracial American Indians did not identify a specific tribal affiliation compared to one-sixth of those who identified only as American Indian. See Carolyn A. Liebler and Meghan Zacher, "American Indians Without Tribes in the Twenty-First Century," *Ethnicity and Race Studies* 36, no. 11 (2013): 1910–34. Another study found that people are more likely to join and leave the American Indian category than any other racial category, indicating that American Indian race-shifting is constant in the US Census. See Carolyn A. Liebler, Renuska Bhaskar, and Sonya R. Porter, "Joining, Leaving, and Staying in the American Indian/Alaska Native Race Category Between 2000 and 2010," *Demography* 53, no. 2 (Apr. 2016): 507–40.

60. Michelle R. Jacobs and David M. Merolla, "Being Authentically American Indian: Symbolic Identity Construction and Social Structure among Urban New Indians," *Symbolic Interaction* 40, no. 1 (Feb. 2017): 63–82.

61. Fitzgerald, *Beyond White Ethnicity*.

62. Jacobs and Merolla, "Being Authentically American Indian," 72–73.

63. Jacobs and Merolla, "Being Authentically American Indian," 74.

64. See Michelle R. Jacobs, *Indigenous Memory, Urban Reality: Stories of American Relocation and Reclamation* (New York: New York University Press, 2023). These ideas are reiterated again and again in Jacobs's interviews with reclaimers; see especially chapter 4, "Being and Becoming Indian."

65. See Jacobs, *Indigenous Memory, Urban Reality*, 198–99. Jacobs notes the *production* of memory that occurs through the repeating of these stories, absent evidence of their veracity. "This story, in one form or another, is repeatedly recalled and retold and passed from one generation to the next. It *becomes* recollection to people who hear it, learn it, and are socialized to believe it. . . . As such people can share memories that never happened. . . . It is foolish to insist [stories] about a Native family in hiding never happened. Indigenous peoples have been dispossessed of territories, communities, and identities for centuries. But it is equally foolish to accept this collective memory as reality for all people, or even a majority of people espousing it."

66. Jacobs, *Indigenous Memory, Urban Reality*, 207.

67. Jacobs, *Indigenous Memory, Urban Reality*, 189–90.

68. Jacobs, *Indigenous Memory, Urban Reality*, 240.

69. This history is well-documented. See especially Margaret Jacobs, *A Generation Removed: The Fostering and Adoption of Indigenous Children in the Postwar World* (Lincoln: University of Nebraska Press, 2014).

70. Jacobs, *Indigenous Memory, Urban Reality*, 79.

71. Jacobs, *Indigenous Memory, Urban Reality*, 82.

72. "About ICWA," https://www.nicwa.org/about-icwa/, accessed Mar. 8, 2023.

73. Cassandra Crandell, "Moving Forward from the Scoop Era: Proving Active Efforts Under the Indian Child Welfare Act in Illinois," *Northern Illinois University Law Review* 40, no. 1 (Nov. 1, 2019): 100.

74. Federal law has long affirmed the right of tribal governments to determine their own citizenship or membership. The qualifications for tribal enrollment vary greatly across tribes. Many have minimum blood quantum requirements that can range from one-half or one-fourth to one-sixteenth, while others require only lineal descent or descent from an ancestor on a government roll, such as the Dawes Rolls. Tribes are increasingly coming to terms with the problem of blood quantum requirements as a process of self-imposed "statistical" or "paper" genocide by either lowering the BQ amounts or abandoning it altogether.

75. Meschelle Linjean and Hilary N. Weaver, "The Indian Child Welfare Act (ICWA): Where We've Been, Where We're Headed, and Where We Need to Go," *Journal of Public Child Welfare* (Oct. 13, 2022), https://doi.org/10.1080 /15548732.2022.2131696, accessed Mar. 12, 2023.

76. Linjean and Weaver, "The Indian Child Welfare Act (ICWA)," 4.

77. Linjean and Weaver, "The Indian Child Welfare Act (ICWA)," 1.

78. Matthew L. Fletcher and Wenona T. Singel, "Lawyering the Indian Child Welfare Act," *Michigan Law Review* 120, no. 8 (2022): 1771, https:// repository.law.umich.edu/mlr/vol120/iss8/7.

79. Fletcher and Singel, "Lawyering the Indian Child Welfare Act," 1771–72.

80. Linjean and Weaver, "The Indian Child Welfare Act (ICWA)," 7.

81. Fletcher and Singel, "Lawyering the Indian Child Welfare Act," 1769.

82. Linjean and Weaver, "The Indian Child Welfare Act (ICWA)," 7.

83. 25 U.S. C. 1902, US Department of Interior, Indian Affairs, https:// www.bia.gov/bia/ois/dhs/icwa.

84. According to market research firm IBIS World, the US' adoption and foster care market size is projected to be $20 billion in 2023. "Adoption & Child Welfare Services in the US—Market Size 2002–2028," Oct. 2, 2022, https://www.ibisworld.com/industry-statistics/market-size/adoption-child -welfare-services-united-states/, accessed Mar. 13, 2023.

85. Kathryn Joyce, "The Adoption Crunch, the Christian Right, and the Challenge to Indian Sovereignty," Political Research Associates, Feb. 23, 2014, https://politicalresearch.org/2014/02/23/adoption-crunch-christian-right-and -challenge-indian-sovereignty, accessed Mar. 13, 2023.

86. The Arizona-based Goldwater Institute has been at the forefront of the anti-ICWA movement, and others include—but aren't limited to—the libertarian Cato Institute, Texas Public Policy Foundation, Project on Fair Representation, and the Wisconsin-based Bradley Foundation, a major funder of the right-wing anti-ICWA "machine." Gibson, Dunn & Crutcher, a corporate law firm notorious for defending fossil fuel companies and casino interests which routinely fight against tribal sovereignty and climate justice, is also integral to the anti-ICWA efforts. For more on the shady linkages between the worlds of Indian adoption, extractive industries, and tribal sovereignty, see Joe Patrice, "Most Firms Don't Advocate Cultural Genocide Pro Bono, But This Biglaw Firm Will!," *Above the Law*, Nov. 8, 2022, https://abovethelaw.com/2022/11 /supreme-court-indian-child-welfare-act-gibson-dunn/, accessed Mar. 14, 2023; and Alleen Brown, "Inside the Oil Industry's Fight to Roll Back Tribal Sovereignty After Supreme Court Decision," *The Intercept*, Mar. 10, 2021, https:// theintercept.com/2021/03/10/oklahoma-mcgirt-oil-industry-kevin-stitt/, accessed Mar. 14, 2023; and *This Land* podcast, season 2, with Rebecca Nagle, https://crooked.com/podcast-series/this-land/.

87. Fletcher and Singel, "Lawyering the Indian Child Welfare Act," 2022.

88. Peter d'Errico, "Cutting Through the US Claim of a Right of Domination over Indigenous People: An Analysis of Haaland v. Brackeen," *Peter d'Errico's Blog*, June 19, 2023, https://blogs.umass.edu/derrico/2023/06/19/cutting -through-the-us-claim-of-a-right-of-domination-over-indigenous-people-an -analysis-of-haaland-v-brackeen/, accessed June 30, 2023. The federal authority argument references the plenary power doctrine whereby Congress is assumed to possess plenary (i.e., absolute) authority in American Indian Alaska Native issues. There are multiple views about what Congressional plenary power means in federal Indian law. In one view, it is seen as (oppressively) unlimited power over Indian lands and lives; in another, it is understood as being preemptive, where Congress preempts the power of states toward tribes, and affirming it as the branch of federal government vested with authority over Indian issues above other branches of the government. See David Wilkins and Tsianina Lomawaima, *Uneven Ground: American Indian Sovereignty and Federal Indian Law* (Norman: University of Oklahoma Press, 2001). In Brackeen, plenary power was affirmed by defenders of ICWA, based on a preemptive view.

89. Nick Estes, "Why Is the US Right Suddenly Interested in Native American Adoption Law?" *The Guardian*, Aug. 23, 2021, https://www.theguardian .com/commentisfree/2021/aug/23/why-is-the-right-suddenly-interested-in -native-american-adoption-law, accessed Mar. 14, 2023.

90. Matthew Fletcher, "A Short History of Indian Law in the Supreme Court," American Bar Association, Oct. 1, 2014, https://www.americanbar .org/groups/crsj/publications/human_rights_magazine_home/2014_vol_40 /vol--40--no--1--tribal-sovereignty/short_history_of_indian_law/, accessed June 28, 2023.

91. "A Significant Win for Tribal Sovereignty—ICWA Survives Haaland v. Brackeen," *Brownstein Client Alert Blog*, June 28, 2023, https://www.bhfs .com/insights/alerts-articles/2023/a-significant-win-for-tribal-sovereignty-icwa -survives-haaland-v-brackeen, accessed July 3, 2023.

92. *Haaland v. Brackeen*, Cornell Law School Legal Information Institute, https://www.law.cornell.edu/supremecourt/text/21-376#writing-21-376 _CONCUR_6, accessed July 4, 2023.

93. Katrina Brown, "Two Lawsuits Could Threaten the Sovereignty of Indigenous Nations," *Crosscut*, Jan. 10, 2023, https://crosscut.com/equity/2023 /01/two-lawsuits-could-threaten-sovereignty-indigenous-nations, accessed July 4, 2023.

94. Pauly Denetclaw, "Another Legal Challenge to Indian Gaming," Indian Country Today, Apr. 23, 2023, https://ictnews.org/news/another-legal-challenge -to-indian-gaming, accessed July 4, 2023.

CHAPTER THREE: WHO'S RUNNING THE SHOW?

1. Alice Littlefield, "Learning to Labor: Native American Education in the United States: 1880–1930," in *The Political Economy of North American Indians*, ed. John H. Moore (Norman: University of Oklahoma Press, 1993), 43.

2. Littlefield, "Learning to Labor," 44.

3. The regimenting and commodification of time, a key organizing feature of discipline into industrial capitalism, was completely foreign to precolonial Indian life. For more on the time organizing aspect of Indian conscription into capitalism, see Kathleen Pickering, "Decolonizing Time Regimes: Lakota Conceptions of Work, Economy, and Society," *American Anthropologist* 106, no. 1 (Mar. 2004): 85–97. The relationship between boarding schools and capitalism has been surprisingly undertheorized, reflecting a larger pattern of disconnect between settler colonial studies and its relationship to the rise of industrial capitalism, but a few have approached it through critical pedagogy and labor studies. For information about identifying this gap in the literature in Canada, see David Camfield, "Settler Colonialism and Labour Studies in Canada: A Preliminary Exploration," *Labour* 83 (Spring 2019): 147–72. For more on the lack of Marxist analysis of Indigenism within anthropology, see Samuel W. Rose, "Marxism, Indigenism, and the Anthropology of Native North America: Divergence and a Possible Future," *Dialectical Anthropology* 41, no. 1 (Mar. 2017): 13–31.

4. Littlefield, "Learning to Labor," 50.

5. Littlefield, "Learning to Labor," 46.

6. L. G. Moses, *Wild West Shows and the Images of American Indians, 1883–1933* (Albuquerque: University of New Mexico Press, 1999), 25.

7. Carter Jones Meyer and Diana Royer, *Selling the Indian: Commercializing & Appropriating American Indian Cultures* (Tucson: University of Arizona Press, 2001).

8. Industrial capitalism refers to "the rapid development of the factory system of production, characterized by much more rigid, complex, and intricate divisions of labor, both within and between production processes" in the nineteenth century, and which depended on the exploitation of a working class that had become separated from their own subsistence modes of living due to the privatization of land (proletarianism). See "Industrial Capitalism," *Science Direct*, https://www.sciencedirect.com/topics/social-sciences/industrial -capitalism.

9. William M. O'Barr, "Images of Native Americans in Advertising," *Advertising & Society Review* 14, no. 1 (2013).

10. Quoted in Kevin Armitage, "Commercial Indians: Authenticity, Nature, and Industrial Capitalism in Advertising at the Turn of the Twentieth Century," *Michigan Historical Review* 29, no. 2 (Fall 2003): 70–95.

11. Armitage, "Commercial Indians," 79.

12. Armitage, "Commercial Indians," 74.

13. Armitage, "Commercial Indians," 196.

14. Armitage, "Commercial Indians," 8.

15. Armitage, "Commercial Indians," 223.

16. Plains Indians accustomed to living free lives before becoming Show Indians would have had an introduction into European modes of exchange in the fur trade and some peripheral exposure to the American economic system, but overall, this was a time that saw their full and complete transition into the cash-based capitalist American economic system. Linda McNenly documents the Indian experience with the Wild West shows as one of agency in a time otherwise characterized by full-scale domination, with Indians legally considered wards of the federal government. Her strenuous archival research unearths copious evidence that hundreds if not thousands of Native people actively sought out employment in the shows as opportunities to earn good pay, to escape oppressive reservation conditions, and to be with families who often traveled together as performers. Further, while Indian people were put in the position of continually reenacting their own defeat—and arguably, trauma—performance was also an avenue to reinforce Native identities through the donning of traditional dress and dancing and singing. See Linda Scarangella McNenly, *Native Performers in the Wild West Shows: From Buffalo Bill to Euro Disney* (Norman: University of Oklahoma Press, 2012).

17. The phrase "the commodification of everything" is often deployed in leftist political spaces and social sciences to critically describe the ways capitalism intervenes into and mediates every aspect of modern life. According to Derek Hall, the phrase was first coined by the American sociologist Immanuel Wallerstein in his 1983 book, *Historical Capitalism* (New York: Verso). Hall quotes from the book: "Historical capitalism involved therefore the widespread commodification of processes—not merely exchange processes, but production processes, distribution processes, and investment processes—that had previously been conducted other than via a 'market.' And, in the course of seeking to accumulate more and more capital, capitalists have sought to commodify more and more of these social processes in all spheres of economic life. Since capitalism is a self-regarding process, it follows that no social transaction has been intrinsically exempt from possible inclusion. That is why we may say that the historical development of capitalism has involved the thrust towards the commodification of everything" (548–49). Hall's point is not to argue against the idea that in capitalism everything is commodified, but that the phrase should be deployed with more precision than it usually is. See "'Commodification of Everything': Arguments in the Social Sciences: Variants, Specification, Evaluation, Critique," *Economy and Space* 55, no. 3 (2023): 544–61.

18. Michelle Raheja, *Reservation Reelism: Redfacing, Visual Sovereignty, and Representations of Native Americans in Film* (Lincoln: University of Nebraska Press, 2010).

19. The literature on the political economy of the film industry analyzes the intertwined processes of cultural production and power in the film industry in which capitalist power controls what films get made and how they get made, constituting how social creativity is mitigated by the calculation of financial risk. Filmmaking also does not exist outside class and other social relations. See, for example, James McMahon, *The Political Economy of Hollywood: Capitalist Power and Cultural Production* (New York: Routledge, 2022); Janet Wasko, "The Political Economy of Film," in a *Companion to Film Theory*, ed. Tony Miller and Robert Stam (Malden, MA: Blackwell Publishing, 1999).

20. H. Glenn Penny, "Not Playing Indian: Surrogate Indigeneity and the German Hobbyist Scene," in *Performing Indigeneity*, ed. Laura R. Graham and H. Glenn Penny (Omaha: University of Nebraska Press, 2014), 178.

21. Moses found that Show Indians and early Movie Indians were always real Indians (250–51).

22. Donald B. Smith, *Chief Buffalo Child Long Lance: The True Story of an Imposter* (Toronto: Macmillan Press, 1982).

23. Smith, *Chief Buffalo Child Long Lance*, 14.

24. Melinda Micco, "Tribal Re-Creations: Buffalo Child Long Lance and the Black Seminole Narratives," in *Re-placing America: Conversations and Contestations; Selected Essays*, Vol. 16, ed. Ruth Hsu, Cynthia Franklin, and Suzanne Kosanke (Honolulu: College of Languages, Linguistics, and Literature, University of Hawaii, 2000), 74–81.

25. See Angela Aleiss, "Who Was the Real James Young Deer? The Mysterious Identity of the Pathè Producer Finally Comes to Light," *Bright Lights Film Journal*, Apr. 30, 2013, https://brightlightsfilm.com/who-was-the-real-james-young-deer-the-mysterious-identity-of-the-pathe-producer-finally-comes-to-light/, accessed Oct. 24, 2023.

26. Liza Black, *Picturing Indians: Native Americans in Film, 1941–1960* (Omaha: University of Nebraska Press, 2020), 213–14.

27. Raheja, *Reservation Reelism*, xii.

28. Black, *Picturing Indians*, 71.

29. Black, *Picturing Indians*, 81.

30. Iron Eyes Cody, as told to Collin Perry, *Iron Eyes: My Life as a Hollywood Indian* (New York: Everest House, 1982), 17.

31. See Angela Aleiss, "Native Son (Italian-American Identity of Iron Eyes Cody)," *Times-Picayune*, May 26, 1996, available at https://www.academia.edu/11282618, accessed Oct. 25, 2023. It's interesting to note that in Cody's autobiography he incorporates the name Abshire into his fictitious account, naming his Cherokee grandfather Randolf Abshire Cody.

32. Morgan Ndlovu, *Performing Indigeneity: Spectacles of Culture and Identity in Coloniality* (London: Pluto Press, 2019), 13.

33. Ndlovu, *Performing Indigeneity*, 19.

34. Ndlovu, *Performing Indigeneity*, 21.

35. Brendan Hokowhitu, "Haka: Colonized Physicality, Body-Logic, and Embodied Sovereignty," in *Performing Indigeneity: Global Histories and Contemporary Experiences*, ed. Laura R. Graham and H. Glenn Penny (Lincoln: University of Nebraska Press, 2014), 275.

36. Hokowhitu, "Haka," 276.

37. Hokowhitu, "Haka," 283.

38. Laura R. Graham and H. Glenn Penny, "Performing Indigeneity: Emergent Identity, Self-Determination, and Sovereignty," in Graham and Penny, *Performing Indigeneity*, 2.

39. Liza Black notes that Graham and Penny's "intention is to undermine essentialist identity performances in hopes of confirming cultural sovereignty, but their articles all treat Indigenous performance enacted for non-Indigenous audiences. This gives the reader the sense that there is no performed Indigeneity outside of the purview of non-Indigenous people." See Black, *Picturing Indians*, 21.

40. Penny wrote that estimates of the number of German hobbyists range from 40,000 to upward of 100,000. See H. Glenn Penny, "Not Playing Indian: Surrogate Indigeneity and the German Hobbyist Scene," in Graham and Penny, *Performing Indigeneity*, 191.

41. Penny, "Not Playing Indian," 185.

42. Penny, "Not Playing Indian," 197.

43. Kara Kovalchik, "Native or Not: True Stories Behind 5 'Native American' Actors," *Mental Floss*, Oct. 6, 2008, https://www.mentalfloss.com/article/19782/native-or-not-true-stories-behind-5-american-indian-actors#ixzz2gQVjl7Dg, accessed Oct. 30, 2023.

44. Adam Beach, "'Suicide Squad's Adam Beach on Why Casting Others for Native American Roles Is So Hurtful," *Deadline*, Sept. 14, 2017, https://deadline.com/2017/09/adam-beach-hollywood-whitewashing-casting-native-american-open-letter-1202169836/, accessed Nov. 1, 2023.

45. Damon B. Akins and William J. Bauer Jr., *We Are the Land: A History of Native California* (Oakland: University of California Press, 2022), 265.

46. Nicolas G. Rosenthal, *Reimagining Indian Country: Native American Migration and Identity in Twentieth-Century Los Angeles* (Chapel Hill: University of North Carolina Press, 2012), 42.

47. See Nicolas G. Rosenthal, "Representing Indians: Native American Actors on Hollywood's Frontier," *Western Historical Quarterly* 36, no. 3 (Autumn 2005): 339. It's interesting to note that Hart himself played at least one Indian character, in the 1916 film *The Dawn Maker*.

48. Rosenthal, "Representing Indians," 339.

49. Rosenthal, "Representing Indians," 342.

50. Rosenthal, *Reimaging Indian Country*, 44.

51. Black, *Picturing Indians*, 74.

52. Black, *Picturing Indians*, 75.

53. Rosenthal, "Representing Indians," 350.

54. See John A. Price, "The Stereotyping of North American Indians in Motion Pictures," *Ethnohistory* 20, no. 2 (Spring 1973): 165. Redwing, known for his stunt work, claimed to be Chickasaw, but after his death in 1971, it

was revealed that he was born Webb Richardson to Black parents in Tennessee, with no known Indigenous ancestry.

55. Beverly Singer, *Wiping the War Paint Off the Lens: Native American Film and Video* (Minneapolis: University of Minnesota Press, 2001).

56. Michael Smith passed away in 2019, but the American Indian Film Festival is still annually held in San Francisco. See www.aifisf.com.

57. Peter Biskind, *Down and Dirty Pictures: Miramax, Sundance, and the Rise of Independent Film* (New York: Simon & Schuster, 2004).

58. Singer, *Wiping the War Paint Off the Lens*, 96.

59. Singer, *Wiping the War Paint Off the Lens*.

60. Yannis Tzioumakis, *American Independent Cinema*, 2nd ed. (Edinburgh: Edinburgh University Press, 2017), 231.

61. Lynette Lobban, "N. Bird Runningwater: Sundance's Native Program Director Believes in the Power of Stories," *Sooner* 36, no. 4 (Summer 2016), https://soonermag.oufoundation.org/stories/n-bird-runningwater, accessed Nov. 7, 2023.

62. Lobban, "N. Bird Runningwater."

63. Heather Rae's IMDb page lists over forty titles that credit her as a producer or director. The appointment of someone with a comparatively narrow range of experience, primarily as a field producer on a handful of modest projects, to the directorship of the Sundance Native Program may appear incongruent with the expectations typically associated with such a large role. It suggests that the selection process may have been influenced by considerations other than a robust and diverse production portfolio. This selection raises pertinent questions about the criteria for leadership within such influential cultural institutions, emphasizing the need for a more transparent approach to hiring individuals with comprehensive experience and the ability to significantly contribute to the advancement and support of Native storytelling.

64. See Gerald Vizenor, "The Pretend Indians: Images of Native Americans in the Movies by Gretchen Bataille; Charles Silet Book Review," *Film Quarterly* 34, no. 4 (Summer 1981). According to Vizenor, the first book tackling Native American stereotypes in films is *The Only Good Indians: The Hollywood Gospel* by Ralph and Natasha Friar in 1972, https://digitalrepository .unm.edu/cgi/viewcontent.cgi?article=1009&context=amst_fsp, accessed Nov. 8, 2023.

65. Quoted in Jean Teillet, *Indigenous Identity Fraud: A Report for the University of Saskatchewan*, Oct. 17, 2022, p. 12.

66. Mack Lamoureux, "New VICELAND Series 'RISE' to Debut at Sundance," *Vice*, Dec. 6, 2016, https://www.vice.com/en/article/7bx3zy/new -viceland-series-rise-to-debut-at-sundance, accessed Nov. 9, 2023.

67. "About Streel Films," https://www.streelfilms.com/about.

68. Vice Staff, "Hey, These VICELAND Shows Just Won Canadian Screen Awards," *Vice*, Mar. 7, 2018, https://www.vice.com/en/article/mb5dn3 /hey-these-viceland-shows-just-won-canadian-screen-awards, accessed Nov. 9, 2023.

69. Ka'nhehsí:io Deer and Jorge Barrera, "Award-Winning Filmmaker Michelle Latimer's Indigenous Identity Under Scrutiny," CBC News, Dec. 17,

2020, https://www.cbc.ca/news/indigenous/michelle-latimer-kitigan-zibi
-indigenous-identity-1.5845310, accessed Nov. 9, 2023.

70. Barry Hertz, "'All I Can Do Is Speak My Truth': Filmmaker Michelle Latimer Breaks Her Silence After Indigenous Ancestry Controversy," *Globe and Mail*, May 11, 2021, updated Apr. 3, 2023, https://www.theglobeandmail.com/arts/film/article-all-i-can-do-is-speak-my-truth-filmmaker-michelle-latimer-breaks-her/, accessed Nov. 9, 2023.

71. The list was extremely controversial, and in May 2021, an open letter posted on the Last Real Indians website publicly denouncing it was signed by hundreds of people. See "Community Members Speak Out Against the 'Alleged Pretendians List,'" May 27, 2021, https://lastrealindians.com/news/2021/5/9/cp3jcylawd83oe095y8npx67n6jng0, accessed Nov. 9, 2023.

72. It's interesting to note the dramatically different responses to Michelle Latimer and Heather Rae in social media. There was a torrent of outrage directed at Latimer whereas there was mostly silence from industry professionals when the story about Heather Rae emerged. There was a noticeable absence of outrage toward Heather Rae from industry professionals with ties to Sundance. See especially the statement posted on X (Twitter) by Devery Jacobs (costar in *Reservation Dogs*), https://twitter.com/kdeveryjacobs/status/1339960923218391040/photo/1; the response from First Nations filmmaker Danis Goulet by Etan Vlessing, "Top Canadian Director Responds to Controversy Over Indigenous Ancestry Claims," *Hollywood Reporter*, Dec. 18, 2020, https://www.hollywoodreporter.com/movies/movie-news/top-canadian-director-responds-to-controversy-over-indigenous-ancestry-claims-4107808/; and Elle-Máijá Tailfeathers, "We Trust Artists like Michelle Latimer to Avoid Harming Indigenous People," *Now Toronto*, Dec. 21, 2020, https://nowtoronto.com/movies/michelle-latimer-indigenous-identity/, accessed Dec. 21, 2023.

73. Attempts to contact the academy museum with questions about the exhibit and the Indigenous Alliance went unanswered.

74. Harmeet Kaur, "The Sacheen Littlefeather Controversy Highlights a Debate over What It Means to Be Native American," CNN.com, Nov. 5, 2022, https://www.cnn.com/2022/11/05/us/sacheen-littlefeather-native-identity-cec/index.html, accessed Nov. 10, 2022.

75. N. Bird Runningwater, "Exploring Ethnic Fraud: An Analysis of Verification Policies for American Indians in Higher Education," May 1996, unpublished thesis, p. vi.

76. Runningwater, "Exploring Ethnic Fraud," 31.

77. Selome Hailu, "Amazon Signs First-Look Deal with Former Sundance Exec Bird Runningwater," *Variety*, Sept. 30, 2021, https://variety.com/2021/tv/news/amazon-studios-first-look-deal-with-sundance-bird-runningwater-1235077998/, accessed Nov. 10, 2023.

78. Erik Pedersen, "Heather Rae Inks First-Look Deal with Amazon," *Deadline*, Feb. 28, 2019, https://deadline.com/2019/02/heather-rae-inks-first-look-deal-with-amazon-studios-1202567340/, accessed Dec. 21, 2023.

79. Rebecca Sun, "Producer Heather Rae Addresses Native Heritage Controversy: 'For Several Years I Have Identified as an Ally' (Exclusive)," *Hollywood Reporter*, Mar. 31, 2023, https://www.hollywoodreporter.com/movies

/movie-features/producer-heather-rae-responds-native-identity-controversy
-1235365089/, accessed Nov. 19, 2023.

80. I recount this story with the permission of those who shared it with me, who will remain anonymous.

81. Rulan Tangan, "Artistic Director's Personal Statement of Identity, Rulan Tangen," https://www.dancingearth.org/news-blog/personal-statement
-of-identity.

82. Jean Teillet, *Indigenous Identity Fraud: A Report for the University of Saskatchewan*, Oct. 17, 2022, https://leadership.usask.ca/documents/about
/reporting/jean-teillet-report.pdf?fbclid=IwAR1TEof-P4myCaWIypGYXNNW
8kVu8BL1KF8zc2geQcfpUncH7reVlxx_s-U, accessed Nov. 11, 2023.

83. Singer, *Wiping the War Paint Off the Lens*, 2.

84. Robert J. Miller, "Tribal Cultural Self-Determination and the Makah Whaling Culture," in *Sovereignty Matters: Locations of Contestation and Possibility in Indigenous Struggles for Self-Determination*, ed. Joanne Barker (Lincoln: University of Nebraska Press, 2005), 123.

85. Indian Arts and Crafts Act of 1990, Indian Arts and Crafts Board, https://www.doi.gov/iacb/act.

CHAPTER FOUR: INDIANS, HIPPIES, AND SHAMANS, OH MY!

1. Adam Elmahrek and Paul Pringle, "Claiming to Be Cherokee, Contractors with White Ancestry Got $300 Million," *Los Angeles Times*, June 26, 2019, https://www.latimes.com/local/lanow/la-na-cherokee-minority-contracts
-20190626-story.html, accessed Apr. 9, 2023.

2. Elmahrek noted that as they were reporting the story, Wages did not renew his minority certification. See Adam Elmahrek and Paul Pringle, "He Claimed Chumash Ancestry and Raised Millions. But Experts Say He's Not Chumash," *Los Angeles Times*, Dec. 23, 2019, https://www.latimes.com
/california/story/2019-12-23/chumash-ancestry-mati-waiya-20191223, accessed Apr. 9, 2023.

3. Among the different Chumash bands are the Coastal Band of the Chumash Nation, the Quabajai Coastal Chumash Keepers of the Western Gate (which splintered off from Coastal Band), the Northern Chumash Tribal Council, the yak tityu tityu yak tiłhini Northern Chumash Tribe (YTT, the people of tiłhini), the Barbareño/Ventureño Band of Mission Indians, and Oakbrook Chumash. The latter three have the most clearly documented lineages, and both Oakbrook and Coastal Bands launched unsuccessful bids for federal recognition.

4. Waiya also sits on the board of the conservation organization Center for Biological Diversity, which is known for its aggressive legal tactics of using lawsuits to create critical habitat for wildlife to prevent development. According to the *Los Angeles Times*, at least one Chumash group clashed with Wishtoyo in the case of a lawsuit against the proposed Newhall Ranch development, which ended in an $8.9 million settlement to Wishtoyo. Members of the Ventura-based Ventureno/Barbareno Chumash argued that Wishtoyo and Waiya wrongly sent a message that they represented all Chumash people and contested Waiya's authenticity.

5. According to the California courts website, 2010 census data shows 720,000 self-identified American Indians/Alaska Natives residing in California, 12 percent of the national Native American population (https://www.courts .ca.gov/3066.htm). There are 109 federally recognized tribes, and figures on unfederally recognized California tribes vary. One UCLA study enumerated more than fifty-five tribes affecting more than 80,000 people (https://www .aisc.ucla.edu/ca/tribes14.htm), while the California Courts site enumerates "about 45 tribal communities who were formerly recognized."

6. Burnett was explicit when he stated, "A war of extermination will continue to be waged between the races until the Indian race becomes extinct must be expected. While we cannot anticipate this result but with painful regret, the inevitable destiny of the race is beyond the power or wisdom of man to avert." See Peter Burnett, State of the State Address, Jan. 6, 1851, available at the Governor's Gallery, https://governors.library.ca.gov/addresses/s_01 -Burnett2.html, accessed Apr. 6, 2023.

7. Kimberly Johnston-Dodds, *Early California Laws and Policies Related to California Indians*, report prepared for California Senate, Sept. 2002, https://www.courts.ca.gov/documents/IB.pdf, accessed Apr. 16, 2023.

8. Akins and Bauer state that by 1930 only a quarter of the Indians living in Los Angeles were California Indians, due partly to the ability of local Indians to maintain permanent reservation residency on one hand, and on the other a desire to disappear in the city. See Damon B. Akins and William J. Bauer Jr., *We Are the Land: A History of Native California* (Oakland: University of California Press, 2021).

9. Joanna Levin, *Bohemia in America, 1858–1920* (Palo Alto, CA: Stanford University Press, 2009).

10. Jay Ruby, "Introduction," *Bohemia in Southern California,* ed. Jay Ruby (San Diego: San Diego State University Press, 2017). For more on bohemianism and surf culture, see in the same volume Kristin Lawler, "San Onofre Surfers: Roots of American Counterculture, 1920–1946."

11. There were other bohemian/counterculture enclaves in the Los Angeles basin not included in Ruby's book. For history on Laguna Beach's counterculture community, for instance, see Nicholas Schou's book and later film adaptation *Orange Sunshine and the Brotherhood of Eternal Love and Its Quest to Spread Peace, Love, and Acid to the World* (New York: Thomas Dunne Books/ St. Martin's Griffin, 2011).

12. Ruby, *Bohemia in Southern California.*

13. P. J. Johnson, "Dharma Bums: The Beat Generation and the Making of Countercultural Pilgrimage," *Buddhist-Christian Studies* 33 (2013): 165–79.

14. Kimberly Teaman, "White Skin, Red Masks: Jack Kerouac and His Mythology of Indigenous American Cultures in *On the Road* and *The Dharma Bums,*" unpublished master's thesis, December 2009, California State University Northridge, https://scholarworks.calstate.edu/downloads/2514nr24g, accessed Apr. 18, 2023.

15. Suzanne J. Crawford, *Native American Religious Traditions* (New York: Routledge, 2007).

16. James Treat, *Around the Sacred Fire: Native Religious Activism in the Red Power Era* (New York: Palgrave Macmillan, 2003).

17. The controversies around Haley's research date at least as far back as 1997 to a journal article he coauthored with Larry Wilcoxon called "Anthropology and the Making of Chumash Tradition," which challenged what they saw as some anthropologists' tendency toward cultural constructivism in their work with Chumash communities, and the creation of a Chumash Traditionalism. The article sparked a flurry of responses from critics, most of whom were professionally associated with neo-Chumash families and groups through archeology projects involving lucrative cultural monitoring contracts. Haley's research has followed in this vein over the years, always provoking spirited debate among his colleagues, and vitriol from neo-Chumash communities.

18. "Chapter 17 Legends: Ascended Masters," Mt. Shasta Bibliography, College of the Siskiyous, https://www.siskiyous.edu/library/shasta/documents /AB_Ch17.pdf. Mt. Shasta was part of a hub that included the mythology of the lost continents of Atlantis and Lemuria which shaped much New Age thought. The Saint Germain material has origins in the late nineteenth century in a book called *A Dweller on Two Planets* (1905), another channeled manuscript that was later argued by Gerald Barbee Bryan in *Psychic Dictatorship in America* (1940) to have been plagiarized by Guy Ballard, the founder of the I AM movement.

19. Faithism is a branch of spiritualism started by an American dentist named John Ballou in the late nineteenth century. He purported to have channeled through "automatic writing" a book known as the *Oahspe Bible* (1882). He channels an entity referred to as Jehovih, as well as "Ormazd," "Egoquim," "Agoquim," "Eloih," "The I Am," and, notably, "The Great Spirit," signaling the influence of American Indian cultures early on in proto-New Age thought.

20. In the article "Craig Carpenter and the Neo-Indians of LONAI," *American Indian Quarterly* 42, no. 2 (Spring 2018), Haley provides references to sources characterizing more precisely the nature of the conflicts at Hopiland, complicating the conventional narrative of a split between progressives and traditionalists.

21. Haley, "Craig Carpenter and the Neo-Indians of LONAI," 219–20.

22. Haley, "Craig Carpenter and the Neo-Indians of LONAI," 222.

23. The *Walam Olum* advanced both a flood and Bering Strait migration narrative and parts of it were supposedly written in the Lenape language. By the early 1950s, however, the *Walam Olum* had been largely debunked by anthropologists as a hoax. See, for example, David M. Oestreicher, "Unraveling the Walam Olum," *Natural History* 105, no. 10 (Oct. 1996).

24. See also Steven Crum, "Almost Invisible: The Brotherhood of North American Indians (1911) and the League of North American Indians (1935)," *Wicazo Sa Review* 21, no. 1 (Spring 2006): 43–59. Haley notes that, in 1958, LONAI's president was Sam Gray Wolf who claimed that he was Lenape and Cayuga and that he was born on a reservation in Oklahoma when, in fact, he had been born Samuel Hannah Jr. to a white Kentucky family and was raised most of his life in Ohio. Haley's research shows no Native ancestry for Gray

Wolf. Gray Wolf was living in Los Angeles in 1958 when he was president. Haley also revealed the false ancestry claims of other LONAI officers, including Frank Tom-Pee-Saw Kirk, Howard Shupshewanna La Hurreau, John Pope/ Rolling Thunder, and, since the original article was published, James Ridgley Osapana Whiteman.

25. Pope married a woman named Helen Spotted Fawn, who was Western Shoshone and related to the Shoshones by marriage. Ethnic fraud and sexual assault, however, runs in the Pope family. Among their children is Mala Spotted Eagle, who also built a career as a Native American shaman in Europe. Spotted Eagle had a son named Red Wolf Pope, who was convicted of rape in New Mexico in 2017 and charged for the rape of three other women in Seattle in 2022. According to a 2018 story looking into his Native heritage, court records indicated he is a member of the Tlingit tribe, though the tribe denied it. See "Who Is Alleged Rapist Redwolf Pope? Turns Out He Is Not American Indian After All," *Native News Online*, July 28, 2018, https://nativenewson line.net/currents/who-is-alleged-rapist-redwolf-pope-turns-out-he-is-not -american-indian-after-all, accessed Apr. 23, 2023.

26. Brian Haley, "Becoming Semu," in *Unexpected Histories*, forthcoming. Referenced with permission from the author, https://www.academia.edu /51317345/VI_Becoming_Semu_draft, accessed Apr. 24, 2023.

27. This claim was recited repeatedly throughout his life. See, for instance, this obituary: https://idyllwildtowncrier.com/2004/11/30/obituary-grandpa -semu-huaute/. In this video clip, he refers to himself as the "only full blood Chumash left" with "only quarter bloods and half bloods left," at the one-minute mark: https://bit.ly/428q0NH.

28. Haley, "Becoming Semu," 30.

29. Haley, "Becoming Semu," 13. On the mission records that Haley analyzes, Monica Mora is only identified as "criada" and "Indian," with no tribe specified. Criada indicated a child who was orphaned, captured, or ransomed from Indian captors.

30. Semu maintained that the name *Semu Huaute* was Chumash for "brave, wise like owl," but Haley notes that scholars of the Chumashan language family have long quietly dismissed the name and interpretation as inaccurate and linguistically impossible.

31. The 1928 California Indian Act passed by Congress allowed California Indians to sue the federal government for lands wrongfully taken by the eighteen unratified treaties and resulted in the 1933 census roll. Applicants only needed to assert direct or collateral descendancy from a California Indian in 1852, not from a specific tribe.

32. Haley, "Becoming Semu," 28.

33. Haley, "Becoming Semu," 43–44.

34. Elena-Marie Koster, "Standing Alone," *Outpost*, Nov. 21, 1975. Other news reports show Marlon Brando deeding forty acres of land he owned, which was heavily mortgaged in Agoura in 1974. See "People," *Time*, Jan. 13, 1975, https://content.time.com/time/magazine/article/0,9171,917071,00.html, accessed Apr. 25, 2023.

35. Koster, "Standing Alone."

36. David Middle Camp, "Native American Settlement Near Santa Margarita Draws Scrutiny," *The Tribune*, May 3, 2014, https://www.sanluisobispo.com/news/local/news-columns-blogs/photos-from-the-vault/article39475008.html, accessed Apr. 25, 2023.

37. The source is a personal and professional acquaintance of mine, highly respected in Indian country. This may be the first time someone has ever come forward publicly with an account of this nature about Red Wind. Because of the sensitive nature of his story, I am protecting his identity.

38. Quotations from the interview are edited for clarity and readability.

39. I first heard about Red Wind from members of the YTT Northern Chumash and Barbareño/Ventureño bands, who disclosed that they knew women who'd experienced sexual exploitation there when they were young and had been so traumatized that, even as adults, they were unable to talk publicly about it.

40. It's interesting to note the difference between Semu's "traditional" Chumash appearance and Mati Waiya's. Semu's manner of dress and regalia have a more Southwestern flair (silver and turquoise, braids, cowboy hat, headband, and moccasins), due likely to his time spent with Laguna Pueblo people. At times it seemed more pan-Indian and tribally nondescript (ribbon shirt, beadwork, and feather headdress). Waiya, ostensibly representing a younger generation of Chumash, seems to draw on more of a historical Chumash or California Indian look, with a nose piercing and less clothing in general, but incorporating fur, feathers, and elaborate face and body painting.

41. Semu and Rolling Thunder's brand of traditionalism was part of a trend that still circulates in California urban Indian and neo-Indian spaces today, as we saw reflected in Sacheen Littlefeather's journal. They are often Lakota-centric, such as "inipi" sweat lodge ceremonies and pipe ceremonies, and draw from pan-Indian concepts like the Red Road and the medicine wheel. Sometimes the ceremonies will incorporate a mix of tribal practices, languages, and songs, or are completely made up.

42. Peter Matthiessen, the prolific, eloquent award-winning writer, is notable for his outsized influence on the counterculture's beliefs about Indians. *Indian Country* did an exceptionally good job of spreading the gospel of the Indian traditionalists since it was Craig Carpenter who first brought him to Indian country and Hopiland. The book is dedicated to Carpenter, who had Matthiessen convinced about his own feigned Indian identity and the so-called last traditionals. Matthiessen wrote about one aspect of the Hopi prophecy that spoke powerfully to hippies, foretelling a time when "help would come from white people who shared certain characteristics of traditional peoples everywhere, such as long hair, their own style of clothing and language, a holistic sense of identity with nature and—because of peaceful attitudes—a name similar to Hopi" (p. 82; *Hopi* means "people of peace"). Matthiessen had no idea how hoodwinked by Carpenter he'd been. If Carpenter hadn't been his primary source, and Matthiessen had a deeper understanding about Indian country, he would never have written the following passages. He credits Carpenter, Rolling Thunder, Semu, and a Hawaiian kahuna named David Bray with marshaling "widespread support for Indian causes among young white Americans;

much more important, it brought thousands of young Indians out of hiding." Quoting Carpenter, "The hippies were the first ones to respond to us. It took those Agency Indians and city Indians, all those powwow Indians a hell of a lot longer" (p. 83). Here, Matthiessen is dangerously close to a white savior narrative proffered by Carpenter, a white man posing as an Indian. There is a substantial body of scholarship on this era of Native American youth activism and no empirical evidence suggesting that Native youth mobilizing can be attributed to this group of neo-Indians, so Carpenter's assertion is ludicrous. Furthermore, it begs the question: Who are the young Indians "in hiding"?

43. The most notorious of the pseudo and neo-Indian communes include Rolling Thunder's Meta Tantay, Vincent LaDuke's (or Sun Bear's) Bear Tribe Medicine Society, and Harley's Swift Deer Reagan's Deer Tribe, which began in California and is associated with fake Cherokee "sex rituals" aired in a 1993 HBO series.

44. Miles Corwin, "Heritage of Indians Questioned: Genealogists Cast Doubt on Background of Chumash Group," *Los Angeles Times*, May 26, 1987, https://www.latimes.com/archives/la-xpm-1987-05-26-mn-2824-story .html, accessed Apr. 28, 2023.

45. John Johnson, personal communication, Oct. 6, 2022.

46. Oteil Burbridge, "Reuniting with Dr. Kote," July 7, 2017, https:// oteilburbridge.com/reuniting-dr-kote/, accessed Apr. 28, 2023.

47. Center for Biological Diversity, "Mati Waiya, Chumash Leader, Joins Center for Biological Diversity Board of Directors," press release, Mar. 9, 2017, https://www.biologicaldiversity.org/news/press_releases/2017/mati -waiya-03-09-2017.php, accessed Apr. 28, 2023.

48. Neo-Chumash rejection of genealogical searches that turn up no Chumash ancestry mirrors that of many neo-Cherokee who cannot document Cherokee ancestry as research on urban reclaimers from Circe Sturm and Michelle Jacobs shows. The lack of documentation is often attributed to ancestors who evaded the Trail of Tears or otherwise avoided government enrollment processes. A similar story is commonly heard among undocumented Chumash, where ancestors are said to have avoided the mission system. It is worthy of discussion here. The use of the term *Chumash* is a more recent phenomenon dating back to the late nineteenth century. It describes a constellation of at least 150 villages in the region of people who spoke dialects of the Chumashan language but could not be thought of as a unified "tribe" in the sense others often are. It is not a term the people historically used. One report constructed for the National Park Service in 1999 by several historians and Chumash people is helpful in explaining the complicated history of the Chumash. The over four-hundred-page report shows all Chumash enumerated in a matrix of records including mission baptisms, marriages, deaths, confirmations, Spanish military garrison records, census records from Spanish, Mexican, and American periods, and other ways people were kept track of. The study painstakingly identifying all the ancestors of today's Chumash also dispels the argument that many Chumash people evaded the six missions in Chumash territory, accounting for why so many neo-Chumash cannot document their ancestry. Addressing this concern they write: "We have searched for

evidence that would show that sizeable Chumash groups moved away from their traditional territories to avoid being proselytized. There is no evidence that this happened…[b]y the 1820's all independent Chumash towns had been abandoned and their populations absorbed into the mission system" (p. 181). In other words, it is virtually impossible for the argument about Chumash ancestors avoiding the mission system to have any basis in reality. See *Cultural Affiliation and Lineal Descent of Chumash Peoples in the Channel Islands and the Santa Monica Mountains*, vol. 1, December 1999, Sally McLendon, principal investigator and John R. Johnson Ethnohistoric Research Coordinator.

49. Haley and Johnson's work on Chumash genealogy demonstrates that the majority of neo-Chumash reclaimers descend exclusively from Spanish and Mexican colonials. There is also a rich literature in Chicano studies tackling the intersection of indigeneity and Mexican identity in California (Haley writes on this phenomenon as well), so neo-Indianism cannot be said to be a strictly white phenomenon.

50. A perfect example of academics who rallied to support neo-Chumash is the conflict that ensued after Haley and Wilcoxon's article "The Making of Chumash Tradition" and their assessment of the Western Gate (Point Conception), which neo-Chumash claim is the place the dead pass through on their journey to the afterlife. Point Conception was the site of a major Chumash protest in 1978 to prevent the building of a liquid natural gas plant based on the sacredness of the Western Gate. Haley and Wilcoxon argued that Point Conception as the Western Gate was a modern construction not supported by ethnographic data of earlier generations of Chumash people. In one rebuttal to the article, for example, Jon Erlandson rejects Haley and Wilcoxon's arguments as "unconvincing," "as is their suggestion that its modern significance is primarily the product of anthropological intrigue and recent Chumash myth making." Erlandson, "Replies to Haley and Wilcoxon," *Current Anthropology* 39, no. 4 (Aug. /Oct. 1998): 447–510.

51. "About the Native American Heritage Commission," State of California Native Heritage Commission, https://nahc.ca.gov/about/, accessed May 1, 2021.

52. "Proposed Initiation of Rulemaking Most Likely Descendants," Native American Heritage Commission Memorandum, Jan. 10, 2017, https://landuse .coxcastle.com/files/2017/02/Proposed-Initiation-of-Rulemaking-Most-Likely -Descendant-Regulations-and-Definitions-Regulations1.pdf, accessed May 1, 2023.

53. Wishtoyo's website is a wealth of information showcasing their environmental work, which includes links to several lawsuits the organization has filed in recent years. The legal battles reflect the influence of Mati Waiya's relationship with the Center for Biological Diversity, known for its litigious approach to environmental protection through critical habitat enforcement, sometimes opposing tribal projects that I documented in my previous book *As Long as Grass Grows: The Indigenous Fight for Environmental Justice from Colonization to Standing Rock* (Boston: Beacon Press, 2019).

54. "The Chumash Peoples," Wishtoyo Chumash Foundation, https:// www.wishtoyo.org/chumash-village-1, accessed May 2, 2023.

55. "Chumash Heritage National Marine Sanctuary Nomination," June 2015, https://nmsnominate.blob.core.windows.net/nominate-prod/media /documents/nomination_chumash_heritage_071715.pdf, accessed May 2, 2023.

56. Chumash Heritage National Marine Sanctuary, "30,000 People Weigh In to Support the Proposed Chumash Heritage National Marine Sanctuary," press release, Feb. 22, 2017, https://chumashsanctuary.org/2022/02/28/30000 -people-support-proposed-chumash-sanctuary/, accessed May 2, 2023.

57. Steven L. Rebuck, "The Perils of Approving a Marine Sanctuary," Coastalnews.com, Feb. 9, 2017, https://calcoastnews.com/2017/02/perils -approving-marine-sanctuary/, accessed May 2, 2023.

58. "Resolution 1042: Support the Chumash Heritage National Marine Sanctuary," https://carbajal.house.gov/uploadedfiles/1043_-_chumash_heritage _national_marine_sanctuary.pdf, accessed May 2, 2023.

59. I obtained a copy of the original genealogical report compiled by Lorraine Escobar, certified genealogist, dated March 26, 2013. The twenty-one-page report outlines Fred Collins's lineage, which clearly shows his paternal line as of Anglo extraction with no origins in California, eliminating the possibility for Chumash ancestry there. The maternal line is more complex, with lineage tracing to the mission system and Mexico but showing no Chumash ancestry. Escobar's work, controversial among some California Indians, was not the only genealogical study on Collins; John Johnson's own genealogical study of Fred Collins also showed no Chumash or other Native American heritage. See personal communication, Oct. 6, 2022.

60. Collins v. Salinan Heritage Pres. Ass'n, 2d Civil No. B267301, 6 (Cal. Ct. App. Aug. 3, 2017). *Case Text*, https://casetext.com/case/collins-v-salinan -heritage-pres-assn, accessed May 2, 2023.

61. The Northern Chumash Tribal Council is a misleading name since it does not appear to function as a tribal government. The "tribe" does not have an official membership roll or governance structure other than that of a nonprofit organization. See https://northernchumash.org/, accessed May 2, 2023.

62. https://chumashsanctuary.org/wp-content/uploads/2022/09/ Environmental-Campaign-Manager-Sept-2022.pdf, accessed May 2, 2023.

63. The list of partners can be found here: https://chumashsanctuary .org/partners/. Tax documents from 2021 show total revenue generated was $480,154. In 2020, total revenue was $383,821, thus 2021 shows a 20-percent increase in fundraising from the prior year. Likewise, 2020 shows a 43-percent increase from 2019.

64. The Coastal Band of the Chumash Nation's website proclaims: "We are proud to be expressing our culture through many ways and we use this tribal organizing body as one way we express our sovereignty as Indigenous peoples." https://coastalbandofthechumashnation.weebly.com/, accessed Apr. 29, 2023.

65. Vine Deloria Jr. and Clifford M. Lytle, *The Nations Within: The Past and Future of American Indian Sovereignty* (Austin: University of Texas Press, 1984), 254–55.

66. See Vine Deloria Jr., *Custer Died for Your Sins: An Indian Manifesto* (Norman: University of Oklahoma Press, 1969), 18.

67. A huge array of "spiritual teachers" and "shamans" were on the speaking circuit in the 1990s; they seemed to be coming out of the woodwork and the Bay Area was a magnet. I had heard of Rolling Thunder because of his close association with the Bay Area–based Grateful Dead, but I never encountered him. I had also heard of Semu, but not Red Wind. Thomas Banyacya was by then a patron saint of the New Age and pan-Indian movements. I did personally encounter Wallace Black Elk, descendant of the famous Nicholas Black Elk and numerous other Lakota and non-Lakota medicine men, most of whom catered to New Agers. I crossed paths with the notorious fakes Hyemeyohsts Storm and Brook Medicine Eagle, who came to town on book tours. There were endless books about "traditional Native American wisdom" and shamanism, and I have read many of them. Not all the medicine people were fakes, but it was a crowded field and often hard to tell the difference between the real ones and imposters.

CHAPTER FIVE: KILL THE INDIAN TO SAVE THE PER CAP

1. Wilkins and Wilkins make a distinction between disenrollment and banishment. Banishment and exile are much older cultural forms of tribal community expulsion that was rarely used and only in cases of grave offenses. Disenrollment, the "legal and political termination of a tribal member's citizenship," (p. 4) is associated with modern tribal governments as conceived after the Indian Reorganization Act of 1934, and has become far more common since the advent of Indian gaming. See David E. Wilkins and Shelly Hulse Wilkins, *Dismembered: Native Disenrollment and the Battle for Human Rights* (Seattle: University of Washington Press, 2017).

2. Vanessa Rancaño, "How a Coast Miwok Group Is Buying Back a Piece of Their Ancestral Land," KQED.com, July 31, 2023, https://www.kqed.org/news/11956856/how-a-coast-miwok-group-are-buying-back-a-piece-of-their-ancestral-land-in-marin, accessed Nov. 24, 2023.

3. I was familiar with none of the other three male council leaders, and a contact in the tribal leadership of Graton Rancheria told me they had no knowledge of kinship ties of two of them to Coast Miwok.

4. Clark Mason, "Indians Challenge Tribal Ousting: Candidates for Pomo Leadership Spots Appeal to Board," *Press Democrat,* Jan. 8, 2013. Archived at ProQuest, document number 1268567421.

5. Gabriel S. Galanda and Ryan D. Dreveskracht, "Curing the Tribal Disenrollment Epidemic: In Search of a Remedy," *Arizona Law Review* 57, no. 2 (2015): 409.

6. *Dismemberment,* 151.

7. See *Dismemberment.* This number differs dramatically from Galanda and Dreveskracht who write that only one fourth of gaming tribes distribute per capitas (p. 409). The discrepancy is likely a reflection on the difficulty of gathering tribal gaming data and a lack of transparency from the tribes.

8. Ernie Stevens Jr., "IGA Report: Record Growth Continues for Indian Gaming in FY2022," *Indian Gaming,* May 4, 2023, https://www.indiangaming.com/iga-report-record-growth-continues-for-indian-gaming-in-fy2022/, accessed Nov. 25, 2023.

9. "California Gambling Control Commission, Tribal Casino Locations, Alphabetical by Tribe as of August 31, 2023," http://www.cgcc.ca.gov/documents /Tribal/2023/List_of-Casinos_alpha_by_tribe_name.pdf, accessed Nov. 25, 2023.

10. See American Gaming Association, https://www.americangaming.org /state/california/, accessed Nov. 25, 2023. In 2016, Indian gaming generated $31.2 billion nationwide, according to the National Indian Gaming Commission, https://www.nigc.gov/news/detail/2016-indian-gaming-revenues -increased-4.4.

11. Adam Crepelle, "The Tribal Per Capita Payment Conundrum: Governance, Culture, and Incentives," *Gonzaga Law Review* 56, no. 3 (2021): 483.

12. Crepelle, "The Tribal Per Capita Payment Conundrum."

13. Crepelle explains the link between tribal governance and per capita payments through public choice theory. Public choice theory surmises that elected political leaders are motivated primarily by the desire to remain in power. Thus, increasing per capita payments is a logical way for tribal politicians to remain in power, which can be easily accomplished by lowering the number of tribal members who share in the tribe's wealth.

14. Crepelle, "The Tribal Per Capita Payment Conundrum."

15. Crepelle, "The Tribal Per Capita Payment Conundrum," 507.

16. These numbers suggest that about 13 to 14 percent of all federally recognized tribes have engaged in disenrollment. Gabe Galanda's research finds closer to one hundred tribes that have disenrolled, constituting 17 percent of federally recognized tribes.

17. *Dismemberment*, 78. See Tables 5.1, 5.2, and 5.3, pp. 68–77.

18. See *Dismemberment*, 153. Given the skyrocketing tribal gaming revenue since the publication of Wilkins and Wilkins research in 2017, it's not unreasonable to assume that in some tribes per caps are even higher.

19. Kenneth N. Hansen, "Uncivil Rights: The Abuse of Tribal Sovereignty and the Termination of American Indian Tribal Citizenship," *IAFOR Journal of Cultural Studies* 5, no. 1 (Spring 2020).

20. David Wilkins, "Re-Membering Native Citizens in an Age of Native Terminations," in *Making Citizenship Work: Culture and Community*, ed. Rodolfo Rosales (New York: Routledge, 2023), 160–75.

21. Wilkins, "Re-Membering Native Citizens in an Age of Native Terminations," 164.

22. Wilkins, "Re-Membering Native Citizens in an Age of Native Terminations," 165.

23. Wilkins, "Re-Membering Native Citizens in an Age of Native Terminations," 154.

24. For complete accounts of California's history of genocide, see Benjamin Madley's *An American Genocide: The United States and the California Indian Catastrophe, 1846–1873*, and Brendan C. Lindsay's *Murder State: California's Native American Genocide, 1846–1873*.

25. See Sean Milanovich, "The Treaty of Temecula: A Story of Invasion, Deceit, Stolen Land, and the Persistence of Power, 1846–1905," unpublished dissertation, University of California, Riverside, Sept. 2021, https://escholarship.org/uc

/item/6dw0w21v#article_abstract, accessed Nov. 28, 2023. The site was also known as Rancho Little Temecula or the Little Temecula Ranch.

26. Leland E. Bibb, "Pablo Apis and Temecula," *Journal of San Diego History: San Diego Historical Society Quarterly* 37, no. 4 (Fall 1991), https://sandiegohistory.org/journal/1991/october/temecula-3/, accessed Nov. 28, 2023.

27. Milanovich, "The Treaty of Temecula," 320.

28. See Gomez, personal communication, Nov. 29, 2023. Gomez is a direct descendant of Manuela Miranda, who was the granddaughter of Pablo Apis.

29. Bibb, "Pablo Apis and Temecula."

30. "The Eviction of the Temecula Indians," Pechanga Band of Indians website, https://www.pechanga-nsn.gov/index.php/history/temecula-eviction, accessed Nov. 28, 2023.

31. Joanne Barker, *Native Acts: Law, Recognition, and Cultural Authenticity* (Durham, NC: Duke University Press, 2011), 165.

32. Barker, *Native Acts*, 166.

33. Barker, *Native Acts*.

34. Gomez, personal communication.

35. The rhetoric of "original Pechanga" Indian is challenged by Gomez. Referring to Pechanga as a distinct band of Luiseño is a misnomer, he told me, because there was no such thing as a Pechanga band until the formation of the reservation. Pechanga simply referred to a place where the Temecula Luiseño Indians lived, and translates to "the place where the water drips," a local spring. The Indians of the village of Teméeku (Temecula) were thus the Temecula Indians, and Pablo Apis was unquestionably a tribal leader of the Temecula Indians.

36. Barker, *Native Acts*, 167–68.

37. Barker, *Native Acts*, 171.

38. See Rick Cuevas, "Is Pechanga's Violation of the ICRA What You Thought Self Reliance and Tribal Sovereignty Was About?" *Original Pechanga Blog*, Oct. 26, 2008. Cuevas is one of the disenrolless from the Paulina Hunter line and has written the blog for many years, helping to raise the issue of Pechanga and other tribal disenrollments. Cuevas writes in this entry that 25 percent of the Pechanga membership has been disenrolled, https://www.originalpechanga.com/2008/10/is-pechangas-violation-of-icra-what-you.html

39. Marc Cooper, "Tribal Flush: Pechanga People 'Disenrolled' En Masse," *LA Weekly*, Jan. 2, 2008, https://www.laweekly.com/tribal-flush-pechanga-people-disenrolled-en-masse/, accessed Nov. 30, 2023.

40. Tom Gorman, "Tribes Behind Prop. 5 Seek State Recognition of Casinos," *Los Angeles Times*, Nov. 5, 1998, https://www.latimes.com/archives/la-xpm-1998-nov-05-ss-39699-story.html, accessed Nov. 28, 2023.

41. Tom Gorman, "Prop. 5's Pitchman Has Starring Role," *Los Angeles Times*, Oct. 25, 1998, https://www.latimes.com/archives/la-xpm-1998-oct-25-mn-36084-story.html, accessed Nov. 28, 2023.

42. Barker, *Native Acts*, 160.

43. "Yes on 1A: Californians for Indian Self-Reliance," https://www.courts.ca.gov/opinions/links/S238544-LINK6.PDF.

44. Cooper, "Tribal Flush."

45. "Disenrollment Background Papers and Resolution," *News*, Association of American Indian Physicians, Oct. 22, 2015, https://www.aaip.org/news /disenrollment-background-papers-and-resolution, accessed Dec. 18, 2023.

46. See Dayna Barrios, "Citizenship and Inequality in Native California," unpublished master's thesis, California State University Sacramento, Spring 2016. The name of this chapter is attributed to one participant in the study, Emilio Reyes, who was quoted as saying that disenrollment is about "killing the Indian to save the casino" (p. 90).

47. Barrios, "Citizenship and Inequality in Native California," 102.

48. Barrios, "Citizenship and Inequality in Native California," 103.

49. One study in the earlier days of California tribal gaming success showed the direct correlation between the rise of political influence and tribal gaming in California. It can be seen, for instance, in the establishment of the Native American Caucus within the California Democratic Party in 1998 on the heels of the Prop. 5 victory. Money was also shown to accomplish multiple goals; one tribal chairman was explicit that political donations "assured access" to politicians who were woefully uninformed about American Indian issues, and donating to campaigns thus provided the opportunity to educate them (pp. 158-9). The study suggested the wealth achieved through gaming launched American Indians into the political mainstream. See Joely De La Torre, "Interpreting Power: The Power and Politics of Tribal Gaming in Southern California," unpublished dissertation, Northern Arizona University, 2000. ProQuest, https://www.proquest.com/docview/304650198?pq-origsite=gscholar&fromopen view=true, accessed Dec. 2, 2023. Another study published twenty years later demonstrates the dramatic expansion of tribal influence in the California political landscape through increased lobbying power. See Frederick J. Boehmke and Richard C. Witmer, "Representation and Lobbying by Indian Nations in California: Is Tribal Lobbying All About Gaming?" *Interest Groups & Advocacy* 9, no. 2 (Mar. 2020), https://www.researchgate.net/publication/339062118 _Representation_and_lobbying_by_Indian_nations_in_California_Is_tribal _lobbying_all_about_gaming, accessed Dec. 2, 2023.

50. https://markmacarro.com/bio/. Macarro was sworn in as first vice president of NCAI in October 2021.

51. See Trish Abalo, Adam Engwis, and Tory Martin, "Philanthropy Is Entering a New Era of Engagement with Native Communities," *Community Philanthropy Blog*, Dorothy A. Johnson Center for Philanthropy, Jan. 18, 2022, https://johnsoncenter.org/blog/philanthropy-is-entering-a-new-era-of -engagement-with-native-communities, accessed Dec. 16, 2023. The authors note the increase in philanthropic dollars to Native organizations since the Standing Rock protest and the racial reckoning movement of 2020, with new pledges reaching into the billions of dollars.

52. "Native Forward Scholars Fund Featured on MacKenzie Scott's New Yield Giving Website," *Native News Online*, Jan. 2, 2023, https://nativenews online.net/education/native-forward-scholars-fund-featured-on-mackenzie -scott-s-new-yield-giving-website, accessed Dec. 16, 2023.

53. "First Nations Receives Transformative Gift from Philanthropist MacKenzie Scott," *News*, First Nations Development Institute, July 30, 2020, https://www.firstnations.org/news/first-nations-receives-transformative-gift-from-philanthropist-mackenzie-scott/, accessed Dec. 16, 2023.

54. *Decolonizing Wealth* naively makes the case that money can heal the wounds of colonialism if it eschews racism. It reinforces Nativeness as race and evades an analysis of capitalism's relationship to colonialism.

55. "Our History," About IllumiNative, https://illuminative.org/about-illuminative/, accessed Dec. 21, 2023.

56. Influence Watch, https://www.influencewatch.org/non-profit/illuminative/, accessed Dec. 21, 2023.

57. Katja Vujić, "Crystal Echo Hawk Strives to Be Like Water," *The Cut*, Nov. 6, 2023, https://www.thecut.com/2023/11/how-crystal-echo-hawk-gets-it-done.html.

58. Vujić, "Crystal Echo Hawk Strives to Be Like Water."

59. "IllumiNative Announces a New Chapter of Exciting Growth and Expansion," IllumiNative.org, n.d., https://illuminative.org/a-new-chapter-of-growth/, accessed Dec. 21, 2023.

60. Resolution #PDX-20-001, the Tribal Citizenship Policy and Protection Task Force, from a Twitter post by Gabe Galanda, Nov. 13, 2020, https://twitter.com/NDNlawyer/status/1578399462476877824, accessed Dec. 16, 2023.

61. Acee Agoyo, "False Claim to Native American Heritage," Indianz.com, Oct. 6, 2022. The claim was made by Gabe Galanda, an Indian rights attorney who represents disenrollees, https://indianz.com/News/2022/10/06/false-claim-to-native-american-heritage-pechanga-band-takes-stand-against-noted-educator/, accessed Dec. 16, 2023.

62. Tom Holm, *The Great Confusion in Indian Affairs: Native Americans and Whites in the Progressive Era* (Austin: University of Texas Press, 2005).

63. Holm, *The Great Confusion in Indian Affairs 52*.

64. Thomas Constantine Maroukis, *We Are Not a Vanishing People: The Society of American Indians, 1911–1923* (Tucson: University of Arizona Press, 2021), 10.

65. Richard D. Gwydir, *Recollections from the Colville Indian Agency 1886–1889* (Spokane WA: Arthur H. Clark Co., 2001). Number 247 of 500 copies published.

66. For example, a book titled *Eureka Gulch: The Rush for Gold, A History of Republic Mining Camp 1896–1908*, published in 1985, consists of a collection of biographical sketches of early settlers in the town of Republic, Washington, which was originally within the boundaries of the North Half of the Colville Reservation. The North Half, around one million acres, was removed from trust status and thrown open to homesteading under very dubious conditions after the discovery of gold and silver. The book is a perfect example of colonial historiography. Little mention is made of the Colville reservation in the book, but the bios include many members of the Colville tribes, including many of my ancestors whose allotments were there within the boundaries of ancestral Okanogan and Sinixt territory, assigned before the

removal of the North Half. The sketches avoid talking about the tribal status of these people, and in some cases they are framed as "settlers." The sketches focus predominantly on the economic status of each individual, lauding the productivity of ranches, farms, and logging and milling operations. Their indigeneity is literally erased in lieu of their accomplishments as producers within a settler capitalist economy. Edward M. Walter and Susan A. Fleury, *Eureka Gulch: The Rush for Gold; a History of Republic Mining Camp, 1896–1908* (Colville, WA: Don's Printery, 1985).

67. See Vine Deloria Jr. and Clifford M. Lytle, *The Nations Within: The Past and Future of American Indian Sovereignty* (Austin: University of Texas, 1984). Citing a 1931 US Senate hearing questioning a Yuma tribal member about tribal decision-making processes, the authors note that the senators were concerned that there lacked a formal tribal organization to represent themselves to the government, not that the tribes should be able to govern themselves (48).

68. See Deloria and Lytle, *The Nations Within.* The authors note, however, that while the Meriam Report is often said to be the main force behind the Indian policy reforms of the New Deal era, there is little evidence to support this conclusion since the report emphasized the upgrading of the BIA but reinforced an assimilationist approach (42–43).

69. Deloria and Lytle, *The Nations Within,* 170.

70. US Department of the Interior, Office of Self Governance, https://www.bia.gov/as-ia/osg.

71. Deloria and Lytle, *The Nations Within,* 236.

72. Donald L. Fixico, *The Invasion of Indian Country in the Twentieth Century: American Capitalism and Tribal Natural Resources* (Niwot: University of Colorado Press, 1998), ix.

73. See *As Long as Grass Grows: The Indigenous Fight for Environmental Justice, from Colonization to Standing Rock* (Boston: Beacon Press, 2019).

74. For more on Original Instructions, see Melissa Nelson, ed., *Original Instructions: Indigenous Teachings for a Sustainable Future* (Rochester, VT: Bear & Co., 2008).

75. Leanne Betasamosake Simpson, *As We Have Always Done: Indigenous Freedom Through Radical Resistance* (Minneapolis: University of Minnesota Press, 2017), 80.

76. Eric Cheyfitz, *The Disinformation Age: The Collapse of Liberal Democracy in the United States* (New York: Routledge Press, 2017).

77. Taiaiake Alfred, *Peace, Power, Righteousness: An Indigenous Manifesto,* 2nd ed. (Ontario: Oxford University Press, 2009), 138–39.

78. Clint Carroll, *Roots of Our Renewal: Ethnobotany and Cherokee Environmental Governance* (Minneapolis: University of Minnesota Press, 2015), 8.

CHAPTER SIX: SLIPPERY POLITICS

1. Marie Garroutte, *Real Indians: Identity and the Survival of Native America* (Berkeley: University of California Press, 2003), 16.

2. The affirmation of federal non-interference into tribal membership practices are most closely associated with the 1978 Supreme Court case *Santa*

Clara Pueblo v. Martinez. Santa Clara tribal member Julia Martinez sued the tribe who refused to enroll her daughters, alleging sexual discrimination because the tribe's enrollment rules allowed the enrollment of children based on patrilineal descent, denying membership to those of Santa Clara matrilineal descent. Martinez lost the case when the Supreme Court ultimately affirmed the tribe's right to determine its membership however it wanted. The case is often hailed as a win for tribal sovereignty, but left intact what many saw as a discriminatory colonial patriarchal structure.

3. See D. Rodriguez-Lonebear, "The Blood Line: Racialized Boundary Making and Citizenship Among Native Nations," *Sociology of Race and Ethnicity* 7, no. 4 (2021): 527–42. The most common blood quantum minimum is one-quarter.

4. For a good discussion on tribal citizenship, see Jessie Young, "Tribal Citizenship and Indian Identity," in *American Indian Identity: Citizenship, Membership, and Blood*, ed. Se-ah-dom Edmo, Jessie Young, and Alan Parker (Santa Barbara, CA: Praeger, 2016).

5. Faith Roessel, "Federal Recognition—A Historical Twist of Fate," *Native American Rights Fund Legal Review* 14, no. 3 (Summer 1989): 1, https://narf.org/nill/documents/nlr/nlr14-3.pdf, accessed Aug. 18, 2023.

6. Roessel, "Federal Recognition—A Historical Twist of Fate."

7. "American Indians and Alaska Natives—Federal Recognition," Administration for Native Americans Fact Sheet, https://www.acf.hhs.gov/ana/fact-sheet/american-indians-and-alaska-natives-federal-recognition.

8. National Archives Code of Federal Regulations Title 25, Chapter 1, Subchapter F, Part 83, Subpart B, 83.11, https://www.ecfr.gov/current/title-25/chapter-I/subchapter-F/part-83/subpart-B/section-83.11, accessed Aug. 18, 2023.

9. These numbers do not include tribes with active petitions. As of this writing there are eleven groups at some stage of the application process. Every case OFA has considered since its inception is on its website, the documentation on the decisions the agency has handed down, and status of current applications are a matter of public record. See https://www.bia.gov/as-ia/ofa.

10. *Federal Funding for Non-Federally Recognized Tribes.* The GAO report revealed that of the four hundred federally non-recognized groups it identified, twenty-six received $100 million in grants from twenty-four federal agencies on the basis of being a nonprofit organization or a state recognized tribe, https://www.gao.gov/assets/gao-12-348.pdf, accessed Aug. 19, 2023.

11. States with formal recognition processes are Alabama, Connecticut, Georgia, Louisiana, Maryland, Massachusetts, New York, North Carolina, South Carolina, Vermont, and Virginia. California maintains a list of tribes and individuals that it endorses for the purpose of identifying and handling cultural resources (such as human remains and burial artifacts), but does not have a legislative or administratively based process of formal recognition. There are two exceptions, however, where tribes were the subject of legislative action. In 1993, the US Congress issued proclamation AJR 48, which states: "This measure memorializes the President and Congress of the United States to declare the Juaneño Band of Mission Indians, Acjachemen Nation, to be the aboriginal tribe of Orange County." A similar proclamation,

AJR 96, was issued in 1994, and recognizes the Gabrielino as the "aboriginal tribe of Los Angeles." There are currently several bands of Gabrielino and Tongva that claim to be original tribes, and three separate groups claiming to be Juañeno/Acjachemen. A few of these groups have applied for federal recognition through OFA, but to date, none have achieved it. The NCSL notes that since 2010, at least twenty states have considered legislation that would adopt a formal process for recognizing tribes. *State Recognition of American Indian Tribes*, https://www.ncsl.org/quad-caucus/state-recognition-of-american -indian-tribes, accessed Aug. 19, 2023.

12. Examples include the Tennessee-based Central Band of Cherokee (denied in 2012), the Georgia Tribe of Eastern Cherokee (denied in 2018), Lower Muskogee Creek Tribe (denied in 1981), Missiquois Abenaki Tribe (Missiquoi St. Francis Sokoki Abenaki Nations, denied 2007), Eastern Pequot and Paucatuck Eastern Pequot Tribes of Connecticut (denied 2005), among others. See OFA's complete list of denied applications at https://www.bia.gov/as-ia/ofa /petitions-resolved/denied.

13. One legal analysis found four different categories of state recognition: state law, administrative action, legislative action, and executive action, not all equally rigorous. The author argues that the federal government should ratify all state recognized tribes to confer federal recognition, which honors the relationship between individual states and tribes. See Ama Lee, "The Two Classes of Tribes: Unifying the State and Federal Tribal Recognition Systems," *Columbia Human Rights Law Review* 54, no. 1 (2022): 249–308.

14. Darryl Leroux, "State Recognition and the Dangers of Race Shifting," *American Indian Culture and Research Journal* 46, no. 2 (2023), https://doi .org/10.17953/aicrj.46.2.leroux, accessed June 7, 2024.

15. Ryan Blessing, "Narragansett Tribe Opposes State Recognition Bills," *Westerly Sun*, Mar. 13, 2023, https://www.thewesterlysun.com/news/charlestown /narragansett-tribe-opposes-state-recognition-bills/article_b5528e44-c1d3 -11ed-89b5-2f2a494ed7eb.html, accessed Aug. 19, 2023.

16. *The Testimony of Principal Chief Richard Sneed Eastern Band of Cherokee Indians, Hearing on H.S. 1964, "The Lumbee Recognition Act," Before the House Subcommittee for Indigenous Peoples of the United States*, Dec. 4, 2019, https://www.congress.gov/116/meeting/house/110282/witnesses /HHRG-116-II24-Wstate-SneedR-20191204.pdf, accessed Aug. 19, 2019.

17. Tavis Snell, "Non-Recognized 'Cherokee Tribes' Flourish," *Cherokee Phoenix*, Jan. 19, 2007, https://www.cherokeephoenix.org/news/non-recognized -cherokee-tribes-flourish/article_ac02834f-35d3-5bc3-bd2c-ad2b69101baf .html, accessed Aug. 19, 2023.

18. McKenzie Richmond, "Cherokee Nation Seeks to Correct Mistake in Federal Law," KTUL News Channel 8, Apr. 5, 2023, https://ktul.com/news /local/cherokee-nation-seeks-to-correct-mistake-in-federal-law, accessed Aug. 19, 2023.

19. Patrick Richardson, "Fake Tribes Bilk Millions from Taxpayers," *The Sentinel*, Aug. 22, 2023, https://sentinelksmo.org/fake-indian-tribes-bilk -millions-from-taxpayers/, accessed Aug. 26, 2023.

20. The 1928 census resulted in a 1933 judgment roll and became the basis for the issuing of Certificate of the Degree of Indian Blood (CDIB) cards to many of those applicants after 1972 when the BIA first began issuing them. In other words, the suggestion here is that the 1928 application process lacked rigor and appears to have sometimes recognized people's claims to being Indian based on no more than unverifiable personal stories. That set up a situation where now, a century later, many people believe they are California Indians, or they believe they are Indians from particular tribes when they are actually from other tribes, based on faulty information given by their ancestors. Evidence of this can be found in OFA documentation. Specifically, proposed findings to applications for federal acknowledgment submitted by the Muwekma Ohlone tribe and by two factions of the Juaneño Band of Mission Indians, also known as Petitioners 84A and 84B, all contain explanations of the problematic 1928 applications and the resulting 1933 judgment roll. For instance, in the Proposed Findings for 84A, OFA notes that while "[t]he acknowledgment regulations list a variety of sources of acceptable evidence of descent . . . [b]ecause the evidence in the record for the Juaneño petitioners often contradicts the claims made in the 1928 Applications, appearance on the 1933 Census Roll *in this case* [my emphasis] is not considered sufficient evidence of Indian descent or of descent from the 1852 ancestor(s) claimed on the 1928 Applications" (p. 185). It also notes that Fred Baker, the government agent charged with collecting and evaluating the 1928 applications, "was instructed to rely primarily on applicants' self-identification" (p. 184). Thus, appearance on the 1933 roll and CDIB cards later issued to descendants of people enumerated on the 1933 roll were considered one form of evidence OFA considered for 84A federal recognition, but alone, without other acceptable forms of evidence, were considered insufficient to show descent from the historic tribe (p. 186). The Muwekma and both Juaneño groups were denied federal recognition for different but similar reasons; for 84A and 84B, the denial was based in part on the fact that many of their members could not show genealogical descent from a "historic tribe," in OFA's language. Historic tribe in that case meant an identifiable tribal group as it existed in 1852.

21. "Fake Tribal Chief Sentenced to Nearly 3 Years in Federal Prison for Selling Membership to Non-Recognized Native American Tribe," *U.S. Immigration and Customs Enforcement Newsroom*, Oct. 11, 2016, https://www .ice.gov/news/releases/fake-tribal-chief-sentenced-nearly-3-years-federal -prison-selling-membership-non, accessed Aug. 26, 2023.

22. "Man Gets 5 Years for Selling Tribal Memberships," *Sun Journal*, Dec. 13, 2008, https://www.sunjournal.com/2008/12/13/man-gets-5-years -selling-tribal-memberships/, accessed Aug. 27, 2023.

23. See, for example, the website http://ancestorstealing.blogspot.com/. A Google search using any number of search terms related to Native American ethnic fraud turns up a growing list of articles outing people, particularly academics, as frauds. Many of them are right-wing tabloids that frame the stories in ways that reflect the current trend of vitriolic partisan politics.

24. The *Chronicle* article, "Sacheen Littlefeather Was a Native American Icon. Her Sisters Say She Was an Ethnic Fraud," was posted Oct. 22, and the Hoover statement was released Oct. 20. For the latter, see "Native Food Sovereignty Figure Comes Clean about 'Identity,'" https://indianz.substack.com/p/native-food-sovereignty-figure-comes.

25. Elizabeth Hoover, *Letter of Apology and Accountability*, May 1, 2023, https://www.profelizabethmhoover.com/identity.

26. *Report of the Investigative Committee of the Standing Committee on Research Misconduct at the University of Colorado at Boulder Concerning Allegations of Academic Misconduct against Professor Ward Churchill*, May 9, 2006, https://web.archive.org/web/20060523111342/http://www.colorado.edu/news/reports/churchill/download/WardChurchillReport.pdf, accessed Sept. 17, 2023.

27. There are too many examples of Native American ethnic fraud in academia to name, but the University of Kansas (KU) is one worthy of mention. KU came under fire in 2023 for three professors with reportedly false Native American claims. Among them is Kent Blansett, known for his scholarship on the Red Power era, including the critically acclaimed book *A Journey to Freedom: Richard Oakes, Alcatraz, and the Red Power Movement*. Blansett, who is white presenting, asserts himself as an "Indigenous descendant" from five different tribes (Cherokee, Choctaw, Creek, Shawnee, and Potawatomie), none of which he can demonstrate any current association with. He was hired under the prestigious Langston Hughes professorship program whose purpose is to bring a "prominent or emerging minority scholar" to the university. Blansett's university bio includes a seven-page, single-spaced narrative explaining his family's oral history of Native heritage. I reviewed *A Journey to Freedom* for the *Los Angeles Times* positively when it first came out in 2018. At the time I blindly accepted his Native claims, but as concerns have been increasingly raised by others, I have also reevaluated my assessment. In my opinion, his narrative lacks convincing evidence. Most of the tribes he claims are lineal descent or low blood quantum tribes (including five American Potawatomi bands and three Shawnee bands), and it seems strange that there would be no documented ancestor he could trace to from at least one of them. Also, the research I've also done for this book has changed my thinking on "intertribalism," as Blansett has written about it in his research. He juxtaposes intertribalism with pan-Indianism, favoring the former over the latter, but fails to consider the ways pan-Indianism was complicating intertribalism through growing ethnic fraud. My point is that we must be far more precise with how we understand intertribalism and acknowledge that, because so many people claiming to be Indians during the Red Power era were not Indians at all, it's more accurate to see them in the light of generic urban pan-Indianism. For more on the KU controversy, see Anna Spoerre, "3 KU Professors Are Accused of Faking Native American Ancestry," *Kansas City Star*, July 26, 2023, https://www.kansascity.com/news/article277464123.html#storylink=cpy, accessed Jan. 5, 2024.

28. All University of California employee salaries are publicly available as a matter of policy and can be found at https://ucannualwage.ucop.edu/wage/.

Hoover's pay at UC Berkeley is reported as $193,394. The site shows Andrea Smith's salary in 2020 as $155,648.

29. Philip Deloria, *Playing Indian* (New Haven, CT: Yale University Press, 1998); Shari Huhndorf, *Going Native: Indians in the American Cultural Imagination* (Ithaca, NY: Cornell University Press, 2001), 5.

30. Joane Nagle, *American Indian Ethnic Renewal: Red Power and the Resurgence of Identity and Culture* (New York: Oxford University Press, 1996).

31. Kathleen J. Fitzgerald, *Beyond White Ethnicity: Developing a Sociological Understanding of Native American Identity Reclamation* (Lanham, MD: Lexington Books, 2007), 12.

32. Fitzgerald, *Beyond White Ethnicity*, 13.

33. Fitzgerald, like most sociologists, understands identity as "fluid, constantly being negotiated, constructed, and reconstructed" and is "somewhat contingent" (p. 16). Identity is viewed as consisting of how one sees oneself and the influence of how others see them. Her analysis of American Indian reclaiming, however, rests on a racialized framing of Indianness outside the bounds of Indianness as political belonging to a tribal community.

34. Darryl Leroux, *Distorted Descent: White Claims to Indigenous Identity* (Winnipeg: University of Manitoba Press, 2019), 28.

35. Leroux, *Distorted Descent*, 30.

36. Pamela D. Palmater, *Beyond Blood: Rethinking Indigenous Identity* (Saskatoon: Purich Publishing, 2011).

37. In her important study, *Native American DNA*, Kim TallBear uses the phrase "biological essentialism" to describe the idea of cultural knowledge as "inhering in the physiological properties of blood," *Native American DNA: Tribal Belonging and the False Promise of Genetic Science* (Minneapolis: University of Minnesota Press, 2013), 64.

38. The study surveyed people who took health-related genomic tests where ancestry results were optional. Of the 3,466 surveyed, 1,317 elected to access the results and 322 responded to the survey querying their interest in the ancestry portion of the tests. See C. K. Rubanovich et al., "Impacts of Personal DNA Ancestry Testing," *Journal of Community Genetics* 12, no. 1 (Jan. 2021): 37–52, Epub Aug. 13, 2020, https://www.ncbi.nlm.nih.gov/pmc/articles/PMC7846620/, accessed Sept. 10, 2023.

39. The authors of the study point out that the lack of genetic testing in uninterested populations results in the underrepresentation of those populations (particularly Asian and recent immigrant Black populations) and have implications for the validity and reliability of genetic ancestry databases that are probability-based to begin with. See Adam L. Horowitz, Aliya Saperstein, Jasmine Little, Martin Maiers, and Jill A. Hollenbach, "Consumer (Dis-)Interest in Genetic Ancestry Testing: The Roles of Race, Immigration, and Ancestral Certainty," *New Genetics and Society* 38, no. 2 (2019): 165–94, https://www.tandfonline.com/doi/full/10.1080/14636778.2018.1562327, accessed Sept. 10, 2023.

40. See Cheryl L. Harris, "Whiteness as Property," *Harvard Law Review* 106, no. 8 (1993): 1725.

41. Harris, "Whiteness as Property," 1726. Consider also the following statement in an opinion delivered by Justice Henry Brown in *Plessy v. Ferguson* in 1896: "[T]he reputation of belonging to the dominant race, in this instance, the white race, is 'property,' in the same sense that a right of action or of inheritance is property" 163 U.S. 537, 549 (1896).

42. Aileen Moreton-Robinson, *The White Possessive: Property, Power, and Indigenous Sovereignty*, Minneapolis: University of Minnesota Press, 2015: xxi.

43. See Kevin Bruyneel, *Settler Memory: The Disavowal of Indigeneity and the Politics of Race in the United States* (Chapel Hill: University of North Carolina Press, 2021).

44. See Khaled A. Beydoun and Erika K. Wilson, "Reverse Passing," *UCLA Law Review*, 64, no. 282 (2017): 324. The authors note several examples where students feigned a race they were not born into, including a survey in 2004 finding that "73 percent [of white students questioned] would lie about their ethnicity on college applications if there was no way for colleges to refute their claims" (329). More recently, a 2021 survey found that 34 percent of students in fact lied on college admission applications, falsely representing themselves as racial minorities. A total of 77 percent of white students who racially misrepresented themselves on their college applications were accepted into those colleges. Notably, 48 percent of those who lied claimed to be Native American. "More Than a Third of White Students Lie About Their Race on College Applications, Survey Finds," *The Hill*, Oct. 21, 2021, https://thehill .com/changing-america/enrichment/education/577722-more-than-a-third-of -white-students-lie-about-their/, accessed Sept. 13, 2023. I would like to note here that anti-DEI (diversity, equity, and inclusion) warriors should not mistake my critique of reverse passing as in any way endorsing their misguided objectives, but only to reiterate the phenomenon as an unintended consequence of policies I otherwise support.

45. See "Plastic Shamans and Astroturf Sundances: New Age Commercialization of Native American Spirituality," *American Indian Quarterly* 24, no. 329 (Summer 2000): 336. This conversation just touches on a literature that theorizes late stage capitalism's impulse to commodify the self in a world where everything is commodified.

46. This comment is from TallBear's blog post in which she summarized a talk she gave at the Unsettling Genealogies Conference: Unmasking Pseudo-Indians, an online conference series in 2022 hosted by Michigan State University's English Department. Kim TallBear, "Native 'Identity' Fraud Is Not Distraction, but the Final Indian Bounty: Opening Remarks, Unsettling Genealogies Forum," *Unsettle*, March 27, 2022. I recommend viewing her talk embedded in the post, https://kimtallbear.substack.com/p/native-identity-fraud -is-not-distraction, accessed Sept. 15, 2023. The entire conference proceeding can be viewed on YouTube.

47. Tuck and Yang are careful to accredit the phrase "moves to innocence" to a master's thesis written by Janet Mahwinney in 1998.

48. Eve Tuck and K. Wayne Yang, "Decolonization Is Not a Metaphor," *Decolonization: Indigeneity, Education & Society* 1, no. 1 (2012): 10.

49. Tuck and Yang, "Decolonization Is Not a Metaphor," 11.

50. There are exceptions even to this rule. Case in point is Kevin Stitt, current governor of Oklahoma, who is an enrolled Cherokee Nation citizen. However, an investigation into his lineage found that Cherokee Nation attorneys showed that the ancestor from whom Stitt's Cherokee membership is derived, Francis Dawson, was actually a white man who pretended to be Cherokee and bribed Dawes commissioners to gain citizenship and access to hundreds of acres of land around 1880. Dawson paid hundreds of dollars for commissioners to enroll other members of his family. The news story reported that the Cherokee Nation had tried unsuccessfully to disenroll the Dawsons in 1900, and notes that because Cherokee citizenship is not based on race, it is not "necessarily unusual for a Cherokee Nation citizen to lack genetic ties to the tribe." "The Cherokee Nation Once Fought to Disenroll Gov. Kevin Stitt's Ancestors," *High Country News*, Feb. 24, 2020, https://www.hcn.org/articles /indigenous-affairs-the-cherokee-nation-once-fought-to-disenroll-gov-kevin -stitts-ancestors, accessed Sept. 19, 2023. A mention of Freedmen is appropriate here as well. Freedmen are racially Black descendants of slaves who may or may not be of genealogical American Indian descent. Histories of slave-owning in the Five Southern Tribes (Cherokee, Choctaw, Chickasaw, Cree, and Seminole) resulted in this category of tribal membership and has been the source of contentious battles within those tribes. Treaty agreements between the US and the tribes at the end of the Civil War stipulated that the slaves previously owned by the tribes be granted full citizenship rights but have not always been honored. Whether biologically Indian or not, citizenship confers legitimate tribal identity on those of Freedmen descent, but does raise questions about Freedmen tribal belonging within the context of a particular historical moment.

51. "Largest Population of American Indians in the U.S.," *Los Angeles Almanac*, n.d., https://www.laalmanac.com/population/po15c.php, accessed Oct. 2, 2023.

52. Leila Miller, "Zapotec in 90006, K'iche' in 90057: New Map Highlights L.A.'s Indigenous Communities," *Los Angeles Times*, July 7, 2021, https://www.latimes.com/california/story/2021-07-07/la-me-indigenous-map -los-angeles, accessed Oct. 3, 2023.

53. This is another instance where I speak from personal experience. When my mother passed away in 2009, my sisters and I inherited her fractionated interests and IIM accounts were created to keep track of the monies the BIA manages from the leasing of our allotments. When the Cobell lawsuit was settled in 2010 and payments were distributed a few years later, as the oldest child on record, I received the money my mother would have received as federal law dictated. Subsequently, the land buyback program created by the settlement gave landowners like my sisters and me the option to sell our interests to the tribe to consolidate the lands into tribal ownership. I chose not to sell, though I cannot use the land due to the restrictions. As a non-enrolled Colville, I have those tiny allotment interests that tie me to my ancestors and our homeland. Having been raised during a time when the Colvilles were wrestling with termination, I grew up hearing the phrase "never sell your land" because without the land, you lose who you are as an Indian. It has stuck with me my entire life.

54. Jessica McDonald, "The Facts on Elizabeth Warren's DNA Test," Fact-check.org, Oct. 30, 2018, https://www.factcheck.org/2018/10/the-facts-on-elizabeth-warrens-dna-test/, accessed Sept. 25, 2023.

55. In February 2020 a letter signed by two hundred prominent Chero-kee and other American Indian leaders was sent to Warren. The final para-graph reads: "You have done some good things for Indian country during your time in political service. You have also done real harm. Right now, you have the platform and the opportunity to stand firmly on the side of justice. This is not about politics or your career. This is about the well-being of our nations. The time has come for you to show true leadership and make this right." War-ren responded with a twelve-page letter, once again apologizing and outlining what she would do to protect Indian country if she were elected president. See Jacob Knutson, "More Than 200 Native Americans Urge Elizabeth Warren to Fully Retract Ancestry Claims," *Axios*, Feb. 26, 2020, https://www.axios.com/2020/02/26/elizabeth-warren-native-american-ancestry-apology, accessed Sept. 25, 2023.

56. *Native American DNA*, 179.

57. Harley Swift Deer Reagan, a white gun-toting martial artist and self-proclaimed "half breed cowboy" from Texas who died in 2013, is nota-ble for the New Age institute he created called the Deer Tribe Metis Medicine Society. It operates worldwide teaching bogus Cherokee sex rituals and other pseudo-Native American spiritual practices, based on his supposed apprentice-ship with a Navajo medicine man named Tom Two Bears Wilson. A year after Reagan died, freelance journalist Friedrich Abel did some digging to find out the veracity of Reagan's story, going to the Navajo reservation to track down Wilson's family in his research. Wilson, who turned out to be real, had passed away in 1981. Abel found the Wilson family, who told him that Reagan visited the elder Wilson (who spoke no English) a few times over a couple of years, allowing him to camp on his land, but never shared any traditional Navajo knowledge with him; Reagan's fabricated story about Wilson was constructed conveniently after Wilson's death. Over the years, the family became aware of the hoax being perpetrated and capitalized on by Reagan, and they told Abel once in a meeting with him, trying to convince him to stop. At the meeting in a restaurant in Flagstaff, Reagan showed up with a revolver tucked provoca-tively in his belt, only expressing annoyance and that he did nothing wrong. The family then banned him from their land and the reservation forever. See "Harley Swift Deer Reagan's Theft of a Spiritual Lineage from a Navajo Fam-ily," Friedrich Abel, https://www.tapatalk.com/groups/sustainedreaction/harley-swiftdeer-reagan-s-theft-of-a-spiritual-lin-t6850.html, accessed Jan. 2, 2025. Hyemeyohsts Storm (birth name Arthur Charles Storm) became famous for the book *Seven Arrows*, a New Age staple since its 1972 publication. Storm claimed to be Northern Cheyenne and took credit for exposing the world to "Native American medicine wheel" teachings, but the Northern and Southern Cheyenne tribes filed a complaint with his publisher Harper and Row about inaccuracies in the text. The offending text was edited out and a cash settle-ment was paid. Erica Prussing, *White Man's Water: The Politics of Sobriety in a Native American Community* (Tucson: University of Arizona Press, 2011),

45. The lack of credibility of Storm's claim to Native American heritage (Cheyenne, Sioux, Crow) has dogged him for years.

58. Simon and Shuster, the publisher of Castaneda's fifteen books, maintains that they have "sold eight million copies worldwide and were published in seventeen different languages. In his writing, Castaneda describes the teaching of don Juan, a Yaqui sorcerer and shaman. His works helped define the 1960s and usher in the New Age movement. Even after his death in 1998, his books continue to inspire and influence his many devoted fans." "Carlos Castaneda: About the Author," https://www.simonandschuster.com/authors/Carlos-Castaneda/415702, accessed Oct. 5, 2023.

CONCLUSION

1. Jay Miller, in the foreword to Mourning Dove's *Coyote Stories*, 1990, p. x. Christine Quintasket, who wrote under the nom de plume Mourning Dove, was one of the first American Indian women to become a published author. Born in the 1880s, she was witness to a time of great change as the old ways of life gave way to the new under the pressures brought first by the fur trade, the Jesuits, and finally, the Americans. Her second book, *Coyote Stories*, was released in 1933, five years after her novel *Cogewea: The Half-Blood*, and had been a project several years in the making. Quintasket was raised hearing the stories told in a traditional way during the wintertime, the time reserved for storytelling.

2. Mourning Dove, *Coyote Stories*, 23.

3. The University of Saskatchewan's Indigenous Identity Fraud report considered strategies for curbing the hiring of pretendians and is a useful tool in educating about what to look for in Indigenous identity claims, what constitutes Indigeneity and so on, but because Canada is a different country with different laws, not all the report's suggestions may be applicable in the US context. See https://indigenous.usask.ca/documents/deybwewin--taapwaywin--tapwewin-verification/jean-teillet-report.pdf.

4. For a useful discussion on funding tribal charitable organizations, see First Nations Development Institute's study *Charitable and Sovereign: Understanding Tribal 7871 Organizations*, https://www.firstnations.org/wp-content/uploads/publication-attachments/2009_Charitable_and_Sovereign_7871_Report.pdf.

5. Gabriel Galanda, "In the Spirit of Vine Deloria, Jr.: Indigenous Kinship Renewal and Relational Sovereignty" (Mar. 20, 2023), available at *SSRN*, https://ssrn.com/abstract=4338913 or http://dx.doi.org/10.2139/ssrn.4338913, p. 13.

6. Graton Rancheria has publicly touted the constitutional amendment it passed in 2013 banning disenrollment, but it does not completely disallow it, and it also disingenuously obscures the fact that its enrollment criteria are so restrictive it effectively constitutes a moratorium. Criteria for enrollment in Graton Rancheria is contained in two clauses in Section 2: "(A) [A lineal citizen is] the biological child of a tribal citizen, whether living or dead, for whom an enrollment application is submitted within six months of the child's birth, or within six months of their parent being enrolled as a citizen; provided that

neither the child nor the parent is otherwise disqualified pursuant to Section 3 of this Article. (B) Those persons claiming biological lineage through the father shall be required to submit to blood or DNA testing pursuant to policies established by the Tribe. The Tribe may also require blood or DNA testing where there are no medical records or other clear and convincing evidence that a child is a biological child of a mother through whom tribal lineage is claimed." Sections 3-6 stipulate all the ways tribal enrollment is restricted. It's also noteworthy that Graton would be so outspoken on disenrollment given that longtime tribal chairman Greg Sarris has for decades been dogged by allegations that he does not have Coast Miwok heritage. Graton's amended constitution can be found at https://gratonrancheria.com/wp-content/uploads/2018/08/Amended-Constitution-7.2012.pdf.

7. William R. Norman Jr., Kirke Kickingbird, and Adam P. Bailey, "Tribal Disenrollment Demands a Tribal Answer," *Human Rights* 43, no. 1 (2017): 12–15.

8. Galanda, "In the Spirit of Vine Deloria, Jr."

9. Wilkins, "Re-Membering Native Nations."

INDEX